The Violets Are Mine
Tales of an Unwanted Orphan

PENNY-FARTHING BIKE

by Lester Morris

The Violets Are Mine
Tales of an Unwanted Orphan

Javelina Books

Copyright © 2011 by Lester Morris

Javelina Books
P.O. Box 93152
Austin, Texas 78709
SAN 850-8046

Visit our web site at www.javelinabooks.com

FIRST EDITION: May 2011
This book is a memoir; however, some names, characters and incidents are used fictitiously.

Lester, Morris
The Violets Are Mine – Tales of an Unwanted Orphan/Lester Morris –
   1st Ed.

ISBN 978-0-9785221-3-1

Library of Congress Control Number: 2011930173

Printed in Canada on acid free paper.

Cover photo credit: *Orphans* by Thomas Kennington (1856–1916). Currently on display at the Tate in London.

For orders other than by individual consumers, Javelina Books grants a discount on the purchase of 10 or more copies of single title for special markets or premium use. For further details, please write or e-mail Javelina Books, Attn: Premiums, P.O. Box 93152, Austin, Texas 78709
premiums@javelinabooks.com

For orders by individual consumers, write or e-mail Javelina Books, Attn: Sales, P.O. Box 93152, Austin, Texas 78709
sales@javelinabooks.com

DEDICATION

I dedicate this book to my wife; Valerie-Dorman Morris, who through all the years she has known me, has been behind me all the way in completing this book. With her skills, knowledge and guidance, she urged me to get this book done.

She helped me with my first book, 'Did You Knows? Of England.' She encouraged me to stick with it and offered her educational skills, which were of great help. After 'Did You Knows?' was done, I got back to working on this book which also I could not have completed without her.

ACKNOWLEDGMENT

"What greater tragedy can there be than is presented by the spectacle of a child whose life prospects and hope are smashed at the very outset of its existence."

Sir Winston Churchill

To all the brave people who helped me with this book which took me thirty-six years to complete. Some gave up on me and died without notice, while others forgot what the hell I was writing anyway. But to these good friends who hung in there with me, I want to thank very, very much.

While I can't mention everyone who helped, here are a few of the most notable,

William D. Buckman. He was the gentleman who told me to write this book in 1975. We still keep in touch, I consider William as a very good friend.

Mrs. Woodley. She spent most of her life looking after us orphans. Died recently at the age of 103, and plays a prominent role in the book and in my life.

Douglas Morris. My brother with no hair, who helped me regurgitate some of the early memories with me, although going back that far to my early life, took some severe memory jogging. He's not only my brother but an exceedingly decent chap.

Margaret Bliss. Known as Maggie the Bitch. Who has been an inspiration to me and helped me, and even typed my manuscript for me. So, if you find any errors in this book, don't blame me, its Maggie's fault. You know she's well read. You can read her like a book!

Debbie Starr. An extraordinary editor and very good friend, she went and got married and is now living the good life. She was a great help in putting my book together, thanks.

Rae & Bev Kilby. They have given me support in everything I have done. Bev has been a true Brit in helping and suggesting ideas for my books and other events. They are both incredible people and are without doubt true friends.

Denny Bolton. He's an incredible author of many books and a jolly good friend, and has helped me tremendously to publish my book, and has given me sound advice. Incidentally we both have been to many events selling our books together. A fun and decent chap.

Darrel Meyers? Gave me lots of encouragement and advice on writing and was the chap who advised me to change the title of the book from, "*The Green Penny Farthing Bike*," to the present title "*The Violets Are Mine – Tales of an Unwanted Orphan.*" Readers always assumed my book was about bikes. He helped clear up the confusion on that one.

Jason Dietrick, or commonly known as Zippy. This tall handsome chap was a great help answering my many cries for help as regards to my computer. His fingers never left his hands except for drinking the milk and eating all the food in sight. But definitely another decent chap.

Bobby Post. An extraordinary English chap who has helped me tremendously in the course of writing this book. He is also helping me with another book I'm working on, and boosts my morale with his wonderful English humour. When we are together there is laughter.

Church of England Children's Society. Besides being a caring organization, they furnished me with dates and information from their archives in London regarding my time in their care. I would like to emphasize that I do not put blame in any way regarding the Society. They, I believe, were unaware of any of the incidents that are mentioned in this book. In general I was very well looked after, even after leaving the Society, they came to my rescue at the age of 17. Now that is what I call dedication to the children they have taken into their care. I thank them for my care.

Thomas Kennington (1856–1916). The painting of the two boys on the cover of this book was done by him. It's called *Orphans* and the original is currently on display at the Tate in London.

And of course, my wife Valerie to whom this book is dedicated.

NOTE: The original title for this book, at least for the first 35 years I put into it, was *THE GREEN PENNY FARTHING BIKE* but as Darrel pointed out, when the book is published and people read the title, they may get the impression that the book is about Penny Farthing bikes and show no interest. I said there will be a picture of an old Penny Farthing bike on the cover and Darrel said, "I don't want a book on old bikes. Can't thank him enough for finally getting me off that one.

Table of Contents

FOREWORD

We all have reasons or motives for reading a book. We want to be entertained. We want to learn. We want to be informed. Let us laugh. Let us cry. Take us from our mundane lives, O Author; and transport us to a place where we can get lost, at least for a little while.

Lester Morris does all this with his memoir, *The Violets Are Mine – Tales of an Unwanted Orphan*.

I've known Lester for some decades now, first when we both were members of the South Texas Professional Speakers Association back in the last century, and later as someone to pal up with, and share a booth with, at various book signing and selling venues around Austin, Texas. For three years now we have sold books together at the Texas Book Festival, and have had a blast. He's a talker. I'm a talker. And the combination of our personalities has allowed us to sell lots of books. He tells folks he hangs out with me merely to teach me English, and I tell them I'm trying to make a Texan out of him and teach him how to pronounce "Manchaca and Buda."

Before Violets he has written and published by The British Connection, *The Did You Knows of England* which covers about every interesting and obscure fact about England and English history you can imagine. For years now I've heard him ask the ladies who stop by our booth,

"Madam, do you know the origin of the phrases, 'loose woman,' 'sleep tight,' 'ring around the rosy' or where the story of Humpty Dumpty comes from?"

"Well no," answers the unsuspecting, soon to be book buyer.

"It's in the book," replies Lester, with a big grin on his face, and the sale has begun.

Ever since I first met him, he's told me he has been working on a book chronicling his early years as a waif and orphan in Church of England orphanages and ensuing years in foster care beginning in World War II in England. When I asked to read his manuscript many years ago, he'd tell me it wasn't yet ready for human consumption, even though it has taken him 30 plus years to write. He merely told me that soon he'd give me a crack at it.

It wasn't until a few months ago that I actually got a chance to read it. I took in all in with one sitting and when I came back up for air, there was but one Anglo-Saxon word I could utter, and even though it wouldn't be appropriate to utter that word at this juncture, roughly translated the word was,

WOW!

Why, you may ask, did it take him so bloody long to write the book? As a tour director in England and Europe, and subsequently as a public speaker, the book has its roots as he began to relate tales from the events and experiences of his childhood to the captive audience on his tours. He was encouraged by his listeners to put those stories in book form.

What he went through as an orphan and foster child was so touching, yet at times so dismal and heart-wrenching, it was difficult for me to relate to some of it. Even though Lester is perhaps one of the funniest blokes I know, he had buried much of what he had gone through under the countless layers of his subconscious. Getting it out became his first step toward getting it down on paper.

But there is a quest for perfection inherent in the man as well, and he has spent all those decades not only dredging it up, but with the desire to make a jolly good presentation of it. He wanted to get it right. And what has emerged is both a timeless and priceless slice of life.

I do believe you will love The Violets Are Mine. It is tragic and at the same time comical, whimsical yet severe, and it remains a wonder how he kept his sense of humor throughout it all. For a glimpse of what transpired in those days, the book is not only his life but as well a personal look at a bygone era. Rest assured it will warm your heart and clear out your tear ducts, and roll you in the aisles with laughter. I would suggest you pour yourself a snifter, a shot, or cup of tea to warm you, light a fire in the fireplace, put on your robe and slippers, grab a box of tissue and begin Lester's journey.

Denniger Bolton
Author of the B. B. Rivers Mystery Series

Introduction

See me now as I was then
See the child behind my eyes
See my hopes, my loss
See my hurt, my pain
See me longing for love —
love that never came.
See my courage.
See my strength
See the will to survive
See my struggle and my triumph:
See my pride
See all this and stand amazed — at
The glory of spirit and soul.
Look again and see me as I was
Then see the child behind my eyes.
Celia McNicholas

On several occasions people have asked me. "Why have you written a memoir; only famous people write such books…and you're not famous…are you"?

My reply has always been, "Well no not famous, but I have a story to tell, and believe it or not, I was told to write it." And not being a writer, I had no idea that it would take me over 36 years to complete?

It was the early part of March, a Wednesday, and it was raining, and the year was in 1975 while in the Lake District that William D. Buckman (whom I will refer to as Bill) told me over a nice cup of afternoon tea and a sticky bun, that I should write a book about my life in an English orphanage during World War Two. I gave him an expression of surprise and informed him that I was not a writer, and because I had very little education I wouldn't know where to start.

After more tea and another sticky bun, we had a long chat and Bill actually convinced me to write some of my stories down, and he would on my next tour want to see a start on my manuscript. Bill Buckman had a travel agency in Chicago and put together some incredible European tours and because of the considerable cost for his custom tours, his passengers were of course, wealthy. His tours to Great Britain were mine. Bill and I got along very well and fortunately his regular passengers were also fun people.

Two chapters were written, so you see I was going through the motions of writing although it was by hand. While I was rewriting the story on a primitive typewriter when lo and behold, I got a long distance call from Bill reminding me of our next tour. He asked how my manuscript was going.

"Bring it with you on our next tour," was his message. He was looking forward to seeing me, but even more excited to see the start of my book.

Bill was impressed with what I had written, and each time I saw him he encouraged me to keep at it. It wasn't until another year has passed, on the traditional Christmas tour at Brocket Hall where we dressed in tuxedos and evening gowns every night for cocktails and dinner. It was at Brocket Hall that I made my mind up to earnestly pursue the writing of this book. A woman named Viola from New York asked me if she could read my manuscript, to which I was hesitant as I believed my grammar and spelling were not for anyone else's eyes but mine. After much persuasion on Viola's part, I gave in and gave it to her.

On Christmas Eve of 1976, Viola read my manuscript aloud to the group while having cocktails at Brocket Hall, and everyone including myself just stared with mouths wide open as she read my tales as we sat in front of the fire. You could hear a pin drop. Viola was an actress and read my manuscript far better that I wrote it. The ladies in attendance were drying their eyes. When she finished, everyone including Bill, told me to get the book finished.

Sadly many of those kind people who first heard my tale have since died, because I was never told *when* to get it finished.

So, that's how **The Violets Are Mine – Tales of an Unwanted Orphan** began.

The Violets Are Mine

Chapter One
A Very Unforgettable Day

All Saints Home was an orphanage, and was subjected like all of England to the *Blackouts* during World War II. It was a bit like a large bird cage having to be covered over at night, due to the relentless all night bombings performed by the Germans.

No, they didn't bomb us, but they made enough noise when flying over to cause some of the youngsters to cry, which in turn made it difficult for chaps like me to sleep. But the next day was Saturday, and I for one was ready to go outside and let off some steam.

What a miserable day that was. Another loud clap of thunder made us children jump yet again. The rain was pouring down, the tree I could see from the window, had branches blowing in every direction, and I had my nose pressed hard against the playroom window making the glass very foggy with my continuous heavy breathing and sighing.

I gave a big sigh, and as quick as I could, put my hands over my ears as soon as the assistant matron covered up hers. That was her signal to us little chaps that another bunch of noisy planes were about to fly over the orphanage. Sure enough, the noise was deafening.

"There must be a hundred planes," one of the boys shouted. We all looked hard at the matron, and seeing her hands drop to her side, we all did the same.

I ran up to the assistant matron and looked up at that puffy little face with her black hair that just flopped over her head, with not one little curl.

"What do you want Morris?" she snapped.

"I...er...was..."

"Well?" she snapped again, putting her face right down to mine.

I asked her, "Is the sun going to take its hat off today Matron?"

She pursed her lips up like she had tasted something nasty, like... our morning thick lumpy unsweetened porridge, and shook her head sideways saying, "NO, it looks like you're going to have to play in the playroom, all day."

As I slumped away, back to the windows, she continued by saying, "As soon as it stops raining young man, you can go outside, but not before."

For the rest of the morning, I had my nose pressed hard up against the playroom window, waiting and waiting, for that last raindrop to fall, so I could go outside to play, by now the window was all fogged up.

Occasionally, I would give a loud sigh, and furiously rub on the window, squinting to see if it had stopped raining. Sometimes when I rubbed the glass hard it would make a loud squeaking noise, and that would immediately get the attention of the assistant matron, as she did not like loud squeaky noises. Once again without thinking, I rubbed very hard, making that irritating sound, and immediately the assistant matron let out her cry.

"Who is responsible for that awful, revolting noise?"

All the children immediately pointed at me. The assistant matron marched over to me and grabbed my ear. My ears used to stick out more than other children, and they very often were too convenient in matters like that. She said in a snappy voice.

"How many times do I have to tell you not to make that infuriating noise?" After letting go of my ear, I cowered, expecting her to cuff me one like she always had in the past, instead she stormed away to terrorize another young lad for something he was up to, so I was relieved.

After wiping the glass again and again, then sitting on the play lockers sulking and staring at my shoes, I heaved another big boredom sigh and wiped the window again. I blinked and blinked, a smile was creeping across on my face.

I frantically rubbed another window and shouted that I just witnessed the last raindrop. My head hit the window, as I had to be sure it had stopped, I muttered excitedly to myself,

"It has...yes it's stopped...yes...it, it has stopped!" I pulled myself away from the steamed up window and went running up to the assistant matron. Looking up at her I shouted-

"Matron...Matron...it's... it's stopped raining, I just saw the last drop fall. Can I go outside to play?" I said in one short breath.

She looked down at me with one of those disbelieving looks, and with squinted eyes promptly marched over to the fogged up window. After a brisk wipe and that matron-like stare, she swung around, and said, "Yes."

Stooping down towards me waving her index finger in my face, she said with that voice of authority. I think she was thrown out of the SS for being too rough.

"You may go outside young master Morris..." She grabbed hold of my ear again and pulled me towards the back door, which was wide open, and she pointed directly at the green penny-farthing bike, and continued,

"Young Morris, if you intend riding that green "thing," keep it off the grass."

Still holding my ear and still pointing she went on, "Look at that grass; it looks like a plowed field where you have been riding that penny...bike...thing all over it." She was still holding my ear as I answered,

"Yes...er...a...matron."

Then I got to hear the usual golden rule when playing in the yard, the matron's finger now swung in the direction of the big double gate from the road to the play yard.

"Do not go out of that gate."

How many times I have I heard that announcement?

"Erm. No matron…now can I go outside?"

"Yes, young Morris and remember what I have told you."

Finally the assistant matron released my ear and I flew out the door like a ferret.

The orphanage was perched on top of a very steep hill. The gate the assistant matron referred to was the big doublewide gate that gave access to the orphanage from the road, and the gate was used for the delivery people, who were given strict instructions to always close it behind them. There was even a sign nailed on the gate.

On that particular morning, things turned out for the better regarding the gate, or should I also say the worst.

The green penny-farthing bike is the type that features an outsized front wheel and a minuscule wheel at the rear. The large wheel represented the large penny coin, and the small sized rear wheel represented a farthing coin, which was a quarter of a penny. The bike was painted green.

As I was going around and around the small tarmac area, and not on the grass as instructed, I become bored, because all the puddles were dry, and there didn't seem to be any more snails, worms or twigs to run over. And then something dramatic happened.

A local delivery van called at the orphanage. After he opened the gate and backed his vehicle in and made his delivery, I was still going around with my legs getting tired. I found myself going slower, but had to pick up speed to stay upright, so I peddled faster. I was hoping that one of the smaller lads would come outside so I could terrorize him. Now that would be fun. No, I was the only person out here except for the deliveryman and he had just driven away. Round and around I went until something caught my eye. And yes it was true.

The gate was still open. He had forgotten to close the gate! My neck was straining each time I circled around, causing me to nearly fall off the bike. I did notice that I was getting nearer to the gate each time I went round. Oh, the driver will return when he remembers he's left the gate open. But no, maybe one of the staff will notice it open and will come and shut it. Still nobody came outside. Maybe it was too cold for them?

By then, my neck was really hurting as I strained to look at the gate, wondering what was going to happen. Surly someone would come outside. But no. I did notice that the green penny-farthing bike seemed to be getting closer and closer to the gate. I thought, "I do believe I can get this bike through that gate in a hurry." After a final look around to see if anyone was watching and the coast was clear, I put all my effort into pushing those pedals around and would you believe it, the green thing was doing what it was built to do, riding like the wind. I pedaled as hard as I could and periodically would cock my head to one side, expecting my name to be shouted out by one of the staff. However the only sound I heard was the constant hum of the great big front wheel with its solid rubber tire.

I headed towards the vicarage and not down the hill. That would have been dangerous. It was a very steep hill. Now and then a raindrop fell from the trees that hung over the road. The cracking of small twigs and squishing of leaves, snails and tall grass that had flopped over onto the road, was great fun. The air was cold but fresh and I had the biggest smile on my face; I was now a happy little orphan. Faster and faster I pedaled and the humming of the front wheel was getting louder and louder. It was a bit frightening because I had no idea that it made that sound. I was approaching the vicarage driveway, which had a wide graveled driveway, just right to turn around without stopping.

After a cautious turnaround I looked back to see the distance I had traveled.

"Wow," I shouted, "that beats that little tarmac area I have been riding around on. I had better get back before I'm missed." So I although I didn't stop, it was hard work to build up the fast pace for the return trip. The scary humming soon started up again, and I figured, I'll get back to the orphanage even faster than I just came. So pedaling even faster created a noisy affair. And yet another clacking noise started up which I couldn't work out what it was, as I picked up speed, I noticed that one of the wooden blocks on the right hand pedal was flopping around every time it was in the down position.

Now the orphanage gate was in view and the speed I was going meant early braking. I stuck my legs out and squeezed hard up on the brake lever, and the metal plate pressed hard onto the solid front wheel. The humming sound was toning down and in turn the bike was slowing down. However, the gate was getting closer and closer. I squeezed even harder, but the whole brake lever just broke away.

I HAD NO BRAKES!

"NO!" I shouted as the gate went flying by me. I was now at the apex of the narrow, 1 in 10 country hill, picking up speed dramatically.

My eyes stuck out like chapel hat pegs. My hands ached as I held onto the handle bars. My knuckles were white gripping them. My bum was sore from sitting on that uncomfortable seat for a long time. My mouth was dry trying to scream, but nothing would come out.

The bike I was sure, had never moved so fast in all its life, and neither had I.

The steepness of the hill made my body lean way back. Then one of the blocks of wood flew off the pedals, which were going around at a tremendous rate, barely missing my head.

The green penny-farthing bike was going faster and faster, and I started to panic because I knew what my fate was, and there was nothing I could do about it. At the bottom of the hill there was a tee junction road, and across the road on the other side of it is a grass bank, and beyond that was a cold rocky brook. I started to fidget around wondering if I should jump, but when I got ready to jump, the bike wobbled out of control, so I froze to steady it up again. The wind howled around me ears. The tall grass lying across the road was squished by the big front wheel. My mouth was still dry as it was wide open trying to scream. My eyes squinted as bits of debris coming off the tires flew into them. Tears tried to flow, but they didn't stand a chance with all that was going on.

I was careening down the hill at a tremendous rate of speed, and before I knew it, there it was; the bottom of the road was approaching and the cold rocky brook was waiting for me. Within seconds the green penny-farthing bike went straight across the road, and as soon as the front wheel hit the grass bank, my scream bellowed out.

It was the longest and loudest scream I have ever produced which must have been heard by the whole village of Ashdon.

I flew over the handlebars through the air like a rag doll, and landed in the brook, with my body bouncing across the hard rocks. I was panicking and coughing up water which was cold, my eyes wide open wondering if that was it.

"Am I all right?"

I was looking around thinking that I had survived, but my whole body told another story. It ached and I felt bruised all over, and saw traces of blood flowing down stream. I sat in the cold water up to my chest gasping for air and choking, trying to get my breath back.

I looked over to the bike, seeing the front wheel was bent, the handle bars twisted, and the saddle dangling. One of the blocks from the pedals was floating but still attached with copper wire. I couldn't bear to look at it anymore, for the life of the green penny-farthing bike was over.

The next thing I heard was a ringing sound in my ears, which was getting nearer and nearer. Low and behold it was the local village policeman. He promptly leaned his bike up against a tree, took off his bicycle clips, rolled his trouser legs up, removed his helmet, and waded into the water to help me.

Although my vision was blurry because by now I was crying, not so much from my wounds, but because I knew I was in deep, deep trouble with the master and matron and now with the police. The policeman was saying something to me, but I had no idea what he was talking about. By then some of the villagers had turned up to see what was going on.

The policeman was now towering above me and thrust out his arms towards me and said, "I'd better get you out of there before a big fish gobbles you up."

I jumped up into his arms and as he dragged me out of the water, I was frantically looking out for a big fish that would gobble me up.

"You're one of the Home Boys aren't you?"

As he helped me up the bank of the river, I looked up at the policeman and with my lips quivering; I nodded and said, "Yes."

There were a half dozen villagers standing and talking. I looked up at an old lady who had her hair in curlers, her arms folded and an empty wicker shopping basket in her hand, shaking her head, saying to her friend,

"I wouldn't like to be in his shoes when he gets back to that big orphanage...they will knock some sense into him believe me. I know, I used to work up there."

The policeman gave her a look of disapproval, shaking his head from side to side. We started our long climb back up the hill.

Walking in wet clothes on a cold damp day was a struggle. My shoes made a squelching tone with each step, and the policeman's made a similar sound. Under different terms it may have been an entertaining sound. But that event was far from entertaining.

"What made you go down this dangerous hill on the green bike? It's bad enough driving a car down it."

I shivered the words out by saying, "I didn't want to go down the hill, but the brake lever fell off...and I couldn't stop?" He stopped to get his breath back, and said,

"You know you're lucky you were not hit by a car. You could have been killed...do you realize that?"

My head hung in shame, but he lifted my chin up.

"I'm sorry. Come on," he said "we've got to get you out of those wet clothes."

We heard a voice from down the hill calling up to us. The policeman and I both looked together and lo and behold it was a villager carrying "Exhibit A" – One bent, buckled up, green penny-farthing bike. My eyes filled up looking at it.

"Come on," said the policeman, taking my hand as we squelched further up the hill. As we neared the top, there was a welcoming committee waiting for us.

The whole of the orphanage, including staff, was waiting for me at the big gate out on the road. I could see some of the lads pointing and some were laughing at me, but matron was the one to come and greet me, immediately followed by the master. I started trembling even more, and it wasn't from the cold.

The matron gave me one her looks – one that would *stun a Doberman at 50 yards*. She reached out to grab me but the policeman pulled me towards him.

"He's been through quiet a fright...so I think you should..."

He stopped talking when the master came over and took over the situation.

"Right Master Morris, I think you owe this policeman an apology for getting him into this mess."

"He's already done that," said the policeman. So the master grabbed my hand and led me on through the welcoming crowd. My head was hung low and lads were shouting that I was in big trouble. Just before I went through the door, a lad shouted.

"Look at the green bike!"

The villager had carried it into the play yard, and all the lads gathered around to examine Exhibit A – one bent up, un-reparable, green penny-farthing bike.

The matron escorted the policeman through to the big bathroom, and after sitting him down on a chair, asked the assistant matron to make him a nice cup of tea. (*In England everything is always sorted out with a nice cup of tea.*) I wondered if I would also get a hot drink.

By then, I was shivering with cold, but it was mainly from fear, knowing that when the policeman left, I would then suffer. The assistant matron stripped me naked and counted aloud all the bruises. It was only then that I noticed how much blood and scratches I had over my body. No wonder I was hurting. I was plunged into more water, which was cold but not as cold as the brook, and I was being washed all over by a day staff who was using a great big bar of red carbolic soap to bathe me. I could hear the master and matron saying goodbye to the policeman, and I felt like shouting.

"No don't leave me."

But suddenly I had a big flannel filled with the awful soap rubbed vigorously all over my face. I knew it wasn't the day care lady. No, the matron had taken over and was viciously scrubbing my face which was already sore. I screamed out at her and got a hard slap across the face.

"You haven't felt anything yet, Master Morris. Oh no, we have only just begun."

Then the master came into the bathroom shouting,

"Where is he? Where is that horrible child who is giving the orphanage a bad name?"

The matron asked in a quieter tone, "has the policeman gone?"

"Yes I drove him down the hill to his bicycle, he said he would not report the incident, for which I thanked him," then looking back at me in the tub, he said,

"Get him out of there."

I was dragged out of the bath kicking and saying, "No, No please don't hit me master I said I was sorry."

Wallop went his hand across my face. He then dragged me across his knee and started slapping my bum, which was already sore. I was now screaming. The master told the matron to go and get his cane from his study.

I now knew that I had really done something bad to get the cane, and I begged him not to but that got him even angrier.

"You'll regret the day you learned to ride that green bike."

The next thing the matron came into the bathroom with the swishy cane and she willingly gave it to the master. I screamed as loud as I could and he hadn't even hit me but with the first squish it made my bum numb with pain.

But then it happened. The bathroom door opened and who should walk in? The policeman.

"I left my wet socks here." He started frowning when he spotted the master with the cane raised high, ready to put another mark on my bum. He quickly pushed me off his knee onto the hard stone floor

"Is all that really necessary?" asked the policeman.

"This young man is a disgrace to the orphanage…and he must be punished."

The policeman retrieved his socks and pointed to me, saying.

"Look at his body full of cuts and bruises. Don't you think he has suffered enough? I gave him a lengthy talk bringing him up the hill and asked questions, and from what I understand he really understood how serious and dangerous his escapade was."

The master stood with the cane behind his back motionless. Nobody said a word. The policeman walked towards the door, but before he left he turned.

"I don't know if you are aware of it, but there is a war going on out there and many people are being killed and severely wounded. I didn't expect to see severely wounded children in an orphanage." Just before he left, he looked at me and gave a faint smile and then winked. The master was furious, as soon as the policeman left, the master shouted in a demanding voice.

"Who let that policeman back in?"

"One of the day staff may have done…or it could have been one of the children…" said the assistant matron.

She was cut off by the matron, who said,

"Get him up to the sick room out of our sight, and with no food… and put some Iodine on his wounds."

"Lot's of it," shouted the master, "and no food until tomorrow night."

As I walked past, the master he slapped me on the back of my head and muttered something. Then the matron followed suit by giving me a slap across my face and then shouted, "Get that horrible child up to the sickroom now."

The assistant matron took me up there and gave me another lecture as to what a naughty child I was, and then she found great delight in dabbing my cuts and wounds with Iodine and watching me scream again. I had to stay in the sick room for a whole week, eating mainly bread and powdered warm milk.

One day the assistant matron came into my room with some more horrible powdered milk stuff, which actually made me feel sick at the sight of it. Involuntarily I blurted out, "No more of that bloody milk stuff…"

I automatically cowered, expecting a slap across the face. But no. She simply put my tray on my side table and disappeared without a word. Within minutes the sickroom door opened quickly, and in walked the matron, towering over me saying.

"Why did you use a swear word to the assistant matron?" My face was bright red and I sat up staring at matron wondering what she meant.

"What swear word?" I asked. The matron turned around and said to the assistant matron in a commanding voice. "Bring him to the bathroom, now." I had no idea what was going to happen.

Once in the bathroom, I heard the sound of a running tap. By my arm, I was dragged to the sink and the matron told me in her official voice.

"Do you know what happens to children who swear in this orphanage? They have their mouths washed out with SOAP and WATER to clean out the vulgar language in them."

As I was trying to say something, a large well soaked bar of carbolic soap was rammed into my mouth, and was being twisted backwards and forwards from side to side so that my teeth collected a quantity of the stuff. The assistant matron was holding my head and the matron was shouting at me saying what a bad boy I was using foul language and that the treatment would help me to remember that I was not to swear at all.

Then she gave a final twist and pulled the soap out, making sure she scrapped more soap on my teeth. The matron was still talking to me while I was coughing and spluttering in the sink. While rinsing my mouth out with water, I never heard a word she said, and with the swishing of their outfits, they both disappeared. As soon as they left I shouted,

"Bugger…Bugger…Bugger," but thank goodness they never heard a word of it.

Chapter Two
My Home on the Hill

It appears I was brought into this world at a very early age, and have a piece of paper to prove it. The piece of paper clearly states that on February 10, 1940 I was born into a very unpredictable world at a place called Woburn Green, in Buckinghamshire, west of London. Apparently, I only lasted one year before being dumped by my father into St. Agatha's Nursery, Princess Risborough, also in Buckinghamshire. I was too young to remember those days, but what I do know is that I was left in the capable hands of the Church of England Children's Society as a "waif and stray" orphan.

You know, I never did find out whether I was a waif or a stray. I do know what I was called at times, but it was neither of those!

The Church of England Children's Society is a charitable organization still dealing with children to this day, but they no longer operate homes. Sadly, most of the homes have left their hands, just like all the thousands of children that were raised in them. These days, the Society places children in the care of foster parents throughout Great Britain.

Some of the homes that had the pleasure of my presence have since closed or been demolished. I stayed in a total of four homes; two are still standing, and no doubt carry the echoes of my shouting, some laughing, and some echoes of screaming.

By now you may be wondering what happened to my parents to make me an orphan? I had absolutely no idea when I was a young lad, and didn't find out until much later in life. So I hope you don't mind if I keep you in suspense for a while, just like I was for many years. You, however, will only have to wait a few pages.

What qualifies me to write the memoir of my life? Well, that was what I asked the people who said I should write it. The main person who encouraged me to do it was a highly recognized business man from Chicago. You see, after telling him and all the tourists I was involved with as a tour guide in the U.K. and Europe, stories about my childhood, these new friends from the USA, where I live now, and in England, encouraged, even nagged me, to get on with it.

I was only knee-high to a grasshopper, aged three, when I was transferred on October 27, 1943, from St. Agatha's Nursery to one of the many orphanages run by the Society. That particular one was called All Saints Home, and was tucked away in the tiny village of Ashdon, near Saffron Waldon, Essex. The village was so small that it had hump-backed mice.

The home was perched on top of a very large hill in the middle of nowhere, surrounded by lots of countryside. The road leading from the village up to the home was long, steep, and narrow, with tall hedges on either side. It had sharp banks with all types of weeds and grasses towering up, trying to compete with the tall hedges. That was the hill that I, at the tender age of seven, had careened down on the green penny-farthing bike.

Just up the road, through the trees, you could see one of our neighbors, the vicarage, which had a well-manicured grounds spread out in front of the building. There was another house beyond it that always looked a bit on the creepy side. It was possibly due to the presence of a large bloodhound that roamed the grounds. When it barked or howled the sound echoed around the dense woodland that surrounded the house and sent shivers down your spine.

The orphanage accommodated 24 children, so the building was quite large inside, or at least it seemed that way to me. Upstairs there were two big dormitories, one for the younger boys and one for the older ones. The sick room was in between the dormitories, tucked away next to the upstairs toilets and washrooms. Up a few more stairs was the assistant matron's bedroom. The master and matron's bedroom was situated between the two dormitories.

At the end of each dormitory there was a wooden hatch built into the wall with a sliding door that could only be opened from inside the master and matron's bedroom. That was to check on us. If we were making too much noise or misbehaving, they could shout and give orders without coming into the rooms.

There were some places that were strictly out of bounds for us little chaps: the master and matron's bedroom, of course, and the master's study, which was also his office and private lounge. Others were the kitchen, unless you were on jobs duty; the sick room, unless you were sick or on punishment.

The fire escape was the first thing that would strike you when you saw the home, apart from its bright-red brickwork and the black slate roof. It was a heavy, wrought-iron affair with several coats of thick black paint on it. The whole thing twisted and turned like a creeping plant and appeared to be taking over the house. The only time we children were allowed on it was during the once-a-month fire drill, when we all had to walk down the iron steps to the ground. It vibrated and made loud clanking sounds when you stamped your feet hard on each step. Sometimes we overdid it and got shouted at. But we actually looked forward to it, since the stairs were out of bounds at any other time.

Whenever a new boy arrived at the home, he was issued some clothing, shown to a bed, and assigned a play locker in the play-room, which was on the ground floor near the rear of the home. The play lockers were floor-level boxes built around the walls of the play-room with seating on top. That was where we could put all of our worldly goods like toys, books or whatever. I didn't have anything to put in my locker, but just the thought that it was mine made things seem all right.

Actually, I was given one thing – a teddy bear. It was a pathetic-looking creature, made of very faded sacking material, and had been handed down from what looked like a hundred previous boys. It had no eyes, except for some that were heavily crayoned in, no right arm, and hardly any fur. Little bits of wood shavings kept falling out of the holes, which were badly stitched. It looked like it had been through hell.

But it was mine, and as I had never owned a teddy bear before, I made it my friend. The other lads teased me about it and called it all sorts of names. I remember boldly thrusting it out at arm's length in the playroom one day, staring at it for awhile, and then shouting so all could hear:

"I'll call him Henry, and I'll look after him for the rest of my life, because he's mine!"

One of the things I remember most about the playroom was that it had paintings on the walls. All around the room there were hunting scenes in oils, with horses and hounds painted with incredible detail and heavily varnished. I had heard they had been painted by one of the previous masters. I used to stand on top of the lockers and gaze at them, sometimes reaching up to touch them, hoping they would move because they looked so real. I even gave names to some of the horses and dogs.

In the far corner of the room was another eye-catcher: a large, intricately carved rocking horse, which in its early days must have looked very impressive. The horse made a sort of squeaking sound when it was in motion; it was in bad need of a good oiling. The color, which was supposed to be gray and white, was very faded, and where the tail should have been, there were just a few strands of hair sticking out.

The hair for its mane was in short supply as well. There were a couple of long straggly bits that looked like they had been curly at one time. The leather saddle was badly torn, and the original leather stirrups had been replaced by some thick pieces of rope. Still it kept many of the children happy sitting on the thing.

All the new children were immediately attracted to that large horse. The very first thing they wanted to do was jump up on it, and I was no exception. I climbed up and had fun rocking it backwards and forwards, until an older boy came over and told me to get off; it was his turn.

Well, you don't argue with someone bigger than yourself, so I jumped off and gladly let him get on. In return, he gave me one of those big boy smiles.

The only other notable features of the playroom were a built-in fireplace with a heavy iron guard to stop us from getting too close, and lots of windows, which made the room, seem big and bright even on a dark and miserable day, of which there were many.

The playroom had all sorts of things to keep us children entertained and we were allowed to play in there any time it was raining, which as I said, was often. But when it was not raining, they turned us all outside. No doubt by allowing us to run around and let off steam, we would tire ourselves out, and be eager to sleep at night and not fool around. We had cars to push around, trains with a few pieces of track, and a large yellow dump truck that I used to play with for hours. One of the wheels was a bit wobbly, so it clunked when you pushed it. I'd get bored tipping it with nothing inside, so I used to sneak outside and get some sand from the sandpit to put in the back. Then I happily loaded and unloaded it, pushing it around and tipping the sand out onto the floor.

Although the dump truck made me happy, the staff was not. Several times, one of them loudly asked, "Who is responsible for all this sand on the playroom floor?"

Everyone would go deathly quiet, including myself, but for some reason the staff member would automatically walk up to me. After the second time, I realized that was because all the other children were pointing their fingers at me, which seemed to be a habit with these children. I was told that in the future I could use sand only when playing outside.

The playroom also had a large biscuit tin filled with lead soldiers of all shapes and sizes, some had traces of blue lead paint on them and the others were red. Little did we know then about the health threats of lead. A lad named Robin Peck and I would often lie on the wood floor, positioning out our soldiers to play a game of war. Things would go well for awhile, but then he kept ordering me to knock over my soldiers because he had shot them. I would reluctantly knock some of my men over. Now if the assistant matron were nearby during one of our "discussions" she would come over and sort the war out by scooping up all the lead soldiers and putting them in the tin.

"And that's the end of that!" she would say. But, she was not around one particular day when I had told Robin that I had shot some of his men. He wouldn't knock them down, so we ended up in a big argument over the game. Robin flatly refused to knock his men down when I ordered him to, sitting there with his arms folded, shouting,

"No...No...No."

I immediately scooped up four of his men, bit their heads off, spat the heads down in front of him, and then threw down the bodies.

"Now they're dead," I shouted.

He went into a rage and ran as fast as he could to report me to the master, who came storming into the playroom as I was trying to put the heads back on. I gave him my best innocent look. That, of course, never worked with him.

Robin stooped down and picked up two of the soldiers and handed them to the master. The master looked at the pieces in his hand and then looked at me.

"What happened here, Master Morris?" he asked in a stern voice. He always used the word "Master" when he was angry or trying to impress someone.

I stood up and stuttered, "Erm, well...they, er, the heads...they just fell off, Master."

The master rolled the heads between his fingers, then looked at the bodies, putting his face right up to mine, "These heads did not just fall off, Master Morris. It is just as Master Peck stated. They were *bitten* off by you, Master Morris, which means that you are not allowed to play with the soldiers any more. Do you understand?"

I reluctantly replied that I understood. He then gave me quick slap on the side of my head then stormed off. I glanced up at Robin, who had the biggest grin on his face. While I was holding my throbbing head I decided to go hide in the toilet.

The toilets were just outside the playroom near the back door. They weren't the best place to hide because they had no doors, but it was where children who were sulking could go to cool off. They also had no toilet paper. Whenever you wanted to do "big jobs," you had to get hold of a member of staff and request some paper. But if it happened to be too late for that, you just had to go and sit on the toilet and keep shouting to get attention or send another child to find some. On a busy day, you could sit there for a long, long time waiting for that bit of paper. I remember once dropping off to sleep while waiting. Also, I remember all of us running around like penguins at one time or another, holding up our trousers and shouting for paper. But most of the time the staff was on hand.

During the war, we didn't have the soft paper-tissue stuff that we use today; it was newspaper, cut up or torn into handy-size sheets. That part was fine; at least we had a picture to stare at or something to read, although I couldn't read yet. The problem was that they didn't give you many pieces of paper, which meant you'd often have to sit and shout for more. If you were an older chap, you would check all the six toilets and steal the paper from a smaller chap. The he'd have to do his own shouting instead. So some days we little chaps ended up with a sore bum and a sore throat.

The dreaded big bathroom, which was also the main washroom, was downstairs. The only good thing about it was that it had more paintings to look at. The master who had painted the playroom had painted tadpoles and frogs around that room, which brightened it up a bit.

Most of us children learned to hate the washroom because of Bath Night, which was held each Wednesday after tea whether we needed it or not. Three large sparkling white baths stood high on bowed, cast-iron legs right in the middle of the room. Each tub had its own wooden slatted drip board leaning up against it, waiting for the next torture session. In between each set of shiny chrome taps was a large white-enamel water jug, also proudly waiting to be used on us poor little beggars.

When you climbed into the bath, which was always cold and slippery, you would sit there and gaze up at the staff members towering above you, anxiously awaiting your fate. Each time they spoke, their voices echoed around the hollow tub.

Bath night was rather like an assembly line, with one member of staff washing hair and continuously telling us to sit still and stop that screaming, and one or more others doing the rinsing. You would sit there and cringe with eyes full of that awful red carbolic soap which they also washed your hair with, waiting and waiting for someone to fill the jug with COLD water, which seemed to take an eternity.

Then it would come crashing down over your head. You would gasp in shock and end up with a mouthful of water, sometimes soapy water that would make you gasp, cough and choke before you got your breath back. And then another big jug-full would come crashing down. That process was repeated several times, enough so you thought you were going to drown, all while you were being told to keep your hands down and not to rub your eyes.

The enamel jugs were branded the "dd jugs," short for "dreaded drowning jugs." But once you survived that, you were squeaky clean and could relax until the next Wednesday, when you had to suffer the same process again.

After our baths, we would be sent upstairs to bed. Our beds were made of iron, and were a bit like military beds so they could withstand the pounding of little chaps like me who would jump up and down on them. The annoying thing about the beds was the springs that made noises whenever there was any movement. What with children tossing and turning all night, it always sounded like someone was knitting a barbed-wire fence.

My bed in the bigger chap's dormitory was just behind the door to the little chap's dormitory, with the head of my bed right by a window. One of the first things we learned regarding the beds was not to run your hand under the metal sides. The reason was quite simple. That was where children stick their buggers, and yes, my bed was covered with these things – big ones, small ones – all clinging on like limpets and barnacles.

Each of us was responsible for the making of his bed upon arising, which was normally at 6:30 am on school days 7:00 am on Sundays and school holidays. As soon as you got up you stood by your beds waiting for a quick inspection by a member of the staff to see that we had, or had not, wet the bed.

There was a correct way to make the bed, which included not forgetting to do the envelope corners. We were always reminded not to make our beds on Wednesdays. On that day, the bedding had to be left neatly pulled back to allow for a good airing. Sheet change was every two weeks, but during the war it sometimes dragged on a bit.

The large dining room had six tables with four chairs to each table spread throughout the room, with a larger table positioned in a prominent position for the staff to sit and keep an eye on us during meal times. None of the three, sometimes four staff sat with their backs to us. It was part of their job making sure we ate what was placed in front of us, and not to waste or swap food with each other.

The master and matron had their spoiled little dog with them at meal times and he was also under stick control. He sat under the table and if you tried to lure him out for scraps, he was promptly told to get back in his place, and with that voice of command from matron, he did as he was told just like us children.

Because it was during the war, we had a restriction on all foods, so sometimes we had good meals other times we had whatever the staff could produce. With twenty four hungry children and staff to feed every day, it must have been very difficult.

For breakfast, it was normally the dreaded bowl of porridge, which sounds all right but was thick and very lumpy. It had no sweetening or flavor. You could load up your spoon up with the stuff and turn it upside down, and the porridge would remain clinging to your spoon refusing to drop. Sometimes you would bite into a hard lump of that stuff and inside the lump would be the dry porridge, causing you to choke. The assistant matron would come to the rescue and take shear delight in slapping you on the back, especially if she didn't like you.

The windows overlooked the outdoor play area, which was a small, rough area of tarmac with a sandpit next to it. We also had a large field with a set of swings and a seesaw, with plenty of room to run around in and let off steam. At the far end of the tarmac was a large storage shed that resembled a barn.

We weren't allowed to go into the shed part that was normally locked, but the other end without doors, we would go and hang around in there. That is where we played when it was raining because they didn't want us dragging wet, muddy feet and drippy clothes through the house. We also weren't allowed in the front of the house because it didn't have a gate; just a pull-in for cars and a fancy front door. Most people would use the back gate, where you could walk directly into the kitchen. That was where all the deliveries came through.

Now that back gate was a large wooden one with big, heavy hinges that opened inwards. It served two main functions in regards to us children. First, and most important, was to keep all of us lads in. Second was to keep the village children out. You see, as with most homes, we were known as the "Home Boys," and they were known as the "Village Kids," and there were always rivalries between us. Let's face it, the village children could spot us a mile off. Our clothes were the giveaway. We attended school in the village, and for school we always wore blue jackets, gray trousers, gray shirts, and gray socks–all hand-me-downs. For church on Sunday we would wear, yes, our best gray clothes, and for playing, we wore our rough grays. So there was no hiding the fact that you were a Home Boy.

Sometimes the local children would stand outside the large gate and call us names and mock us. Naturally, we shouted back. Then the master would come out and ask them to leave, in a polite sort of way.

The master and matron who ran the orphanage was a married couple in their mid-forties. He was a very neat chap of medium height who had the appearance of a very official person, which he was. The matron looked like, well, like a matron, the sort you see at a hospital. She always wore a blue uniform with starched white cuffs and a white hat thing, which sat on her head and fanned out on each side like she was getting ready for take off. Like the master, the matron was very neat at all times.

Then there was the assistant matron, who was quite the reverse. She was a dumpy little woman with short black hair of no particular style. She had certain peculiarities about her. When she was angry at you she would draw her puckered lips to the side of her mouth and talk in a peculiar manner. These manners we would have fun imitating, when she was not around of course.

She wore a blue nurse's outfit, but it wasn't neatly starched, and was maybe a little too large for her. When she came after you for what ever reason, you could hear the loud rustling of her outfit long before she got to you. She was very stern, especially if the master or matron were around. She seemed to put on a show just for them. If they weren't around, she would simply box your ears and go off and terrorize the next child.

There were other helpers at the home, the staff, who would come in now and then, along with two daily helpers that were more warm and friendly toward us. If we were in trouble, we were inclined to go to them for a little bit of sympathy.

One of them I remember very well. Her name was Mrs. Woodley. She was like a fairy godmother, and is locked in my memory forever. She died in 2009 aged 103, and I've spent many a grand moment with the dear lady throughout my life. During our years in Ashdon, she took a special interest in my brother and me.

Oh, didn't I tell you I had a brother there? I didn't know it either for awhile. This was how I found out I had a brother: One day, when we were both having a rough and tumble over that big toy yellow dump truck which I always liked to play with, the assistant matron heard the commotion and rushed to sort the situation out. And after Douglas told his story, she took the truck from me and gave it to him to play with. As the assistant matron was walking away I shouted to Douglas,

"She only let you have the truck because you're big and ugly."

The assistant matron swung around, waiving her finger in my face and shouted, "That's no way to talk to your brother, now you apologize to him right now." Doug and I just stood and stared at each other frowning. We both looked up at the assistant matron and asked.

"What's a brother?"

The assistant matron looked at us both and said with her lips all twisted. "It means that you're both related to each other." She then promptly walked away muttering to herself. We both looked at each other and said,

"Brothers?"

I still had no idea what a brother was, but I said I was sorry to Doug, and he gave me back the truck. He was three years older than I was. So that's how I found out I had a brother. By the way, he was the older lad who told me to get off the rocking horse so he could get on. Later in life, he at first denied the rocking horse incident, but later confessed.

Mrs. Woodley used to collect some of the kitchen scraps, like potato peelings, cabbage stalks, and any leftovers that couldn't be reused, and take them home. She would then boil them in an old cauldron, adding a bit of this and a bit of that with some sort of wheat mixture which included the rejected left over porridge. She would take her concoction and feed it to her chickens.

Sometimes she would take Doug and me to her lovely old thatched cottage down in the village, and allow us to feed the chickens. To get there, we would cut through a vast, golden-brown cornfield, trying to scare out rabbits along the way. The bit I liked best was when she would let us go hunting in her garden for fresh eggs. We used to look forward to that, and got all excited whenever we found one, holding it up for inspection like it was a rare prize. Once I went to reach for an egg and stepped on another I didn't see, I thought I was in big trouble.

Douglas shouted, "Mrs. Woodley, Les has just trod on an egg."

But Mrs. Woodley merely replied, "Oh…that's all right," and scooped it up and added it into the chicken feed. Doug, being the oldest, used to collect the most. No, my brother and I will never forget that lovely lady.

I arrived at the home in Ashdon during the war. Yes, the Second World War.

Although I can't remember too much about those early years at the home, the one thing that sticks in my mind was the loud noises from the planes when flying directly over the home. The big bombers that flew low used to vibrate everything in the orphanage, and some of us smaller chaps used to latch on to one of the staff for comfort. If Mrs. Woodley was nearby most of the children, including me would run up to her for a group hug. She would pat us on the heads and say,

"Now, now there's nothing to worry about, they are just big old noisy old planes flying over us."

But it was the Spitfire planes that without warning would zoom over at such a speed that would make the littlest chaps cower in the corner of the room. It took some time to encourage them to come out and join the rest of us.

The worst time for me was during the night. A plane would suddenly fly over without warning and wake us all up. Some children would just lay there and cry, some would scream louder than what the plane had.

At last, everything would settle down to peace and quiet again. An hour later more planes would roar overhead, and the commotion started all over again. Eventually, most of us got used to it all.

It was the *Blackouts* that added fear and mystery to what was going on. Each window in the home by law had to be blacked out. A black pull-down blind or some dark material was pinned up over it to avoid showing the enemy where the buildings were. Obviously, you didn't want to make the bombing of a house too easy by having it all lit up. Very few lights were used, and those that were used were normally very dim. Not even the slightest crack or hole in the material was allowed. These were put in place every evening at dusk before any lighting was switched on.

It was a bit frightening for us little ones because the only nightlight we had in the dormitories was the faint glow from a light that was left on in the hall. The darkness was bad enough, but there were also a lot of strange war noises going on outside.

Anyway, when people ask me how far back I can remember, those blackouts are as far back as I can go. You see, one night, instead of going to sleep like all the other children, I couldn't settle in, so I kept peeping behind the blackout blind, which was conveniently located at the head of my bed. The assistant matron, who seemed to be constantly on patrol, had already told me several times to go to sleep like a good boy.

Well I tried, but I couldn't sleep because of all the noise. After awhile the temptation was too great, so I had to get up to see what on earth was going on outside. I mean, nobody had told me there was a war on, as if I even knew what a war was anyway. I could hear planes going over and the sound of what must have been a large convoy roaring along a road in the distance. I knelt on my pillow with the blind pulled to one side, staring at the flames in the distance, and the lights flashing in all different directions. I kept turning my head from side to side, looking intently but not knowing what I was seeing.

All of a sudden, I felt a sharp pain across my left ear. I let out a loud howl, which must have woken the entire house. As I spun around, I found the assistant matron leaning over me and waving her finger as her mouth soundlessly opened and closed. She was telling me off, but I couldn't hear a word she was saying because my ears were ringing from the boxing I had just received.

I sat there holding my ear, tears rolling down my face. Then the assistant matron dragged my bed into the center of the room, away from temptation. I remember sitting in the middle of the dormitory with the other lads laughing at me, but I had no idea why. What had I done wrong?

Not long after that, I managed to get whooping cough and then German measles, so I was confined to the sick room. Everyone, no doubt, gave a sigh of relief, as they now were able to get a good night's sleep.

That was the first time I was in the sick room for actually being sick. It was a miserable experience. None of the other children were allowed to visit, and I hated the sick room diet – hot powdered milk in a cereal bowl with great dollops of soggy bread floating around in it. Not even a spoonful of sugar. And if you didn't eat it the matron or assistant matron would on their periodic visits, see that you weren't eating and wake you up. I tried to fake sleep, hoping that they would go away, but they woke me up anyway.

They would then launch into a lecture about wasting food when there is a shortage during the war, and then start shoveling it down you, including the dreadful skim that was lurking on top of the milk.

To me, the sick room was also a punishment room, because I was sent there often when I knew I wasn't sick. It was scary being in that very small room all alone, which only had one window that was too high to look out of. It didn't even have a picture hanging on the wall. Well, it did, but it was a frame of many colors which if you stared at it long enough, you could find a picture in there somewhere.

The one thing the sick room did have, was a handmade quilted bedspread, which I remember to this day because it was full of different materials. There were a few solid colors, but most of the pieces were made up of unique patterns, so when I was bored, which was quite often, I used to count the patterns to pass the time, and if I was still bored, I would look at that picture thing.

Periodically, the assistant matron would stop in to see if I was all right and take my temperature. Mostly I think she was just going through the motions. All the time I was in there, I would look at the door whenever I heard someone and fervently hope it was a friend with food or something nice.

One day, during my convalescence, the door opened and dear Mrs. Woodley came in. She always wore a wrap-around pinnie, or apron, with pockets on the front. I asked her when I was getting out of there, and she said, somewhat hesitantly,

"Soon...soon, I'm sure."

Then she slipped her hand into her pocket and gave me a crust of bread.

"Oh thank you, Mrs. Woodley," I cried, but she put her finger up to her mouth and went,

"Shush, I have something else for you." And then she produced a boiled egg. It was covered in lint and stuff from her pocket, but she told me to eat it quickly before someone came in.

Just after I had gulped it down, who should walk in but the assistant matron, who gave Mrs. Woodley a stern look, and asked coldly,

"Hello, Woody," for that's what the grown-ups called her, "what are you doing here?"

"Oh, hello, well, I have work to do. I just wanted to drop by to see how the little chap was doing," Mrs. Woodley said, and off she went.

"How do you feel, Master Morris?" the assistant matron asked, not very kindly.

"Fine," I said, but just then a little bit of egg flew out of my mouth. The assistant matron frowned and exclaimed, "That was food that came out of your mouth!"

She frantically started looking over the bedspread, which fortunately made the bit invisible. It turns out that she was color-blind anyway.

"It sounds like you can get out of here tomorrow then, if all is well." She tucked my bedding in so she could have another scan over the bedspread for evidence, but she obviously saw nothing, so, off she went with that suspicious look of hers.

As soon as she left, I laid there with a big smile on my face, knowing that with a bit of luck I would be out of there the next day. I think I got to know every square inch of that sick room, like the hand sewn tapestry bedspread which had a total of 37 different patterns of material.

Chapter Three

On a Dare

One fine sunny day, a group of us children were sitting outside on the grass picking daisies, when who should appear but dear Mrs. Woodley.

"What are you going to do with those daisies now that you have picked them?" she asked with a smile on her face.

We all just sat there, staring up at her with our hands full of daisies. Then William asked, "What do you mean? What can we do with them?"

Mrs. Woodley promptly knelt down and took some of my daisies and said,

"Let me show you how to make a daisy chain." We all huddled around her and she showed us what to do. "Use your thumbnail to make a slit in the stalk of one of the daisies. Then get the stalk from another one and thread it through the slit like this, and so on." She started threading, and was going on until she was suddenly summoned into the house.

"Well, looks like I'm needed somewhere else."

As she walked away, I asked, "What do we do with them when they're made?"

"Oh! You have to present them to a lady, of course."

And so, after a bit of muttering about ladies, we all got busy again.

It was during that daisy-chain day that I did my very first "dare." You see, I saw a ladybug beetle crawling around the daisies, so I picked it up, letting it run all over my hands. I was fascinated with the little thing, with its bright-red wings and black spots. I counted seven spots on its back.

"That's their age," said William.

I counted the spots again. "So it's seven years old," I said.

Then everyone started giving their opinions on the matter, and then some of them even tried to take my ladybug from me. To stop all that, I told them that if they kept on I would eat it. I can't believe I even thought of that, let alone said it.

That's when it happened. All the children stood around me and dared me to eat the ladybug or they were going to take it from me. I immediately adopted a mean look and announced that no one was going to take it from me. I slowly uncurled my hand, picked it up between my thumb and my index finger, and put it into my mouth.

At that, the lads all created such a noise that the assistant matron and the matron herself came running out to find out what had happened. The children all crowded around me and screaming that Les, as I was called, had eaten a ladybug.

By then, I was feeling a little queasy, but I had managed to manipulate the bug under my tongue. With arms folded, the matron stood in front of me and squawked,

"What's all this about you eating a ladybug? Didn't you have enough breakfast?"

I tried to mumble something out of the side of my mouth, which didn't come out very clearly. So the matron tilted my head back and commanded,

"Open your mouth, wide! Let me see if we really have an insect-eating child at Ashdon."

After looking all around my mouth, she asked with a strange frown,

"Did you actually swallow that bug?"

With my mouth still wide open, I nodded. The matron turned to her assistant and said, "see if you can see any bugs in Master Morris's mouth," and stepped to one side. The assistant matron held my head back and demanded that I open my mouth even wider. She brought her face very close to mine and gazed hard inside.

"No," she said. "I cannot see any bugs in Master Morris's mouth. If he did put it in, he obviously..." She suddenly stopped talking, because at the same time, I felt a movement on my lower lip. The ladybug was crawling out of my mouth!

Both women put their hands over their mouths in horror.

"Well, well," said the matron. "So it is true we have a bug-eating child at Ashdon."

Then I heard one of the lads shout, "Grab the ladybird! Quick, get it!"

I could feel them crowding me, so without warning, I flicked out my tongue out like a chameleon, drew the bug back into my mouth, gave a couple of chews, and swallowed the thing.

Then I stood there with a faint smile on my face, looking at the matron's eyes, which were sticking out like chapel hat pegs, her mouth wide open. Everyone was looking at me in disbelief. For a few seconds, it was deadly silent, and then all sorts of comments started flying around.

"I don't believe what I just saw!" shrieked the matron. "Open your mouth again, Master Morris."

So there I was again, mouth wide open, ready for inspection. The matron took one look inside, and turned to the assistant matron.

"Yes, he's got bits of bug in his mouth. I don't believe it! I just don't believe that one of my children would eat insects!" she moaned, and turned to walk away shaking her head, still muttering.

My brother Doug ran up to her and said, "Les was eating the bug as a dare! He doesn't normally eat bugs, at least, not that I know of," he added, throwing me a frown.

"Oh," said the matron, who seemed to be a bit relieved that it wasn't a normal thing for me to do. "But don't you come crying to me if you have an upset tummy, Master Morris!"

And away she went, inspecting the daisy chains that the lads handed her as she passed by. When she was out of sight, Doug ran up to me and asked, "Are you all right mate? Do you feel sick? What did it taste like?"

The other lads fired a barrage of questions as well, and Peter, one of the older lads, said, "Here Les, I've got a big snail you can eat."

My bug eating became the topic of conversation that day, and every other time someone spotted a bug. Well, you can guess what happened. When all the lads had gone into the house, I went to the side of the storage shed, out of view, because I thought I was going to be sick. As I stood there waiting, Doug appeared.

"You're going to be sick mate, aren't you?"

"I don't know. It's just the thought that is making me feel funny."

Then he said, "I just saw the biggest, fattest, slimiest looking slug over there that you..."

And without warning, I was sick as a parrot just thinking about that slug.

"Get it up mate! You should feel better now," he said, with the biggest grin on his face. I told him it was his fault I was sick because he started talking about slugs.

He just laughed, and said, "Come on Les, let's go and eat some real food."

We both burst out laughing and went into the house, but on the way I begged him not to tell anyone that I had been sick. I couldn't sleep that night because I kept thinking about that poor ladybug, and what it would be doing right then if I hadn't swallowed it. Maybe it would be running around with its mates or just flying around having fun. I felt terribly guilty until I had a bright idea. If I lay with my mouth wide open, and it wasn't dead, it could crawl out just like it did before. So I settled down. Then my eyes sprang wide open because it occurred to me that I had chewed the poor thing up. How could he or she now crawl out of my mouth?

So I vowed that I would never intentionally hurt a ladybug again, and went to sleep with my mouth open a little bit. I can honestly say that I have not eaten another ladybug since.

Chapter Four

The Discovery of the Green Bike

As I became a bit older, I was allowed to play in the storage shed. On wet days, we older chaps from seven up, could play there or just hang around. The younger chaps had to remain in the playroom inside. We mainly just sat around chatting, waiting for it to stop raining. The shed was more like an old barn, with one end securely locked up, no doubt full of precious stuff. The other end had no doors, so we could go in and out at will.

It was stuffed with all sorts of bits and pieces, mainly broken toys, a swing set that was unsafe to use, broken tricycles, old iron beds, and other odd things, all covered with a thick layer of dust.

That day, I was sitting in the shed because it was raining, and I began poking around in the piles of junk. I suddenly spotted a large, funny-looking object that had a huge spoke wheel with solid rubber around it. It had lots of stuff leaning against it and stuff stacked up on top. I wondered why I hadn't noticed it before, so I asked Peter, who was sitting next to me, "What's that funny looking bike-thing over there?"

"Why do you want to know?" Peter being a little older was not one to converse with us younger lads.

"Well, what is it?" I asked again, now standing.

He promptly got up and said, "It's a 'something' bike, named after some money."

"Well," I demanded. "Can anyone ride it?"

"Of course not," he snapped, "it's far too big for any of us," he huffed, muttering to himself, and walked off with his hands in his pockets, kicking a rock all the way back to the house. After he disappeared, I walked over to the bike-thing and started moving stuff off. Several minutes later, there it was – a monstrous, er, "something bike." I rubbed my hand over the framework, taking off a thick layer of dust. Then I ran my hand over the whole frame to remove more of the dust, and revealed a lovely deep-green coat of paint. The green framework was a thick pipe-work, bent in the shape of half a C, and thin tubing, which had the wheels attached. It was not a highly polished but a sort of rough old looking metal which still retained the green paint over most of the frame.

Once I had wiped the whole thing down, I stood back to admire it, which had a very large wheel at the front with a solid tire that had bits of grit stuck to it and little chunks of rubber missing. There was a smaller wheel at the rear that appeared to be in fairly good condition, although it too had bits of grit and chunks of rubber chipped off.

"What on earth is it?" I asked myself. It didn't look at all like a normal bike. I just kept looking at every part of it, and for some reason, it fascinated me. I was busy clearing more stuff away in order to see it better when the master appeared.

"What are you doing, Master Morris?" he asked.

I stood to one side and said, "I was trying to get this strange bike-thing out and clean it."

The master surprised me by helping me pull the bike out into the open and told me that someone from the village, long before his time, had donated it to the home. Then he stood back with his hands on his hips, looked at it hard, and suddenly said, "You know what this needs, Master Morris? It needs a good brushing down and a good cleaning, but most important, it requires a jolly good oiling." The master didn't hesitate, as he got a broom and flicked as much of the remaining dust off as he could, then searched around for an old cloth, handed it to me, and said, "Here, give it a good going over."

He started to walk away, but I stopped him by asking, "What sort of bike is this, Master?"

"This is called a penny-farthing bike."

"Why is it named after a penny farting?" I asked. Without thinking, I mispronounced the word, but I don't think the master heard me or I would already have been inside having my mouth washed out with soap as punishment for swearing.

The master rested his hand on the handlebars and pointed to the large wheel. "This, being the large wheel, represents the penny coin. Here." He quickly fumbled around in his pocket and held out a penny for me to look at, then continued. "This represents the large wheel, and the other coin, which I don't have, is called a farthing. Now a farthing is equal to a quarter of a penny in value, and that represents the small wheel, so hence," he grinned and pointed dramatically at the bike, "this is a green penny-farthing bike!"

Just as he said that, the matron called him to the house. Before he could leave, I quickly asked, "Has any one managed to ride this thing?"

He turned and shook his head. "Not that I know of, you see, the art of riding this machine is not in the pedaling, but in the getting on and off of it. Once you've mastered that, you're ready to ride."

He started to walk away again, but I asked another question. "Well, can I have a try, Master?"

The master had a faint smile on his face, and I saw that deep inside of him, he was basically a good man. I saw a fatherly side to him that vanished almost as soon as I saw it. He shook his head and turned to walk back toward me. "No, no, Master Morris, you are far too small for the pedals."

But then he noticed the wooden blocks dangling down from each pedal that had been attached by some thin copper wire. Obviously some other children have tried to ride it a long time ago.

"Well, maybe with those blocks. And the seat will have to be adjusted…maybe one of the bigger lads could try. Or maybe you can try when you get a little older." And with that, he walked toward the house, because the matron was still calling him. But he turned around halfway to face me, and walking backwards, called out,

"Forget about riding the bike, because it takes a lot of skill," and as a last gesture, threw his hands in the air and said, "I don't even think I could ride it." Then he disappeared into the house.

I spent a lot of time cleaning and oiling that penny-farthing bike, and even figured out, with a little effort, how to put the blocks back on the pedals.

I was nearly seven years old when I had my first go at it. Although it was cold out, it didn't stop me from playing outside. I got the penny-farthing bike out, and was wiping it off when I decided to actually try to ride the thing.

Having climbed up on it, I immediately fell off again, and the bike crashed to the ground. I quickly looked around and saw that there wasn't another soul outside, so I didn't feel embarrassed. I tried again, remembering that the master had said that the getting on and off was important. It was hard to get up on it, but the getting off was easy. You just fell off.

The next time I climbed on I stayed on, and because I could only just reach the pedals, I had a job to get it moving. And then I fell off again. I was standing there scratching my head when one of the lads came out and asked what I was doing.

"I'm trying to ride this bike, but I can't get it going," I replied.

"Do you want me to push you?" he asked.

My eyes lit up. "What a good idea!" I shouted. He pushed the bike over to a large rock which I used to climb onto the thing. Once I was on it, the lad gave me a push, and low and behold, I was moving! Although my little legs were straining, I was actually riding the thing around the tarmac. Then I fell off. Many of the lads said that I was wasting my time because I was too small. Whenever I did fall, which was quite often, they would all laugh. And when I did stay on for awhile, some of the older lads would run in front of me, causing me to swerve and loose my balance.

My riding the bike created a lot of interest. All sorts of ages of children would try and ride the thing but would inevitably give up and ask me to help them, but I was reluctant because I wanted to ride it myself. I suppose in a selfish way I always considered the green penny-farthing bike to be mine. Douglas, my brother, had a few turns but being a clumsy chap, he soon gave in, which in the long run was fine with me. So, after try, try, and try again I eventually, sort of got the hang of it. I think I used up all the plasters (band aids) at the home in my attempts to ride the thing.

I was always a bit wobbly to start with, but after a few trips around the tarmac, I got the hang of it and started showing off. I started going faster, and found that the bike handled better that way. So I went around the tarmac with a huge smile on my face, and the other lad shouting for me to go faster still, but I was afraid to over-do it.

Eventually it occurred to me that there was a brake lever that would help me to stop, if that didn't work I tried aiming for the rock so I could use that as a stepping stone, but I kept missing it, so I ended up throwing myself onto the grass. It was a bit of a bumpy landing, but I was all right.

I was quite proud of myself and had the biggest smile, but I had to put the bike away when we were told to come in for lunch. After lunch, it was pouring down with rain, so it was some time before I could get back on the bike again.

Then the winter came, and so the penny-farthing bike was tucked away until the spring. After a good oiling, it was practice, practice again.

The master was impressed with how I was doing and even decided to have a go himself, but he waited until he was on his own. I watched him in secret, and lost count of the times he fell off, but eventually he got the hang of it.

After some time of riding the penny-farthing bike, I eventually got quite good at it, and would climb up by way of the rock and push myself off with my foot. For stopping, I now used the brake, which was a bit rickety, but it slowed me down enough to pull up to the rock, where I could climb off.

It turned out that I was the only boy who could handle the thing. Someone told me that in the past, two of the older lads had tried to ride it, but made a right pig's ear of it, so nobody bothered to try it again – until I came along.

After my episode of going down the hill on the penny-farthing bike, the crumpled up green thing had become the main subject in the barn when it was raining. New chaps who came to the home always asked what is it? And the elder children would have great delight in telling them the green penny-farthing saga, and if I happened to be in the barn at the time, fingers were to pointing at me.

It took forever for the saga to settle down, but I was often reminded by master, matron and staff that I was a naughty boy, I was and how lucky I was not to have been run over by a car or something. And they were quite right. The big gate was now padlocked and could only be opened by a member of staff. Because of me, all deliveries now were made via the front door.

As for me? Well, I was upset over the bike for a long time. I used to sit in the barn and look at the crumpled-up frame tucked away in the "not required any more department" near where I first found it. It didn't take long for a thick layer of dust to cover it up again, but I would look at it and sometimes touch it to reveal the green paint. And in a very soft voice, after looking around to see if anyone was nearby, I would tell the green penny-farthing bike how sorry I was, and how much I missed riding it. I swear I could sometimes hear the humming sound that the big front wheel had make, and that would make me think about the good times I had had on it.

Then I would look over at the "replacement thing." It was a home-made wooden scooter, which had been well used and looked like it had had several coats of paint. Someone in the village had donated it. I couldn't tear around on it but there was a mysterious humming sound coming from it. Certainly not from those small funny looking wheels. Anyway, I didn't have to worry about that because, well, I was banned from using it for three whole months.

I wonder why?

Chapter Five

Miss Lorie

Sometimes children from orphanages get taken out for tea, weekends, and even on holidays by their relations or by people who either want to help, or feel sorry for us, or would like to give us and the orphanage a break.

Well, despite my uneven history, it happened to me.

One day, a very nice lady with a friendly smile was sitting in the master's study. I could see her through the open door, as three of us children were lurking about in the corridor spying on the visitor, trying to find out and see who it was.

I had a fit of the giggles, and in the middle of it, my name rang down the corridor, as it frequently did, but that time I was whisked away by a member of the staff to have my face and hands scrubbed. Then I was instructed to put on my Sunday best, you know, my best grays, and the next thing I knew I was transformed into a smart little Home Boy by having dabs of water wiped on my hair and combed flat. Then I was given a crumpled brown carrier bag with posh string handles, which contained some clean gray clothing and of course my teddy bear, Henry. I was instructed to report to the master's study immediately.

Now, while all that was happening, all sorts of things were going through my mind like, "What have I done wrong?" and "Where are they sending me, and why?"

As I made my way to the study, some of my mates shouted, "Where are you going?" I merely shrugged my shoulders and said, quite honestly, that I had no idea. I gave a hesitant knock on the master's door, which was still ajar. I could see the lady with the lovely smile drinking a cup of tea.

When the master said, "Come in, Master Morris," the lady rose to her feet.

I cautiously walked in, dragging the carrier bag, and noticed that the master had a sort of smile on his face. I then looked up at the woman, who towered over me with a friendly smile, and although I didn't know what was going on, I gave her a smile back.

"What a smart young man you are!" she said.

I quickly turned around, thinking she was speaking to someone who had walked in after me, but no, she was actually referring to me. Well, that cheered me up no end. And then she shook my hand, and said, "I'm pleased to meet you. My name is Miss Lorie."

As she shook my hand, I felt all my built-up tension suddenly drain away. I was starting to feel comfortable, so the little smile on my face lingered on. The smile changed into a big grin when she asked me if I would like to spend a holiday with her.

Now to me that was like someone saying you have won the lottery or something. I said,

"Yes!" umpteen times, my head nodding just as fast.

The master took some of my smile away by reminding me about my best clothes, which was code for "You must be on your best behavior," and said that Miss Lorie had been instructed to bring me straight home if there was "any nonsense, and you know what that will mean."

My brother and my mates all watched me get into her car and stood staring with envy, the way I had whenever one of them went away. As I got in the car, it had a nice fragrance with the smell of leather; I couldn't help but stare at everything, as I had never been inside a car before. As we slowly drove off, I sat there with the biggest grin on my face and gave a sort of triumphant wave, for I knew exactly how they all felt.

I kept sniffing that lovely smell of perfume in the car, which was quite pleasant, and I couldn't help but look at that lady. She was very attractive, with blondish hair rolled into a bun at the back of her head. She was tall and very hilly (big breasted). But it was her smile that I will never forget. It didn't matter how down I was, just one smile from her would lift me up and make me smile. At the early age of seven, I was in love.

Throughout the trip to her apartment in Saffron Waldon, Miss Lorie tried to make conversation. She asked me a lot of questions, but I found it difficult to talk to her, as we boys didn't usually have much contact with real people. To have a general conversation with anyone was hard work – for them as well as us.

To get things going, she asked me about the penny-farthing bike. I looked at her and frowned, as much as to say, "How did you know about that?"

But she quickly said, "It's all right, the master told me about it, and I thought it was very amusing!" She laughed when she said it, so I relaxed and had great pleasure in telling her all about my ordeal. We both ended up laughing, which broke the ice and helped me talk to her.

Needless to say, during my week-long stay with Miss Lorie, I was very spoiled. I did what I liked, was never told off, and discovered what bliss it was to have a bath full hot water and bubbles. When she washed my hair, she was very concerned to know if the sweet-smelling soap got in my eyes, and rinsed it out with great care. She didn't tip gallons of cold water over me either, and I could have stood a lot of her treatment!

One thing I remember well was sitting on her veranda on a hot summer day, with a huge dish of strawberries, which I had never eaten before, topped with a spoonful of sugar and a serving of homemade ice cream. Now that was real tongue-moving luxury, I can assure you. How she managed to get that stuff during the war, who knows?

During my stay, I had a nice bedroom next to her room, and each night before going to sleep, she would read me a bedtime story. While she was reading, I would just stare at her and watch her red-ruby lips move up and down and look at her eyes, which occasionally would look down at me to see if I was still interested or had fallen asleep. The words flowing from her mouth were like music to my ears. I had no idea what story she was reading; the thought of her reading a story just for me made me feel great. Then I would shuffle my body around in the big snug bed and drift off into a deep sleep with a great big smile on my face.

It was while staying with Miss Lorie that I discovered that crusts grew on loaves of bread. At the orphanage, all crusts were cut off the bread and used for cooking, perhaps mixed in with leftover meats and put through the mincing machine for the making of cottage pie, or used for making a bread-and-butter, pudding (dessert), etc. So the slices of bread we were given didn't have crusts. Miss Lorie gave me nice warm toast for breakfast, and with crusts, and real butter, not margarine, and strawberry jam piled on, along with all sorts of other tasty stuff.

Miss Lorie was very good to me during the short week I was with her. She took me shopping, and introduced me to her friends not as Master Morris, but as Mr. Morris, which made me feel good. While out shopping, we would pop into a sweet shop, and she would ask me which sweets I liked. Because everyone was on strict rations, the shop assistant would ask for so many coupons with each purchase. But I still would end up with a bag of sweets, and then we would stop at a tea room and have a glass of lemonade and some nice fresh cakes.

On the way home, Miss Lorie would call at the bakery and buy whatever items I pointed to. Talk about being spoiled! One day when we were shopping, Miss Lorie suddenly said, "I have an idea. Come with me, I know just the shop." She grasped my hand and we crossed the busy main road and walked into a little shop on the corner.

I stood looking around at all the stuff that they sold: wool things for knitting and baskets of all sorts of craft things to make and repair. While I was picking up various things and inspecting them, I heard

Miss Lorie ask the shopkeeper, "Do you sell glass eyes for stuffed animals?"

"Well," said the shopkeeper, a little frail-looking woman. She walked over to an old shoebox and pointed to it, saying, "That's all I have. If there is anything in there that you want, it will be just one penny each," and promptly went back behind the counter.

My ears pricked up at the mention of eyes, so I immediately went over to Miss Lorie, who was digging around in the shoebox. All of a sudden, she said excitedly, "Ah, here we are! I have found a matching pair of eyes for Henry!" She thrust the eyes under my nose and could immediately tell that I approved.

Miss Lorie paid the old shopkeeper, and off we went toward home. All the way back she kept telling me how nice it would be to see Henry with real-looking eyes. So after supper that night, we sat down with needle and thread, and she put Henry's eyes back in, and properly sewed up some of his patches before they got worse.

When she had finished, I held Henry up high and Miss Lorie could tell by my smile that I was happy. I cuddled Henry and said, "Henry, you can see again!"

Then I turned him toward Miss Lorie. "Thank you very much for my eyes, Miss Lorie!" I said, muffling the words through my teeth to sound like Henry. Miss Lorie was highly amused by that.

In no time the week came to an end and I suddenly became an orphan again. "Return to sender," I believe is the phrase.

The day I found myself being driven back to the orphanage in Ashdon was a very unhappy one for me, as I hated the idea of going back. The past week seemed like it was only a couple of days and the drive back seemed to take only seconds. Miss Lorie talked and smiled along the way, and although I tried to smile too, I couldn't, as I felt the tears welling up in my eyes. I knew I was going to have great difficulty saying goodbye to her.

The heavy wooden gate of the home was swung open by one of the children when they saw the car approaching. There was the master, holding his pet dog and smiling, as the car drew close. I reluctantly got out, dragging my now-swollen carrier bag behind me and feeling downright miserable.

Miss Lorie had a few words with the master, who was now surrounded by just about all of the children and the other members of the staff, including Mrs. Woodley, who gave me a smile and a personal welcome home. Miss Lorie refused a cup of tea, as she thought that under the circumstances she best be off straightaway. She squeezed my hand hard, and then kissed me on the cheek.

Well, that was it. I couldn't hold the tears back any longer. They came rolling down my face as I cried out, "I want to go back with you!" But alas, the large wooden gates swung back open and Miss Lorie drove away, waving goodbye. Then the gates clanged firmly shut and I never did see Miss Lorie again.

The matron tried to comfort me by telling me that if I was a good boy, I would be able to go for another holiday, but right now I had to act my age, which was seven,

"And stop that silly sniffling," she said as she walked away, shaking her head and muttering to herself, leaving me to get on with it.

My brother and some of my friends came over firing a whole load of questions at me about my week's holiday away from the home, but I just stood there looking through the bars of the big wooden gate and wishing Miss Lorie would come back. My eyes and jaw ached from crying.

Eventually, I found myself alone, and a quick look around, I climbed over the gate, complete with brown carrier bag, and without any hesitation ran up the road, fast as a ferret.

Swapping my bag from one hand to the other, I kept running, expecting to hear my name called across the fields by the master, but heard nothing. I ran faster and faster, with the odd tear still rolling down my face. After a while, I slowed down and wiped my nose on my sleeve. How common I must look, I thought. I have to get control of myself.

I turned left opposite the vicarage, and walked along what was known as Glebe Road. As I trudged along on that lovely summer day, I looked at the open fields that surrounded me and stretched my head to look up in the sky and watched a skylark fluttering and singing. I started walking backwards. I saw other birds singing and flying around about me and tried to whistle like them. But try as I might, nothing would come out.

I stopped when I saw the orphanage across the fields. "They can't see me from there," I thought, so I tried to whistle again. I was right in the middle of a hard blow when I heard the sound of a motorcar. It was coming from the direction I was heading. I looked around, but there was nowhere to hide – not a hedge or a bush or a tree anywhere.

The sound of the car's horn made me jump, and my eyes popped out when I saw who was driving. It was the assistant matron. The expression on her face was enough to tell me that, once again, I was in serious trouble. She flew out of the car as soon as it stopped, ran over to me, and grabbing hold of my ear, demanded to know what I was doing miles away from the orphanage on my own.

I tried to tell her, but I ended up stuttering, as I had not rehearsed what to say if I got caught. Then the tears started, and I could think of nothing but Miss Lorie. Why couldn't it have been her in the car?

As the assistant matron couldn't understand a word I was saying, she simply led me to the car by my ear and sat me in the front seat. She drove speedily back to the orphanage, reminding me all the way that I was in serious trouble, of which I was well aware.

She pushed me into the master's study. He jumped to his feet and flew over to me, grabbed the lapels of my jacket, and was virtually lifting me off the ground as he gave me a hard stare that made me very afraid of him. He let go when the assistant matron stepped forward to give her report, pointing a finger at me as if there was a bounty on my head and she was there to collect.

"Look what I found wandering around the countryside, miles away from home along the top road. This young man, Master Morris," she said, her finger still pointing at me. "It was lucky that I came back from my holiday today instead of tomorrow. Otherwise, goodness knows where he would have been!"

She looked at the master, who gave a big sigh, stared at me hard, shook his head, and said, "What are we going to do with you, Master Morris?"

"Send me back to Miss Lorie in Saffron Waldon," I thought to myself. I stood there in fear, my sweaty hands still clutching my brown carrier bag, waiting for the outcome of my sentence.

After a long pause, the master went to his desk and took something out of a drawer that looked like a small bat. He then gave me a severe telling-off, saying I was a disgrace to the home, etc., but the whole time I kept wondering what he was going to do with that bat. I soon found out. He removed my trousers and smacked my bottom really hard with it, which really did hurt. I was then sent to have the dreaded bath. It was painful sitting in the bath with a sore bum, and nothing at all like the luxury bath I had last had.

And oh, those jugs of cold water! How is it that when you are in trouble you always get about ten jugs of cold water to rinse your hair, but on normal days it only takes two or three? And then, of course, I was sent to bed in the sick room with no food.

It took me weeks to get back to normal. All I could think about was Miss Lorie. That was the sad thing about being given a taste of the good life; it was really hard to go back to normal orphanage life again. I saw it happen many times with the other children as well.

Chapter Six

The Inkpot Incident

The school we went to in Ashdon was situated in the middle of the village on the main road, not far from where I fell into the brook. It was simply called Ashdon Primary School. It would take us lads about ten minutes to walk there and about 15 to walk back home, allowing for the very steep hill, which incidentally, was called Home Boys Lane. As there was no such thing as school meals in those days, we had to climb that hill twice a day, which made school days very tiring.

My classroom was an elevated classroom, with a floor that sloped a bit like those in a cinema, but much steeper. The floors were wood, like the desks and the chairs. Each desk had a large hole in the top part for you to put your inkpot in. When you got into your classroom in the morning, you had to collect an inkpot, which had been filled up for you, and insert it in the hole. You would also collect a large sheet of blotting paper for drying your ink after writing. There was a recess at the top of the desk for the pen to rest in. The pen was made of wood with a sharp metal nib. You just dipped it into the inkpot and it was ready for writing.

It was my inkpot that got me into trouble one day. Apart from dropping it now and then or spilling it over my desk, I always seemed to get ink over my books and on my clothes, which the home wasn't too happy about. The day I'm talking about, I knocked my inkpot over while trying to put it in the hole on my desk. I was frantically trying to mop it up with some blotting paper when a large, ink-soaked bit of paper hit me on my left arm. One of the village lads had flicked it at me with his ruler, so I in turn tore off a piece of my soggy paper, rolled it up, and tried to flick it back at him as he moved about to dodge me.

But guess what? When I flicked my soggy bit of blotting paper at him, it missed him and landed at the feet of my teacher, who was busy writing on the blackboard. The class suddenly went deathly quiet. The teacher stopped writing, slowly looked down at her feet, and saw my soaked piece of blotting paper sitting next to her shoe. She placed the chalk on the chalk stand, brushed her hands together to get the chalk dust off, and turned to face the class, announcing in a stern voice,

"I am going to walk around this class and look at all of your hands to see which one of you has ink all over them."

We all examined our hands. Blotting paper and handkerchiefs were quickly employed, to no avail. Hands were thrust under desks, and some children even tried to leave the classroom. But the teacher told everyone to stay at their desks and started making her way around. I was shaking and trying to wipe off the ink with blotting paper, but it was too late.

"Ah ha! Here we are," she declared, pointing at me before pulling me to my feet by my hair. "I have found the culprit right here. Come with me."

She let go of my hair and grabbed my ear and triumphantly led me to the front of the class. I could hear one or two comments by the other lads whose fingers were just as inky as mine. I felt like saying, "Look at their hands as well," but I was too concerned about what was going to happen to me. She didn't say a word. Still holding my ear with one hand, she reached for the chair behind her desk with the other and dragged it out in full view of the class. Then she pushed me in front of the chair and sat down. In one quick movement, she yanked my trousers and underpants down, and threw me across her knee. With my bare bum exposed to the whole class, she shouted to the room that she would not tolerate any more of that nonsense in her classroom.

Of course, all that time I was dangling there, red-faced and waiting uncomfortably.

Then it happened.

She reached for a large wooden paddle that was under her seat in a rack designed just for it and gave me a thrashing – six hard slaps across my bare bum with the paddle, which really hurt. Now the color of my bum matched my face.

I had tears in my eyes as I pulled my trousers up and followed the teacher's finger, which was pointing to my seat. She was still shouting at me and the rest of the class, but it went in one ear and out the other. I was more concerned about sitting down than anything else, but when I heard her mention the master of the home, I looked up and listened. She looked directly at me and said that she was going to report the incident to the master.

Now if you were in trouble at school, it was also guaranteed you would also be in trouble back at the home, because the school would telephone the master and inform him of what you had done. Then you got punished by the master for the same thing you had been punished for at school, so it was always double trouble.

The bell sounded to tell us it was time to go home, and as usual, the teacher told us to bring our inkwells with us and put them on the table for refilling.

"You may all leave now, with the exception of Morris. Morris, I want to see you before you leave." I stopped short with the inkwell in my hand and in minutes the classroom was empty. I sat down at my desk again. My teacher, Miss Richards, was tidying her desk. When she had finished, she sat down, clasped her hands together, and instructed me to come to her desk. She then gave me a lengthy talk, and to my surprise, mentioned that she had noticed later that one or two other children had ink on their hands also.

I looked up at her and I do believe there was a faint smile on her face. She stood up and told me she wouldn't mention this matter to the master if I promised it wouldn't happen again. I naturally agreed at once, and thanked her several times, I headed out the door when she said,

"For goodness sake put down your inkwell!" I sheepishly placed it on the ink table, and was off like a ferret, running out of school as quickly as I could, thinking that I would miss tea, but oh, I felt so much better knowing that the teacher wasn't going to tell the master! I actually ran up the hill to the home.

As I got to the gate, it dawned on me that a few of the lads in my class – there were about four of them – knew I'd been in trouble. There was always at least one of them who got his kicks by telling the master when someone had been in trouble. With that in mind, I approached the house with caution. Everything was quiet.

"They must be having tea," I thought. "I'll sneak in and have a quick wash," but as I entered the washroom, guess who was standing there?

"Where have you been, Master Morris?" The master snapped.

"Er...well, I..."

"I hear you have been in trouble at school," he said in a sarcastic tone.

See what I mean? Some little bugger had broken all records to get up to the home to tell the master all about me. I tried to tell him that my teacher held me back after school and that she wasn't going to report it, but he wouldn't listen. He stripped off my clothes while the bath was running and well, you know the drill – a drowning, another sore bum, no tea, and to bed in the sick room.

And would you believe it? That weekend I was in trouble yet again, but for some reason, I got away without a hiding that time. The master had a new Morris 8 car delivered. While he was inside sorting out the paperwork or something, I was caught climbing all over the car. He raced out of the house and I ran from him like a scalded cat.

At the time, I wondered why I could see his tonsils when he shouted at me. But now I can understand why.

Chapter Seven

Food, Glorious Food

From what I remember, the food at Ashdon was all right, but because it was wartime everything was on ration, and most of the general food items were in short supply. Milk, for example, was that powdered stuff mixed up with water. In the winter months, breakfast consisted of porridge with no sugar, which was bad enough, but what I really didn't like were the big lumps lurking at the bottom of the dish. We had small enough helpings of that, followed by some thin toast with just a smearing of margarine and no crusts. As I said before, all the crusts were cut off the bread to supplement other dishes.

For tea, we would have something like baked beans and potatoes, or canned peas, or string beans and mashed potatoes. Lunch would be cabbage, a thin slice of meat, some potatoes with a watery gravy, and if we were lucky, a stale cake donated by the village bakery. But you had to have a clean plate before qualifying for that.

And that reminds me of another story. Although the story is very amusing today, it was not at the time, and I remember it very well indeed.

Most of us children had never seen the ocean, let alone been on a holiday, so the master decided that he would like to take us to the seaside for a holiday. He was given permission by the Society to do that, but no money was available. In other words, he was told that he could take us, but he had to raise the money himself. And so he did.

The master and his staff set about writing and producing a play with us children as actors. We were all called "The Ashdon Little Lyricals" which involved us performing short sketches, which included a western show, a farm yard sketch, a wedding and even a ballet. No, I tried to do a pirouette, but landed flat on my bum in the attempt.

I did perform in the play along with my brother Doug. The master painted the scenery and helped with the costumes. The play was performed at the Conservative Club in Ashdon and at the Town Hall in Saffron Waldon, which to us was the big time, if you can believe it.

Through the play, we raised over 100 pounds, which was a lot of money back then. That enabled us to have a summer holiday when our school was closed. We had a whole week at Broadstairs, Kent. A local school allowed us to stay in their classrooms for free, which we used as bedrooms. We had camp beds donated by local scouts. The wash rooms were similar to what we were used to but the difference was we had toilet paper and we didn't have to ask for it. The school library was our dining room.

It was all very exciting. A big motor coach – something we had never seen before – arrived at the orphanage, and after loading just about everything we could think of in it, we all climbed aboard and went off for a long ride through the country to visit the seaside for the first time.

It was during the holiday that I got into trouble again.

Now you may well be thinking that I was always in trouble when I was in the orphanage. Well, yes, you're dead right. But with that particular piece of trouble, I don't think it was really my fault.

You see, I hated fat, and still do. At Ashdon I was always punished if I didn't eat all my food. I know it was wartime and food was scarce, but I think it was wrong to force someone to eat fat when he can't stand the sight of it, let alone the idea of eating the stuff.

The room where we had our meals in Broadstairs was the library, as all down one side were shelves and shelves of books. It had tables for four scattered about, and my table was right next to the bookcase. A large table at one end of the room accommodated the staff in a good position for them to keep an eye on us. Underneath the table sat the master's pet dog. So, it was set up like Ashdon.

On the day in question, we all went into the dining room for lunch, and as usual stood to say grace. When we all sat down, the master remained standing to make an announcement about the afternoon's events. While he was talking, the lads on dinner duty were quietly bringing in the meals, which the staff had already made up on individual plates.

"As it is a nice day today, we will all go to the beach this afternoon and play games, etc., and if we have enough money left, we will treat you all to a ride at the fun fair," the master explained.

Great shrieks of excitement echoed around the room, and the matron told us to be quiet, as there was more. Everyone quickly hushed, and the master continued, "But if we don't have enough money for that, we will certainly treat you all to an ice cream." Then there was more excitement, for ice cream was something we rarely had.

"And," he continued, as we all sat there with watering mouths, "When we return, there will be a special tea party given by our hosts, and as we have two birthdays this week, we will include them with this special meal."

Just before the master sat down he added, "Don't forget to eat all your lunch. Remember, no pudding (dessert) for those who can't eat the main course."

I was sure he was looking at me when he said that, for you see, I missed out on a lot of my puddings through not eating fat. I always looked forward to my pudding, and today it was going to be sponge cake and custard. I was really looking forward to that, but when my meal was thrust in front of me, all the excitement I had built up suddenly drained away just like the watery gravy that was slopping over the edge of my plate. For there, lurking between the mashed potatoes and the boiled cabbage was a slice of beef with the...

Biggest Piece of GRISTLE I had ever seen.

I heaved at the sight of it. My pudding and all the events of the afternoon and tonight's tea party were all depending on a clean plate, and there was that horrible thing lying there. I could see that, once again, I was going to miss out on all the excitement.

The lads at my table all thought that was highly amusing and made various comments about it. As for offering them a piece each, well, that was out of the question, for they hated it too. Perhaps the dog under the staff table? But no, every time the dog moved it got shouted at.

I looked down at my plate, but the terrible thing was still there. I had hoped that it would disappear, but no such luck. So I slowly ate the potatoes and cabbage and carefully cut the meat off that big, hard, shining lump of horrible gristle. If I was to have any pudding, I'd have to get rid of it soon, as most of the other lads had already finished their meals.

And then I had an idea. The lad sitting next to me saw what I had done and promised not to tell. I put my knife and fork together on my clean plate to indicate that I had finished, and looked at it with a big smile on my face. Everyone looked at me with suspicion, including the staff, which seemed to go into a little conference about it. But I sat there triumphantly, mouth watering, waiting for my pudding to turn up. When it did arrive, I ate the lot and could have eaten more.

After we had done the washing up and set the tables for tea later on, we were ready to go to the beach. As usual, we walked down to the town and onto the beach in twos. What fun we had running around on the sand, splashing in and out of the sea! We weren't allowed to go into the water, as none of us could swim, but we built big sandcastles and then took turns jumping all over them.

Although we didn't get our ride at the fun fair, we were treated to a lovely ice cream, which we tried to make last as long as we could. But it disappeared just as fast as the time. Before we knew it, we were all back in twos, marching back to our holiday home. We didn't mind much, as we still had a nice tea to look forward to.

Having all scrubbed our faces, hands and knees, which was the usual procedure before meals, we stood in line awaiting inspection. Suddenly, I felt a pain on my right ear and had the distinct feeling that it was being grasped by fingers and a thumb. I was dead right!

Without saying anything, the master led me away from the queue by my ear, straight into the dining room. He stopped in the middle of the room, and with me wiggling and generally trying to let him know that he was hurting me, shouted so the whole house could hear.

"Where do you sit, Master Morris?"

I half-heartedly pointed to my seat, and without warning, the master tugged on my ear even harder, as he led me to my table. When he finally let go, he placed his hands on the back of my chair and in a sarcastic voice said,

"Now Master Morris, I want you to pass me that brown book," he said, pointing to a large, leather-bound volume. I looked at him with all the surprise and innocence I could muster and said,

"Erm...which book, Master?"

"You know damn well which book," he snapped, then pointed with his finger almost touching it. "That one, Master Morris."

I slowly walked around the table to avoid walking in front of him, and although I was very nervous, I still managed to catch sight of all the food that was laid out for us. And what a mouth-watering lot it was. There were jellies, sandwiches, and all sorts of cakes, and as I reached for the bookcase, I gave a big sigh and looked at the master, hoping for sympathy, as I knew I would miss out on all that lovely food.

My hand trembled as I reached out for the book. I pulled it half out and looked at the master again. He had an expression on his face that I had seen many times before. So I continued the movement and removed the book from the bookcase, nervously handing it to him.

"Now, Master Morris, I want you to turn to page 74," he said, clearing a space on the table for me to place the book on. I slowly set the book down and stood there, looking at it. The tears were slowly building up, and as I glanced up at door, I could see that most of the lads and the staff were watching and waiting to see what would happen. Whatever it would be, I had a feeling it would be bad. Through the tears in my eyes, I looked once again at the master and knew that my audience didn't have long to wait.

"Turn to page 74 Morris; we're all waiting to have our tea." I reached nervously for the book, and it automatically flopped open to page 74. The audience gasped when they saw the bookmark I had placed there – one great, horrible lump of gristle. I heaved again at the sight of it.

The master peeled the ghastly lump from the book and calmly placed it on my plate, having first removed my jelly in a ceremonial sort of way. Then he stared at me and said, "Now you are going to eat that for your tea, and don't let me see you touch anything else on this table until you have eaten the remains of your lunch. I'll deal with you further afterwards." And with that, he stormed off, telling everyone else to get to their places. There was a hustle and bustle as everyone went to their tables, all saying what a lovely tea it was, and of course laughing and joking as soon as they saw what I had on my plate.

Then the master spoke, and there was deadly silence as we all stood behind our chairs. He looked directly at me and said in a dreadfully serious tone, "Master Morris will say grace for our tea tonight."

I raised my head and found that everyone was looking at me. Focusing my eyes on the master, I gave him my best, "if looks could kill" stare, then lowered my head and said the prayer.

"For what we are about to receive," I paused and looked down at the dreadful lump of gristle, and as I pulled a face to match it, I'm sure I saw it move and wink at me. I then gave another heave and continued, "May the Lord make us truly thankful."

And at that, the room exploded with the noise of scraping chairs as everyone sat down and started to eat. As for me, well, I think I was the last person to sit down. All I really wanted to do was run to the bathroom and be sick.

Now in the middle of the table was a large plate of cakes, in all shapes and sizes. To avoid any arguments, the procedure was that whichever cake was opposite you was yours. It just so happened that my cake was the biggest and the most mouth-watering, so the lads at my table, between bites of other luscious treats, were arguing as to who was going to have what of my tea – the jelly, the cake, the sandwiches, and don't forget there was birthday cake as well.

While all that was going on, I just sat there, head down, fiddling with my hands and giving the occasional glance up to avoid looking at my plate. I would sometimes catch the eyes of the staff at their big table and see them talking and looking in my direction.

The children at my table were still arguing as to what part of my cake they were going to get. Someone suggested cutting it into three pieces and then started saying who was going to do the cutting

It got to a point that I didn't care what would happen to me, I knew I wouldn't be allowed any niceties on the table. So, without hesitation I put my index finger right up my nose and twisted it around and then jabbed it into my cake, the best one on the plate, making a large hole in it. After that, I brought my fist down and flattened the thing.

"There you are!" I said in a temper. "I have split it up for you!"

Little did I know that the master had seen what I had done. He shot from his chair and came over to me in a flash. Grabbing hold of my hair, he dragged me out of the room as I yelped that he was hurting me, and he shouted that I was a naughty and horrible boy. Straight into the bathroom we went, where I was stripped off, got a damn good spanking and a cold bath, and was sent straight up to bed, all in a matter of about ten minutes.

Not bad going, eh? The good part was that I didn't have to eat that horrible lump of gristle, and I'm sure that none of the lads had the pleasure of eating my cake. As I lay in bed, a faintly contented smile flashed across my face.

Chapter Eight

A Visit from Santa

Now you may well be thinking that during my time at Ashdon I wasn't happy at all. It was quite the opposite really. I may well have been the cleanest child, owing to the number of baths I had, but during the six years I was there, I can honestly say I was very happy. It was the only life I knew.

The only time I used to get upset – well, not really upset, more envious I suppose – was at Christmas time. You see, the children who had relatives used to get all sorts of presents from their uncles and aunties, whereas those of us who were on our own only got a generic present from the home, and sometimes a gift from the people of the village. Invariably, the gift from the village was a discarded toy that had a fresh coat of paint on it and maybe the odd nail banged in to hold it together, all nicely wrapped up.

The gifts from the orphanage were just about the same each year. You either had a pair of socks, a tie, a belt or a neatly colored handkerchief. After we got our presents, we would try and guess what was in the neatly gift wrapped paper. When a child got a large present from a relative, we would sit and stare at him as it was unwrapped.

The master and matron had everything under control. First we would have a big roast turkey with all the trimmings and a great big helping of Christmas pudding. Once everything was cleared away, the washing-up done, and all the tables laid for the big tea party later on, we would wait to be called to the playroom, which was already set up with a tall, brightly decorated Christmas tree. The tree twinkled and glistened like a beacon right next to the very large and comfortable red cushy armchair that Santa would sit in.

We would sit on the playroom floor and wait excitedly, looking at all the decorations, the fire glowing, and the glittering of the tree, with all the presents under the tree. It was very tempting to see the names on them, and not want to take a peek to see what we got. The assistant matron would stand next to the tree waiting to help Santa. If she slipped out of the room, one of the lads would run over to the tree and read some of the names on presents.

The big clock over the fireplace would be the focus for some of us, although we couldn't tell the time. But we would venture a good guess. An older lad would correct us or the assistant matron would give us a lesson on how to read the clock. Most of us, including myself, would stare at the door and wait for the special visitor in his red outfit.

Then at long last, the door would burst open and the master would shout, "Do you children know who has come to visit our orphanage?"

We would all jump up and yell at the top of our lungs, "It's Santa! It's Santa!"

Now, our Santa that Christmas was a slim chap, with a cushion in front of his costume and a false beard, concealing his mouth. The beard invariably stayed put whenever he turned his head. But who cared? It was Santa.

He would haul a large sack full of gifts into the room and wish everyone a Merry Christmas before finally sitting in his chair, to the relief of all of us children. For it was the moment we had been waiting for ever since we had gotten up that morning.

It was present time.

The assistant matron would call out our names as we sat in eager anticipation. Each boy had a few minutes on Santa's lap to answer the question,

"And what would you like for Christmas, young man?"

While we were on Santa's lap, the assistant matron hovered near-by, watching and listening closely to make sure that no one asked for anything inappropriate.

Suddenly, my name was called out. I ran as fast as I could, jumped up on Santa's lap, and shuffled myself into a comfortable position. Santa looked at me and said, "Well, well, young man, what would *you* like for Christmas?"

I spoke in a soft voice because I didn't want the assistant matron to hear what I had to say. "Santa, I just want to have my own pet," I told him. As soon as I got the words out, the roar of a Spitfire flying over-head, drowned my voice. Scared by the sudden noise, I hugged him.

He clenched his arms tightly around me, and said, "It's all right, it's all right. So, what did you say you wanted?" asked Santa, leaning in closer to me.

I looked up and saw the assistant matron also leaning in and frowning. That was *not* a good sign.

Again I said in a soft voice, "I just want my own pet." Santa glanced over at the assistant matron and saw her fold her arms and hold her lips tight, shaking her head from side to side. That was *definitely* not a good sign. Santa leaned back in his chair and put his hand on his cheeks and said, "I'm sorry, I can't give you a pet. If I gave you one, everyone would want one, and well, it would be more like a zoo here than an orphanage."

By then, I was sulking with my head hung low. Santa lifted my head up with his white-gloved hand and asked, "What *other* gift would you like young man?"

I just shook my head from side to side and said, "Santa, that's all I wanted for Christmas – a pet to look after and call my own."

Just then the assistant matron stepped forward and held out the generic present for Santa to give to me, but Santa put up his hand and said firmly, "Just a minute." He plunged his hand into his sack and rummaged around. Then he looked at me and said, "I have a special gift for you in my bag." He pulled his now-clenched hand out of the bag and said, "How would you like to look after one of Santa's pets?"

I was beaming now, my eyes wide open, and said, "Wow! I would love to look after one of your pets, Santa!" Santa opened his hand just a little bit and asked me if I could see what it was.

"Uh, no, I can't see anything," I said.

Santa opened his hand just a little bit more and said, "It's Harry, my invisible cricket. Can you see him now?"

"Well, erm, I *think* so." I wasn't quite sure what to say.

Santa instructed me to open my hand. He slowly put his clenched hand over mine to place Harry in it, saying, "You can look after Harry until next year. Then I can give him to another child to look after. Now close up your hand – not too tight. There, have you got him?"

"Yes, yes, I have him Santa. Thank you very much!"

Suddenly, the assistant matron gave a loud, fake cough. She was still frowning over the whole incident and holding out the orphanage present for me.

As I slid off Santa's lap, he retrieved my present from her and gave it to me. Then he leaned forward and said quietly, "You know young man, only you and I can see Harry." Then he winked at me and wished me a Merry Christmas.

When I got back to the other lads, they all started asking me questions, but I simply said, "Santa has chosen me to look after one of his pets until next year." I thrust my clenched fist out in front of them, and announced that I now had an invisible cricket to look after, called Harry.

"Let's see him!"

I made all sorts of excuses not to show them, and of course they made all sorts of comments back, when the master walked past. He stopped and looked at me, saying, "Young Master Morris, you haven't opened your present yet?" And then he walked away.

The lads took turns guessing what might be inside, as they did every year. Because I had only one hand free, one of the lads offered to open my present for me. Halfway through, he looked at me and said, "What do you think it is?"

"Oh, I bet it's a pair of socks," I replied.

"No, it's a tie," he said, and sure enough it was.

For the rest of Christmas Eve, I walked around with my right hand clenched, opening it periodically to see if Harry was okay and to show him to the other children on request. And by the end of the day, everyone was exhausted. After a nice cup of hot chocolate, we were all sent off to bed in our dormitories.

After the assistant matron checked to see if we were all tucked in and said her usual "Goodnight," there was very little whispering because we were all very tired. I lay in bed with my right hand on top of the bedclothes. Before dropping off to sleep, I slowly opened my hand to tell Harry a bedtime story, and I actually saw my invisible cricket. But I was so tired that all I could manage was a faint "Wow!" and promptly fell asleep.

When I awoke up the next morning, the first thing I did was look at my hand. I instantly noticed that instead of it being clenched, it was wide open.

"He's gone. Harry has gone. Where are you Harry?" I shouted as loud as I could, waking the entire orphanage, and no doubt, the entire village.

The master and the matron both ran into the dormitory, adjusting their dressing gowns and wondering what on earth was going on.

"Who's responsible for all this noise?" demanded the master, and all the children immediately pointed their fingers at me. The assistant matron also came rushing in, demanding to know who was responsible for the rude awakening.

I found it very difficult to tell the staff what was wrong. I kept stuttering, "I've lost Harry! How am I going to tell Santa I lost one of his personal pets?"

"All right. All right. Let's try to find this, uh, Harry thing, whatever it is," the assistant matron said in a sharp tone. With her in control, the master and matron left the dormitory, muttering about the whole incident.

Everyone went through the motions of looking for Harry, but they all gave up when the assistant matron said at last, "Wait a minute, it's impossible to find the invisible, let's get ready for breakfast." One by one, they all left me sitting on my bed with my head in my hands, wondering what on earth I was going to tell Santa.

My brother came in from the other dormitory and laughed at me, saying it was a good start for a Christmas morning. Then he put his arm around my shoulder and said, "Come on downstairs or you will be late for breakfast. And by the way, Happy Christmas."

I just looked at him and sort of smiled. All the next year, I periodically worried and rehearsed what I was going to say to Santa. What made it worse was that the other boys kept telling me I was going to be in big, big trouble when Santa found out. But Doug said to me, "Maybe a different Santa will come this year," My eyes opened wide and that cheered me up a bit, "Yes, that would be great."

All of a sudden, it was Christmas Eve again, and all of us were sitting on the floor in the playroom awaiting Santa's arrival. Every time the door opened, I looked to see if Santa was there and looked at the big red Santa armchair. Then it happened.

The master opened the door and announced, "Guess who's come to visit the orphanage?" And all the children jumped up and cheered, except me, because I spotted him before he came in. And yes, it was the same Santa as last year. I slumped to the floor, wondering what to say to him.

After Santa's usual round of greetings, he sat in his big chair and the assistant matron started calling out our names so we could run up and sit in his lap. Although Santa looked in my direction a couple of times, I avoided eye contact with him.

Soon everyone was in good Christmas spirit, laughing and tearing open their presents, but all that stopped when my name was called out. Everything went quiet and all eyes were fixed upon me.

Unlike the other children who ran and hopped excitedly on his lap, I walked slowly over to Santa.

"Come on Master Morris, I've been waiting to see you," Santa said. I slowly climbed onto his lap with my head hung down looking at my shoes.

"Well, young man, how did you manage looking after one of my favorite pets?" Santa asked, just before he noticed that both of my hands were wide open. He sat back in his chair and asked, "Where is Harry do you have him with you?"

I turned my face toward Santa and looked him right in the eye before stammering, "Santa, I...I looked after Harry all day...

and when I went to bed...I even told him a story before I went to sleep..." I then swallowed hard and said, "And when I woke up in the morning...my hand was wide open...and he was gone...Harry was gone."

I was about to burst into tears when the assistant matron said, "Yes, Santa, we were all awakened by the disappearance of this Harry thing, whatever it is, and so we all helped look for him."

I looked at her surprised that she even remembered. Then I looked at Santa, and he seemed to be in thought and stoking his false beard, but I think he was adjusting the thing, I then saw a filtered smile through the beard and his eyes lit up. Leaning over to me, he said, "Let me check in my bag." He put his white-gloved hand deep into his big red bag and fumbled around, muttering some sort magical words. And then he withdrew his hand and said, "Well young man, it's all right."

Santa pulled his clenched hand out of the bag, and with a smile and a flourish, said again, "It's all right. Harry is right here, safe with me. You know Harry came back to me. He told me all about you, and how you told him a bedtime story, and how you were so proud to show and tell people you were looking after one of Santa's pets. So you see, have nothing to worry about. Harry is fine."

I let out a contented sigh, and a big smile beamed across my face. "Can...can I see him?" I asked.

Santa put his hand out in front of me and opened it just a little bit, and for a moment, I could actually see him again.

"Wow! I'm glad he's safe, Santa." Santa put Harry back in his sack and settled back again.

"Now then, young man, do you still want a pet for Christmas?"

I shook my head from side to side and told him I didn't want a pet.

"Well, what *do* you want for Christmas?" he asked.

I shook my head again, and said, "Santa, I don't want anything for Christmas. I'm just pleased that Harry is all right and that he's back with you."

The assistant matron handed Santa the generic Christmas present. "Well, here's a little gift for you anyway," Santa said.

After jumping down from Santa's lap, I thanked him, and as I was leaving, he said, "You have a great Christmas, young man!" And so I went off to join my friends, who were soon crowded around, barraging me with questions. But I just smiled and said, glancing up at Santa,

"Harry is back where he belongs."

My brother joined us, and said, "You haven't opened your present. Are you going to open it?"

I picked up the gift, looked at it, and said, "I bet it's a tie."

He said, "I bet it's a pair of socks."

Another lad said, "Come on, open it!"

So I slowly tore off the wrapping paper, and was surprised to find a small red box.

"Ties and socks don't normally come in that kind of box," Doug said.

"Turn it over, there's some writing on the other side," said another boy.

So I turned the box over and there on the lid, printed in large gold letters, was the word "HARRY." I immediately looked up at Santa, who was watching me. I turned back to open the box smiling when I found a beautiful, hand-carved wooden cricket inside, with a note saying, "Have a wonderful Christmas. From Santa and Harry, the Invisible Cricket."

Once again, I looked at Santa and he looked at me over the top of his glasses, and waved his white handed glove to me smiling, as he gave me a wink.

I kept that little carved wooden cricket chap for many, many years, until he disappeared one day in my adult life. I wonder if he went back to Santa?

Chapter Nine

Mother's Day

My brother and I continued to be happy at Ashdon until one Sunday, March 27, 1949. It was a day I will always remember, and a time I will always try to forget. For that was the day that my brother and I were plucked from our happy environment, like two pieces of fruit from a market stall, and taken far away, to live in a strange house with two strange people, whom I didn't like one little bit.

I had just turned nine and had lived in the orphanage for six years with all my orphan friends. The day started out as another normal Sunday. The dormitory was filled with its usual lively talking and giggling, while we all got into our play clothes. Some of the children were going back and forth to the washroom when, all of a sudden, the matron came in.

The room instantly went quiet. The matron marched over to my brother, who dropped the smile he was wearing, and she pointed to him, and then to me, and announced in a military fashion, "Both of you will get changed into your Sunday best. Now."

She disappeared as quickly as she came in, but shouted out whilst leaving that everyone else would remain in their play clothes.

There was deathly hush in the dorm, everyone just stood there and looked at Doug and me, wondering what on earth was going on. We sat on our beds, looking at each other with question marks hanging over our heads. Should we be excited, or what? Why just the two of us? Were we going to another home? Perhaps someone was coming to see us. All these thoughts flashed through our minds as we got dressed. All the other children were asking all the questions we were thinking about. We had no idea that what was about to happen was to change our lives, dramatically.

All through breakfast, the lads at my table kept asking me where I was going.

"I have no idea," I told them.

"Perhaps you are being sent away because of the trouble you've been in," said one little lad.

"No," I said, but then thought, was I?

Another lad leaned over to me and said, "It's because you escaped from the home on that penny bike thing."

I pulled an expression of amazement, and said, "No, no. It can't be, because Doug is coming with me."

"Oh, that's right," said the lad.

I suddenly thought of that lovely woman at Saffron Waldon. Maybe she wanted me to live with her! A little smile came to my face at the idea, but it suddenly dropped because I realized she didn't know my brother.

Then one of the staff walked past the table, I asked her, "Excuse me Miss, where am I going?"

"We shall see all in good time, Master Morris," was the reply.

All through breakfast I had nothing but a barrage of questions from the lads, who also kept regurgitating how many times I had been in trouble. But for the life of me, I couldn't give them an answer.

After breakfast, the staff packed what toys we had and an assortment of clothes into big brown carrier bags with string handles. Doug and I went to the bathroom to wash our hands and who should we bump into?

Dear Mrs. Woodley.

She came up to us and gave us both a little pat on the head. Her eyes were full of tears. She then produced two bundles of violets and gave us each one. "Here," she said, as she pressed them into our hands, "I picked these on my way in this morning. Now give these to the people you're going to, because, you know, today is Mother's Day. It would be a nice gesture." She wiped her eyes and shook our hands, saying in a soft voice, "I hope you will both be very happy where you're going."

My eyes filled up, and I looked up at Mrs. Woodley, and asked, "Where are we going?"

"Ah, there you are," interrupted the stern voice of the master. "I have been looking for you. Now, have you got everything?" he asked, as he straightened my tie.

We both simply nodded our heads.

"Just a minute!" the master snapped. He saw Henry, my teddy bear, tucked under my arm. He quickly snatched it away, and in a loud voice yelled, "That belongs to the home, thank you very much," and promptly tucked Harry under his arm. "Right, now go and sit in my car; I'll be along in a moment."

I stood there begging the master to give me my teddy bear back and even raised my voice in anger. That surprised the master, who frowned. By now, the matron was also on the scene. The master handed Harry over to her and said, "Take care of that will you."

The matron fled to the study with me chasing behind her sobbing, "Please can I have my teddy bear?" She quickly opened the study door, threw the bear in, and just as quickly slammed the door shut. She stood in front of the door, and said,

"That bear belongs to the orphanage. Now go! The master is waiting for you."

The master was shouting my name down the hall. All the other children were standing and staring at Doug and me. It must have looked like a game of tennis; first looking left then looking right, back and forth, wondering what was going to happen next.

"Where are you both going?" shouted one of the lads. The master told them to keep quiet and again ordered Doug and myself into his car.

We reluctantly sat in the back seat of the master's Morris 8, each clutching a bunch of violets and a brown carrier bag. We were now more confused than ever.

"We must be going to another home," My brother whispered.

"But I don't want to go to another home," I said, and started to release some tears that had been building up. "I like it here." I tried to ignore the lads who were all gathered around the car.

Well," said Doug, sighing. "That's what it sounds like – another home. Why can't we stay here?" Although he wasn't crying, I don't think he was far from it either.

The master, having worked his way through the crowd of children and staff who had turned out to wave us goodbye, got into the car. I gave a final plea for my teddy bear, but the master simply shook his head and said, "You might have a better one where you're going."

As the car drove off, I had eyes only for Mrs. Woodley, who I caught sight of. She was standing at the back, doing the same I was, waving with one hand and wiping her eyes with the other. Then I couldn't see her or the orphanage anymore. We drove down the steep hill from the orphanage, the very hill I rode down. Doug leaned towards me and said,

"I bet you went down this hill faster than the master's car?"

As I was nodding my head, I noticed the master looking in his rear view mirror, but he never commented. So, we had left the orphanage in Ashdon Village and we both had no idea where we were going.

During the first part of the trip, the master never said a word about where he was taking us, or even made conversation with us. Finally, Doug boldly asked, "Well, where *are* we going, Master?"

We saw him look into his rearview mirror and give a false smile before he said, "It won't be too long before we are there."

I was about to ask if we were going to another home, but he interrupted me, saying sharply, "Just wait and see. We are driving to Chelmsford, if you must know." That's all we got out of him the entire way.

Doug and I just looked at each other, wondering if we dared ask him anything else. For most of the journey, I simply sat there staring at the bunch of violets and thinking of Mrs. Woodley. When we did speak to each other, it was in a whisper, and each time the master would look into his rearview mirror.

As we drove along the country roads, we saw families with their children, a dog running after a stick and some lads trying to climb a big tree. A thick rope was hanging from one of the trees for children to swing on. It looked like fun. We saw fields beyond the hedgerows with sheep. Young spring lambs were taking their first wobbly steps next to their mothers. I wondered what it was like to be part of a family.

Eventually, we were out of the country, and into an urban are with nothing but buildings all shapes and sizes. We weaved in and out of the winding narrow roads of Chelmsford, only to find ourselves in a dreary landscape amidst hundreds of identical red bricked council houses.

We had arrived at Chelmsford, in Essex. After weaving in and out of the town, we went slowly up a narrow road. The master was holding a piece of crumpled paper in one hand, and was looking at all the houses as we passed them. He finally stopped and said with a sigh, "Ah, here we are: Number 51 Manor Road."

As the master opened his door, the door of Number 51 opened and two figures appeared. Both were wearing big smiles, Doug and I looked at each other in disbelief. Suddenly our door opened, and the master looked in, saying with a faint smile on his face, "Come on you two, this is your new home."

I turned to Doug and we both looked at each other in amazement. Doug muttered to me so the master couldn't hear, "This is a small orphanage." We slowly and reluctantly got out of the car, clinging to our carrier bags with one hand and the violets with the other.

As we walked up to the door, I couldn't help but stare at the two people standing there staring back at us. He was tall and balding, with black bushy hair on each side of his head and big, bushy, black eyebrows. He was thin and scrawny looking. His cheekbones were sunken in because of his thin structure. He wore a black suit with a waistcoat and a bluish tie with a tiny knot. I think the best way to describe him is that he looked like a very stern character from a Dickens novel, or an undertaker. His baggy trousers hung down with the impressions of his knobby knees still sticking out.

The woman was a little on the plump side, with wiry hair that hung in no recognizable style. She wore a baggy flowery dress. But her main feature was her two large, protruding front teeth. They even protruded when her mouth was shut, and they were stained badly. Maybe it was a bit of mildew from the damp weather, I thought.

There was something about her that made me feel uneasy right from the start. She just stood there with that big grin that made her teeth (by the way…did I mention her teeth?) stick out even farther.

As we were ushered into the house, I quickly brushed past her, looking at her the whole time. There was a strong sweaty smell about her. I looked around the place and the front room which was the lounge, had drab looking wallpaper that was badly glued to the wall, and a painting of a sandy beach with seagulls and people walking along the seashore, that hung askew.

Like a frightened dog, I stood behind a chair half hiding. There was a small empty coal fireplace, a great big Marconi wooden radio set, and a Bible the size of a small suitcase next to it. The room was dark and musky smelling with a slight aroma of mothballs in the air.

It was time for the master to introduce these two people to Doug and I.

"This is Mr. Green, who you will call Dad or Daddy, and this is Mrs. Green, who you will call Mum or Mummy. They are now your new parents."

I just stood there frowning and looking at these two people we had never seen before, thinking, I only know Master and Matron. Why do we have to call these strangers Mum and Dad? I don't even know what those words mean. We've never used them before." It took us a long time to drop the "master" and "matron" bit.

Doug went through the formality of shaking hands with both of them, but I remained motionless, as all eyes were on me, waiting for me to do the same.

"Come on Master Morris, where are your manners? Introduce yourself," the master said.

With reluctance I went over and limply shook their hands, but kept my lips tightly sealed and did not look up at her. Doug handed his violets over to Mrs. Green, who then reached out for my violets, which I was clinging to very firmly. I had no intention of handing them over. The violets were mine.

"Thank you for bringing these. That was very thoughtful," she said, but suddenly stopped speaking when I snatched my hand away, and said. "No the violets are mine." I clutched the violets to my chest and turned sideways.

The master stepped between us, instructing me to hand over the flowers.

"But Mrs. Woodley gave them to me," I snapped then put them behind my back and I repeated. "These violets are mine." Shaking my head in her direction I again in a louder tone snapped. "The violets are mine...Mrs. Woodley gave them to me!"

The master snatched them from me and gave them to Mrs. Green, and then gave me a telling-off. It didn't do my ego any good, and as for those tears, they were building up, and I knew it wouldn't be long before they came gushing forth. I stood there staring at that woman who towered above me with those two big teeth (Did I tell you about her teeth?) I was thinking, "How can I call this woman of all people, a mum?"

The master saw it as his cue to leave, and told Mr. and Mrs. Green that I would be all right shortly, and that I wasn't normally like that. He swung around to Doug and me, thrust out his hand, and said goodbye.

I looked up at him with the tears starting to roll down my face and cried out, "I want to go back to the home with you! I don't want to stay here. Please Master, please take me back with you. I'll be good...I'll..."

But he just gave me a pat on the head and said to Mrs. Green, "He'll be all right shortly; it's all a bit strange to him now." And with that, he walked swiftly toward the front door. I tried to follow him, but the master turned around and snapped,

"Just behave yourself and act your age."

"Please take me back with you."

He just gave me a hard stare and off he went. That was the last I saw of the master.

As I listened to the car drive away, crying my eyes out, Doug handed me a handkerchief and showed me a bit of comfort, which was more than I got from our new foster parents.

"Now then," said Mrs. Green, as she pushed me in front of her. "What about a nice cup of tea and a piece of homemade cake? I'm sure you would like one after that long journey, wouldn't you?" She looked at me as if she expected a reply.

I looked up at her and said, "I want to go back to the home."

But she just stared, which was quite frightening because of those teeth.

"You're not going anywhere; now let's have a nice cup of tea and a piece of homemade cake."

The cake was quite good and it wasn't that sweet, but it had plenty of fruit in it. I ate mine in record time and then we had a cup of tea with powdered milk and no sugar, so I only drank half a cup.

After the tea bit, she suddenly pulled me onto her knee, but I gave a bit of a struggle. Doug gave me a nod, so I sat on her knee, and she started telling us both that, "This home was our new home. So you can forget the other home." Pointing to Mr. Green, she added, "This is your new Daddy, and I am your new Mummy, so you can call me Mum and you're Daddy, Dad."

All that time in her lap, I was wriggling and trying to slide off, but the harder I tried, the harder she gripped me. I gave her a heavy frown in response to the whole idea of calling them Mum and Dad.

Then the two of them started talking about it being Sunday and Mother's Day, and my foster father got out the very large family Bible. "As it is Sunday, and we will not be going to church today, we thought you might like to listen to some stories from the Bible," he said. And so our new foster father started to read the enormous Bible out loud.

I glanced in Doug's direction and saw him looking at me with an expression that said, "What on earth have we got ourselves into?"

During that time I was able to get a closer look at those teeth. I had never seen teeth sticking out that far. I found myself twisting my head to get a better look from underneath. She suddenly realized what I was doing and told me to sit still and stop staring at her.

After the Bible reading, which seemed to go on forever, my foster mother asked if I enjoyed that, and I honestly did not know what to say. So she looked me right in the eye and asked me again.

I shrugged my shoulders and said instead, "Do you have a teddy bear for me? The master said you might have one because they kept my teddy bear called Henry."

Both of them just stared at me. Then Doug came to the rescue and told them the story about my bear. She was shaking her head while Doug was explaining why I was so attached to Henry. To which Teeth – I mean my foster mother – responded sharply, "No, we don't have a teddy bear here, so you had better get over that teddy bear nonsense right now."

Her breath smelled somehow worse when she said that. I stood up and gave her a hard look and that was the end of that subject. The false warmth in her voice was rapidly disappearing to be replaced by a more arctic tone. World War II may have been over...but we were about to start a small scale civil war of our own.

We were then taken to the house next door to be displayed to Ted and Joan Gower, who were the neighbors. It turned out that they were very good and kind to both of us, and we ended up calling them Uncle and Auntie. After that introduction, we were eventually shown around our new house, which was very, very small compared with the orphanage. It was a council house, and so was identical to all the other houses on the street. It had three bedrooms, which meant that I slept in a room all on my own. I wasn't very happy about that.

The whole house seemed so dark and creepy, but the main thing I didn't like was the toilet. They only had one, which was OUTSIDE. There was no toilet paper; just the latest copy of the *Radio Times* attached to a nail on the wall with a piece of string. Which was an improvement from the orphanage where we had to ask for paper and had no doors, so in that sense it was all right, but, OUTSIDE? I was visualizing the cold and snowy weather sitting out there.

So, if you had to go during the night, you either held it until daylight, or you braved the darkness of the house, got wet if it was raining or cold if it was winter. The whole idea of the new place and the new foster parents made me feel worse and worse through the night, and I cried myself to sleep. I first dreamed that I was given to a lovely mum and dad...and then was traveling through the stars of the milky way by horse and carriage...and finally imagined I was presenting my bouquet of violets to Miss Lorie.

I awoke in the morning to the sound of my foster mother calling for me to get up. When I fully awoke, I found myself clutching the violets that Mrs. Woodley had given me. I must have gotten up and retrieved them during the night. That led to my second telling-off.

My foster father had gone to work, and when my foster mother discovered the violets in my sticky little hands, she noticed that they had stained the sheets and pillowcase. She gave me a mad stare her eyes wide open and unblinking, her head twitching slightly which made her teeth protrude even more. I slowly tried to crawl under the sheets again, but she pulled back the bedclothes and gave me a sharp crack on my face.

I do believe that that was the moment that she and I decided we were not compatible. She disliked me immensely, and I certainly disliked the pair of them. It was the first battle in our never ending war.

It was Monday morning, and the first job was to introduce Doug and me to our new school, Molsham School in Chelmsford. I did not want to go in. I stood at the front entrance and cried and would not enter the building, the thought of going to another school with new teachers and all the new children was to me frightening. It was a much bigger school to the village school that Doug and I were used to.

It was all very embarrassing for my foster mother. Even Doug was getting embarrassed and flatly told me to get inside the school.

My foster mother finally dragged me behind some bushes and gave me a damn good hiding. That was also my introduction to her name callings. As she hit me, she shouted in no uncertain terms that the reason I was in the orphanage was because I was a "rejected child, and nobody wanted me." That remark took all the wind out of me, and I reluctantly entered the school.

When I look back at all it now, I realize she seemed to take pleasure in beating me, and from then on beat me and bit my arm like it was a hobby of hers. The Greens didn't like me, but they couldn't send me back to the home without sending Doug too, who, incidentally, was the goody good and could never do anything wrong. He seemed to settle down quite well in our new home. In addition, they would lose money if they got rid of me, because they were paid a grant to look after us both. So, it looked like they had to put up with me, and I had to put up with them.

Before I go any further, let's just have a recap on exactly what occurred that Sunday, March 29, 1949. Imagine if you will, two children who were brought up in a large home with lots of other children about the same age. They played, laughed and cried together. They were in a happy environment, but were suddenly plucked away without even being asked or told what was going on. They then found themselves in a small, dark house with two strangers (and did I mention those teeth?), and were instructed to call them Mum and Dad.

Now think about it. You try going up to two strangers and calling them Mum and Dad. It not only feels very odd, but it doesn't seem right. It's very difficult to say it, let alone mean it, especially when you have never used those words before. That's exactly how Doug and I felt about that sudden change in our lives. We felt like we were two UPS packages being delivered to 51 Manor Road and these two people were asked to sign for the package.

Now, many, many months after, when I finally settled down – if you can call it settling down – to our new way of life, by the way, still without a teddy bear, it didn't change my feelings toward my foster parents, although I was with them for several years. When she met people she knew, she seemed to delight herself by saying. "Oh, have you met my two sons, Doug and Les."

She used to get strange looks when I would say, "Oh, this is my FOSTER mother." Instantly I knew I was going to suffer for that later.

I could never bring myself to call them Mum or Dad with any feeling whatsoever. I always referred to them as foster mother and foster father and they didn't like that at all. Douglas, the favorite, oh, he called them Mum and Dad, and I would give him a stare whenever he did. Sometimes he stuck his tongue out at me in return so I would stick mine out at him, and would you believe, I was always the one who was caught with the tongue out, and got the cuff around the ear.

When I look back, it was a great shame. We could have had a great family life together if the whole adoption thing was prefaced with the simple question, "Would you like to be fostered or adopted by these two people?" And after seeing those teeth, I would have given an instant reply: NO.

But back to my first day at my new school.

Chapter Ten

Miss Janie

When I was introduced to my teacher, Miss Janie, I took to her straightaway.

She had a friendly smile and a warm manner, and it was obvious that she cared for her students. She was a very attractive lady; tall, with sort of blondish hair, friendly eyes, and very, very hilly. She always wore the same perfume, an aroma that seemed to cling in your nostrils all day. I have only smelled that same perfume other time in my adult life, and it immediately made me think of Miss Janie, so I started singing, "The hills are alive..."

Miss Janie gave me a test to find out what level of education I had attained, but I made a right pig's ear of it and failed miserably. Not only was I behind in my studies, I hated tests. But she told me she would help me catch up with the other children in any way she could.

Now, Mrs. Green knew exactly how long it took Doug and me to get home from school each day – precisely 17 minutes – and she timed us each day. If we were late, we were punished. You see, she didn't want either of us to mix with the other lads on our street, as she thought they would be a bad influence on us, so our orders were to, "come straight home after school."

The first time I was late from school was when my teacher, Miss Janie asked me to remain and discuss my work because I was way behind in all subjects. She suggested that I take home more home-work, to which I agreed.

All the time she was talking to me, I kept on saying "I have to go, I'll be late," and when I finally did get home, there was hell to pay. My foster mother attacked me as soon as I walked into the house, striking out with both hands at whatever she could hit, but mainly aiming for my face. I noticed that when she lost her temper, her teeth stuck out even farther than normal. Yes, I did tell you about those teeth.

"Get up to your room and wait for your father to come home," she ordered, to which I snapped, "He's not my father," which only added fuel to the fire. She wouldn't listen to the reason why I was late, but just kept bellowing at the top of her voice and swinging her arms around like a windmill. I finally managed to escape and run up the stairs, as her shouting echoed through the whole neighborhood.

I sat on my bed, trembling with fear and unable to do my home-work, and waited for Mr. Green to come home from work, which wasn't long. As soon as he walked in the front door, I could hear her telling him what a horrible child I was and that he was to go and beat some sense into me. I could hear his heavy footsteps pounding up the stairs, so I stood in the corner of the room, feeling sick with fear and knowing that whatever he was going to do to me would hurt.

The door burst open, and as he entered the room, he started tak-ing off his big, thick leather belt. I tried to tell him why I was late, but he totally ignored me and shouted at the top of his voice, "I am fed up with you upsetting your mother. The only way to teach you is to beat some sense into you."

And he did just that. He ripped my trousers down, threw me over his knee, and thrashed the hell out of my bum, making sure that the big, brass buckle got me good. I was shouting at the same time I was screaming my head off, still trying to tell him why I was late from school.

When he finished, he threw me on the floor. While he was thread-ing his belt back through his trouser loops, he started to swear and curse at me. I looked up at him, and then saw her standing at the door. I fixed my eyes on her, and that started another shouting match, which finished with her telling me, "It's no good you looking at me for sympathy, because there's none of that in this house for you!"

Then they slammed my bedroom door, calling me all sorts of names while going down the stairs, making sure I could hear them. They left me sobbing my heart out on the cold linoleum floor. I pulled myself up onto my bed and nursed my sore face, my back and my bum, which were throbbing so much that I could not lie on my back. So I lay there on my stomach and pulled a blanket over myself, because it was very cold and there was no heating. I thought about Mrs. Woodley and the orphanage that we were dragged from, and wondered if it were punishment for the things I had done wrong there.

I must have dozed off, because the next thing I knew it was dark, and I desperately wanted to go to the toilet, and my stomach was crying out for food. Every step I took going downstairs was painful, my body ached that much. I went outside to the toilet and upon my return found everyone sitting around the fire in the living room, listening to the radio. As nobody looked around at me, I just stood there for a few minutes, making little coughing sounds to let them know I was there. Not one head turned around. I plucked up my courage, cleared my throat, and said in a soft, hesitant voice, "Can I have some food, please?"

Mrs. Green spun her head around like an owl and gave me that famous stare of hers. Then she bellowed so the whole street could hear, "Get back to your room and stay there, you horrible thing. None of us want to see you until morning."

I just stood there motionless, hoping she would change her mind, but no, she just shouted "get out of my sight," and started to get up. I repeated, "But I'm hungry; I've had nothing to eat since lunch," which caused her to swing her arms at me in that windmill fashion of hers, and shout, "Someone as bad as you doesn't deserve feeding!"

I tried again to tell her why I was late, but her temper got even worse, and without warning, she grabbed my arm and started biting it.

I was screaming, and it was so bad that my foster father actually came to my rescue and pulled her off me. Doug was very sympathetic, but what could he do? He stood their shaking his head, and I do believe he had tears in his eyes.

My foster father pushed me to one side and shouted at me to get to my room and stay there. As I quickly went upstairs, I felt blood running down my arm and saw the big teeth marks my foster mother had given me. It hurt even more once I had seen what she had done. I put my handkerchief over the wound, but for some time kept taking it off and looking at my arm, wondering what she would do next. All I could do was lie on my bed in pain and misery, and eventually drop off to sleep with the sound of my foster mother still raging downstairs.

The next morning at breakfast, I was really starving and ready to eat everything in sight. Doug was sitting at the table eating cereal and toast and drinking a glass of milk. He asked how my arm was, and I told him how I was awake most of the night with the throbbing pain.

While I was showing him the deep teeth marks with the dried blood around them, my foster mother walked in. My foster father had already gone to work. She frowned and tried to see what I was doing. Then she rested one hand on the table and put the other on her hip, and in a sarcastic voice said, "Are you sniveling to your brother about getting what you deserved? You're lucky that I didn't really lose my temp..." She stopped when she saw what she had done to my arm, and held it, staring in disbelief. Her frown was more sympathetic, but that didn't last long. She was silent for a moment, before saying in her usual stern voice, "Come here to the sink and let me clean that arm." She ran the cold water on it and wiped off the blood with a flannel. I flinched every time she touched me. She had a strange look of amazement on her face.

"Is it all right?" asked Doug, wiping the milk from his mouth.

"Mind your own business and get on with your breakfast," she snapped.

She dabbed my arm dry and used it to pull me over to a little medicine box in the corner of the kitchen. Still holding my arm, she fiddled around for something, saying, "Here it is."

I then understood why she was still holding my arm. The little bottle she was holding contained iodine, and we both knew that it was going to hurt. I immediately tried to pull my arm away, and she shouted at me to stand still "while someone is willing to help you, you ungrateful thing you." Then she ordered Doug to, "come and hold your brother still or you'll both be late for school."

I kept trying to tell her that I didn't need that stuff, but as Doug held me, she took the top off the bottle and tipped it onto my open wound. And did I scream. Doug asked me if I was all right, and as soon as he said that, she slapped my face hard and told me to stop acting like a little baby. Then she grabbed my arm and snapped, "Stand still," as she wrapped a bandage around my wound. "Now eat your breakfast or you will be late for school."

I sat down to a bowl of soggy cereal because the milk had been sitting in it forever. As I was on punishment, there was no sugar, and just two pieces of dry toast and half a glass of milk. My brother winked at me, which meant he had some food in his pocket for me. The thought that he had food for me, made me feel much better.

Before we left for school, my foster mother stood with the front door open and in a stern manner said, "You are not to take that bandage off for any reason. You keep that on all day. Do not take it off for anyone. Do you understand?" I agreed, and she stood there with her arms folded. As Doug went past her, she said to him, "Make sure he keeps that bandage on, and let me know if he tries to show people, right?" Doug agreed, and we both went off to school.

Once we were around the corner, we both stopped and Doug said, "How's the arm? It looks bad. I bet that iodine stuff hurt." I agreed, but was more interested in what food he had. He dug into his pocket and produced some bread with margarine and a thin smearing of jam on it, along with some little bits of rubbish that were lurking in his pocket. After a quick wipe, I ate it all in a matter of seconds.

During the course of the morning activities at school, the bandage on my arm started slipping down. I was pushing it back up again when Miss Janie asked me to come to her desk and told the other children to get on with their work. She reached out for my bandaged arm and I tried to pull it away, but she gave me one of her smiles and said, "Let me redo the bandage on your arm." She said it would be best to undo it and start again, but I pulled my arm away and said it was all right. "No, no, I insist," she said, and again I pulled my arm away. Then I told her that I was instructed not to show it to anyone, and if I did, I would be in trouble.

Miss Janie looked at me and said, "Who on earth told you that?" I told her my foster mother. She gently held my arm and said, "I'm sure she would want me to secure your bandage."

With that, I let her redo it for me. She carefully undid the bandage and then gasped in horror when she saw the big teeth marks on my arm.

"Who...on...earth did this to you? I don't believe...these are teeth marks... Who did this to you?" I hung my head down, reluctant to tell her. But Miss Janie gently put her fingers under my chin and lifted my head up saying, "It's all right, you can tell me. Who bit your arm? Was it an animal? How did it..."

I suddenly spurted out the truth: "It was my foster mother who did this."

"Your foster mother bites you? Why did she do...I can't believe that a person would...I thought it was a dog or...but your foster mother?"

Her eyes were filling up with tears, so she turned her back on the class and said, "Why did she bite you? Why?'" She re-bandaged my arm.

"She always bites my arm when she loses her temper with me."

Miss Janie was making all sorts of comments about how people could be so cruel to children. Then the bell rang for lunch and she dismissed the other children, which left us alone in the classroom.

"What did you do to make your foster mother bite your arm?"

"She just doesn't like me, Miss," I replied.

She sighed and was shaking her head when she noticed someone at the classroom door. She waved her hand and told him to go away, but when I turned around, I noticed it was Doug, and told her he was my brother. She flew up from her chair and ran to the door as Doug walked away. She called him back and asked him to please step into the classroom, and we welcomed each other with a smile. He immediately asked how my arm was, and Miss Janie straightaway asked him what had happened to my arm.

Without hesitating, my brother said, "It was our foster mother who did that. She's always biting his arm, but she got carried away when she did it this time."

Frowning, Miss Janie asked, "But why did she bite him?"

"Oh, because he was late coming home from school," Doug said, looking at me with concern. "Are you all right, mate?" he asked me.

I simply shook my head. Then Doug explained how my foster mother times us coming home from school, and she knew how long it takes and if we are late we get into trouble.

Then Miss Janie said in a faint voice, "Well, that was my fault yesterday. I asked you to stay behind." And with that, she stood up and pulled me towards her, and gave me a big hug. As she was hugging me, I discovered that I felt great. With my eyes wide open and a faint smile on my face, I was in heaven, my face was buried in her breast, and I didn't feel any more pain. I just wanted to throw my arms around her and ask if she wanted to adopt me.

You see, as I mentioned before, Miss Janie was hilly. I found my head tucked right between those hills, and realized that that was the first time in my life that I had ever had a hug. I really liked it. Doug was looking at me strangely, but I loved it and didn't want to move away from her.

"Time for lunch," she said, releasing me from her hills, I mean arms, and off to lunch we went. I had the biggest smile on my face, and Doug was asking me all sorts of questions like, "What did it feel like when she, you know, pulled you into her, you know?" and ended up by saying, "I wish I had a teacher like that."

The problem with Miss Janie's reaction to my arm was that it caused me to take advantage of her friendliness. You see, sometimes when I was in trouble after having a beating from my foster mother, I would bite my own arm very hard and show it to Miss Janie, who would automatically give me a hug, which really made my day. That was fine, until one day she looked very closely at the teeth marks and put her fingers under my chin and lifted my head up and said,

"These teeth marks are much smaller than the first ones. I wonder who made those."

I hung my head in shame, confessing that I just wanted another hug. Miss Janie smiled and gave me a quick hug, then told me anytime I wanted a hug, I should just come and ask her and she would understand.

Once my foster mother found out that the school knew about her biting me, I seemed to be in even more trouble with her. My teacher Miss Janie had sent my foster parents a letter asking why it was necessary to bite my arm. And of course my foster mother did not like that at all.

The major difference between living with the Greens' and living at the orphanage was that when you were in trouble at the orphanage, you were dealt with and then it was over. Not so at the Greens'. They didn't forget about anything, and made sure you didn't either.

For example, for the rest of that week, I was not allowed to have any margarine on my bread. They also stopped my ration of sugar. We each had a small jar of sugar that was topped up at the beginning of each week. If any sugar was used for cooking, equal amounts were taken from each jar, so not having any sugar was yet another punishment.

Although everyone's food was still on ration, we were rationed even more in that house. "To stop any small hands from stealing food," as my foster mother put it, she affixed a very large padlock to the pantry door. During the half-terms from school, whenever Doug and I wanted something to eat and my foster parents were both out of the house, we had to go without until Doug discovered that we could get into the pantry by prying up the staple that kept the padlock in place. After we had gotten some food, he would simply bang it back into position. That's how we got around the problem.

One day, Doug forgot to bang the lock back into position. I couldn't reach it, but he could. When Mrs. Green came home, all hell let loose when she saw the pantry door wide open and the padlock still in place. The way she acted, you would think that someone had committed murder.

In her fury, she asked who had been stealing food from her pantry. Doug shook his head and said, "It wasn't me," which of course left only me. She gave me one of those wicked stares and flew at me like a wild dog. She grabbed hold of my hair and dragged me to the scene of the crime, telling me that I was the most wicked child on earth. "Why we ever got you out of that home, I don't know. You should have been left there to rot."

Then she got stuck for words. So she struck out like a windmill again, hitting whatever part of my body she could, and once again ended up by biting my arms. After that, of course, I had to wait in my room to have more tears wrung out of me by Mr. Green's big leather belt.

That sort of treatment went on most of the time I was with them, although I know I may have deserved some of the punishment.

Chapter Eleven

St. John's Church

I secretly used to play with Smugger Smith, a lovely character about my age, who lived a few houses away from us. He came from a very poor family. Because he always looked dirty and wore rough, tattered clothes, I was told to keep away from him. In fact, I think most of the children on the street were told the same thing, so he ended up with no one to play with.

I first got in trouble over him when I gave him a pair of my shoes. Apparently his parents couldn't afford to buy shoes for him, so he used to wear an old pair of football boots to school and to play. Those boots were all I ever saw him in. Naturally, all the lads at school laughed and picked on him. So, unbeknownst to my foster parents, I gave him my old school shoes, which I never wore because they caused blisters on my heels. I had another pair that I could wear, and if they asked where the other ones were, I could simply say I lost them.

One day, my foster mother saw Smugger wearing what looked like a new pair of shoes. Everyone was so used to seeing him in the football boots that the shiny black shoes he had on now were very noticeable. She stood on the front doorstep with her arms folded and waited for him to come closer. As soon as he passed by, she immediately accused him of stealing the shoes and started waving her finger at him.

I couldn't bear to see him in trouble, so I stepped in and told her that I had given him the shoes. Well, you can guess what happened then. I was dragged into the house and got black and blue all over.

When Smugger learned that I was in trouble and not allowed out, he came to my house with the shoes in his hand to give them back to me. My foster mother opened the front door to find him standing there holding my shoes. She was speechless at first, but then hit the roof so the whole street could hear.

Now Smugger was used to getting a lot of abuse, but that was different, and he nearly fell backwards off the top step. She grabbed the shoes from him, examined them closely, and then threw the shoes back at him, saying scornfully, "Take the shoes! Nobody would want to put their feet in them after you have worn them!"

Smugger slowly bent down to pick up the shoes and muttered the words "Thank you," but she didn't hear what he said. As he stood up, she swiped him across the side of his face. She then pointed in the direction of his house, told him never to set foot in her yard again, and then slammed the front door very hard.

It was worth it to me to get a beating over that incident. The best thing was that Smugger got a nice pair of shoes out of it, and now that the old football boots were gone, it also changed the way that some of the children treated him. I still got to see Smugger sometimes, but it was always in secret, and usually at the church. You see, apart from Mr. Green's normal job as a factory worker at Marconi's, he held the position of verger at St. John's Church. (Verger is a posh word for caretaker.) The main responsibility of his job was to keep the church clean, or to put it another way, the main part of the job was for Doug and me to keep the church clean for him, especially when I was on punishment, which was quite often. I often wondered if that was the real reason for taking us out of the orphanage.

It was much later on that I found out that Mr. Green was an alcoholic and he gambled his money away on horses, so working in the church would take up his valuable time away from the horses. So, that was where we fit into the picture. Mr. Green would take

Doug and me to work at the church, mainly in order to show us what to do and how to do whatever it was. Gradually the job dwindled down to just me working at the church all on my own. In the Green's eyes, I was capable of doing the work without supervision because I could be threatened with punishments if the work was not done, and done correctly. I naturally did the job well. And I was able to meet Smugger there sometimes, and sometimes he would help.

One day, I was sent down to the church and told to clean the entire inside of it thoroughly. I had done something wrong, and I suppose it was a good excuse to get rid of me for the day. I went reluctantly, as I hadn't had a chance to ask Smugger to help me, so I ended up in the big old church on my own. While I was sweeping the long main aisle towards the altar when, I stopped and looked at the dust and bits and wondered what I was going to do with it all. Each side of the aisle along the edge of the red tiles was an iron grill with the heater pipes. I looked at them and decided to flick the dust and bits down the grating, and within seconds it was all gone and a smile was across my face thinking how clever I was.

But, I got the feeling I was not alone in the big, empty church, and that I was being watched by someone, and stopped periodically to look around. I couldn't see anyone. Every sound I made in that church seemed to echo all around the building. My footsteps and the banging of the broom caused a continuous noise, but when I stopped, I still couldn't hear anyone. I carried on, and again I stopped.

"Smugger, is that you Smugger?" I shouted, but when the echo died down, there was no other sound, so I continued sweeping. When I got to the end of the pews, I stopped and looked around again. There was nobody there, but I still had that feeling of being watched. I slowly looked around and eventually found myself looking up. Right above me was a large beam and a life-size figure of Jesus looking down at me from a crucifix.

I stepped back in amazement, and thought for a minute, realizing that it must have been Him looking at me. I looked down at the grill where I had swept all the rubbish, I then looked up at the effigy of

Christ, and stuttered in shame, "Erm, I'm sorry about that. Uh, I'll, uh clean it all out, sir." Well, I didn't know what to call Him, and "sir" seemed to fit. Then I ran to the cleaning cupboard and got the dustpan, and cleaned up my mess, and when I got back under the crucifix. Holding up the dustpan to show him I was true to my word and cleaned all the bits out. When I finished, I replaced the grill and gave a big smile up to Jesus and said, "That's better, I er...won't do that again, er...sir. I'm sorry."

And off I went to finish my jobs. The next time Smugger came to the church I told him all about talking to the crucifix and his immediate reply was "Oh, you mean, J. C."

"What?" I asked in amazement, "Who is J. C.?"

He pointed up and simply said, "Him."

So, from then on and even today, I refer to Jesus as J. C., all because of Smugger. You know, I felt much better after that, and whenever I went back to the church, I would smile at or talk to that crucifix of Christ. I would make a point of saying hello and goodbye, but I would also tell him whenever it was cold or raining out. If anyone was in the church when I arrived, I would look up and whisper hello and tell Him what the weather was doing, and sometimes I would get a strange look from people because of it.

During my time at Chelmsford, I spent a lot of time at St. John's Church. I not only spent numerous hours cleaning it, but also singing in the choir. I had to attend choir practice one night a week, and I had to go to services three times each Sunday, once for morning service, once for Sunday school, and again for evening service. You could say that I got to know the church very well, inside and out.

On the outside of the church there was an old boiler house, which had a small boiler to provide heat during the winter months. It was far too small to do the job successfully. To get to the boiler, you had to go down four steps and duck your head when entering the tiny room. Inside was a large, black metal stove showing signs of age. It had several large patches of rust and a tall chimney, which at some point had been repaired. To the left was a large pile of coke, and a small amount of coal for lighting the fire, plus a big old cardboard box, filled with sticks to start the fire.

On Sundays, when it was very cold outside, the boiler had to be kept stoked all day for both the morning and evening services. Now guess whose job it was to light the boiler and stoke it up? Yes, it was mine.

It was during one very cold spell when I was continuously running back and forth to stoke up the boiler, that I met a very nice old man. That day, I was sitting by the boiler trying to get warm, wondering what my friends at the orphanage were doing and wishing I was back there, when I heard footsteps in the churchyard coming toward the boiler house. I sprang to my feet and made myself look as if I was busy. You see, if I was caught not doing something I would be in trouble. Could it be my foster father or even the vicar?

All of a sudden, the footsteps stopped. I turned toward the entrance and saw the bottom half of a man with dirty old boots standing on top of the steps. I quickly coughed to let whoever it was know that somebody was down there. As I leaned sideways to see who it was, an old man was bending down to see who I was. When our eyes met, he smiled and slowly walked down toward me.

"You gave me a fright there, son. I thought you were one of the church people." He promptly went over to the stove, lifted the lid, and peered inside. "Hmm, I think you had better put a bit more on there, son, or you're going to have it burn out." Then he sat down on the old wooden box that I always used as a seat.

I just stood there and stared at him. He wore a big brown coat that was covered in stains, with large pockets bulging with all sorts of things. His trousers were big baggy corduroys, with the turn-ups turned down and just as many stains on them as his coat. They also had several threads hanging down, and a couple of large rips that must have made them drafty. His boots looked as if they had done a good few hundred miles. It was difficult to see what their original color was. The laces were tightly tied with different thicknesses of knotted string.

As the old man warmed up and the color came into his cheeks, I noticed he had a ruddy complexion and a well-weathered face. It was a kindly face; the sort that should be wearing a fishing trawler's hat, and I took an instant liking to it. But when he gave a big smile, he showed his very badly stained teeth, what few he had.

Pulling an old piece of dirty rag from his pocket, bits of string and paper fell out at the same time. He blew his nose on the rag and said, "When you get to be my age son, the cold really bites into you."

I felt sorry for him, and although I got a whiff of him, I still didn't mind, so I pulled up a bucket and sat next to him. He gave me a warm smile as he put the rag back into his pocket. "I haven't seen you down here before, son. Why are you down here?" the old man asked, as he fumbled around in his other pocket.

"Well, I..."

"I know," he interrupted, "you're hiding from someone."

"No, I'm not hiding. My foster father tells me to come here and keep the boiler going."

At that, the old man sprang to his feet and with a frown said, "Who is your foster father, lad?" He got very fidgety and kept looking up the stairs.

"Well, it's Mr. Green," I replied.

"The verger?" the old man almost shouted, stepping back in surprise. He uneasily fumbled around in one of his large pockets and finally recovered a bent cigarette. While trying to straighten the thing, he said, glancing up the stairs, "You won't tell him that I was down here, will you?"

I immediately told him, "No, honest, I won't say a word."

Then he carefully rolled up a long piece of old paper and put it into the boiler. When it caught fire, he used it to light his cigarette. While he was stamping out the paper, I asked him why I wasn't to say anything.

"Because these church people keep kicking me out of here, but I do no harm. I told them I would look after the boiler for them, but they told me to clear off. You see, they think that would bring other people down here looking for shelter." He paused, puffing on his cigarette. "I'm the only one that knows this place, and you don't think I would tell anyone else, do you?"

"Well, no," I said, wondering who he could be referring to.

Anyway, I sat there for some time talking to him and didn't realize that it was getting dark. I suddenly sprang to my feet and said, "I'll have to go now or I will be in trouble." I picked up the shovel to stoke the boiler once more, but the old man said,

"Leave that, son. You run along. We don't want you to get into trouble. I'll look after the boiler for you." I thanked him and told him that I hoped to see him again, and when I was at the top of the steps the old man said, "By the way, what's your name?"

"My name is Les," I said with a smile. "And what's your name?"

"Well," he said, rustling his hand in his pocket, "They all call me Lonely."

And with that I shouted, "Goodbye Lonely!" and got another quick look at those ugly black teeth of his. He said something, but I had no idea what, because I was running home as fast as I could, repeating to myself. "Please let there be food. Please, please let there be food," because I was starving.

Well, as I expected, I was in trouble again. I was greeted at the back door by Teeth, I mean my foster mother, who without saying anything, swiped me hard across my face. It was then that I learned why. Not only was I late for tea, but they didn't know where I was. They had sent Doug to the church to find me, but he came back empty-handed, saying that I was nowhere in sight.

"So where the hell have you been?" was my welcome. Mr. Green swung his hand across my face as well, and that made me dizzy for awhile. I told them that I was at the church.

"Don't lie to me. Your brother has been down to the church looking for you."

Clutching my face, which was stinging and red-hot, I sniveled,

"I have been at the church all day. You can ask the old man who was down by the boiler." I suddenly realized what I had said. I had promised the old man I would not say anything.

Mr. Green, who had just sat down, sprang to his feet and stared at me. "Is that horrible tramp in the boiler room again?"

I stood there not knowing what to say. With my head hanging down, I mumbled, "I don't know."

"What did you say? Do you want me to beat the answer out of you?"

"No. Yes. I mean no, oh well."

He grabbed the collar of my shirt and pulled me close to his face and in a nicotine-alcoholic enhanced voice shouted again, "Was that tramp in my boiler room?"

As I was trying to pull back from him, I stuttered, "Yes…he was… down there."

My foster father released my shirt collar and threw me across the room. I fell flat on my bum, which really hurt. He went into the hallway to put on his coat and said that he would put a stop once and for all to that tramp using the church like some hotel.

He suddenly waved his finger at me and said, "Don't let me ever catch you near that man," and off he stormed, slamming the front door behind him.

As I predicted, tea was over, but I was just in time to wash up all the dishes. I would have to wait until supper before I had anything to eat, but luckily there were a few scraps left on the plates, which I quickly scooped up and ate before you-know-who came in. Usually if there were leftovers, my foster mother would scrape them all into a bag to throw in the dust-bin, just to make sure that you-know-who didn't get it first.

Supper, when it came, was not very exciting anyway; just one piece of bread with no butter or jam, as I was still on punishment, and a drink of warm cocoa with no sugar.

Once again, I went to bed very hungry. When I climbed into bed cold, hungry, and miserable, my hand went under the pillow and I touched something. I quickly jumped out of bed to put on the light. But there was no nightlight for me, no doubt as an additional punish-ment.

Low and behold, I found that my brother had wrapped up a bread-and-jam sandwich for me in some grease-proof paper. Oh, what a surprise! I ate that sandwich slowly, with my little finger stuck in the air, and nibbled and nibbled until it was all gone. Then I folded the paper up into a tiny little square and slipped it into my shoe, as I didn't want to leave any evidence.

The next day, my foster father gave me a lecture about Lonely the

Tramp. He had no idea that I had really gotten to like him. He told me that if I ever saw him around the church, I had his permission to kick him out, and if he caused any nonsense, I was to come home for help or tell the vicar if he was at the church. In a sarcastic tone, he then told me, "He won't be going into the boiler room anymore, as I have put a padlock on it," and then dangled the key in front of me like it was a trophy of some sort. But he made the big mistake of telling me where the duplicate key was kept, for I had every intention, right or wrong, of telling Lonely where it was and letting him use the boiler room for warmth.

When I went to the church again, which was for choir practice, I went around to the boiler room and found that there was not only a big padlock securely fastened to the door, but a big "Keep Out" notice as well. I felt really guilty for having opened my big mouth about poor Lonely. It was some time before I saw Lonely again, and when I did, I apologized for telling my foster father about him. He understood, but he said he was looking for somewhere else to find warmth, because they had locked up the boiler room. I told him the good news about the key. He slipped the key into his pocket because he had a friend that could make a duplicate of it, and that way he could come and go into the boiler house as he liked, as long as they never saw him. I reminded him to make sure the original was put back in the special place.

I took him food that I salvaged from meals or went without, and even snuck some of the school meal stuff out for him. I would run all the way from school, drop off the food at the churchyard, and then run all the way home to be on time. Sometimes I didn't quite make it and got a beating, but it was worth it. Every so often, Doug and I would do little jobs for the lovely couple who lived next door, Auntie and Uncle. One of the jobs was to run to the little shop up the street called Schillings, and purchase items or get them marked on the book for them. On a couple of occasions, I got some cigarettes in their name, giving them to Lonely. I knew it was wrong, but did it anyway.

One day Uncle and Auntie questioned me about the odd thing that they never asked us to get, cigarettes. I went into great detail about Lonely and told them I would do anything for that man, even though he would never ask me for anything.

What's more, I thought more of that poor old man than I did of the foster people that I lived with. It was always him that I ran to when I was in trouble or even when I got lonely myself, which I did on many occasions.

Uncle and Auntie both told me that they would not mention it to my foster parents, and although they could not afford the cigarettes, they would help me with the odd bit of food now and then. I thanked them, and as I was leaving their house, who should be coming in but my foster mother.

"Has he been pestering you for stuff?" she demanded.

"Why no, Erm, Les was just asking us how we were, as we haven't seen him lately," came the halting reply.

My foster mother looked at all three of us very suspiciously. She then pointed to our house and told me to shovel up the coal, "NOW," so I backed out of Uncle and Auntie's house, keeping a eye out to make sure I wouldn't get slapped, kicked or bitten. Off I went to do my jobs.

Cleaning the church was a full-time job. On Saturdays, which was when I cleaned the brassware – and believe me, there was a lot of brassware – it would take all day. On some days, lots of people would come and go while I was cleaning and other times not even the church mouse would pop out to see me.

But that particular day was very different from the normal brass-cleaning days. First, it was pouring rain, and then a thunderstorm blew in. That made the inside of the church very dark, so I carried all the big pieces of brass over to the side door and swung the door wide open to let in some light. I had been told-off once for turning on the lights during a similar storm so I could see what I was cleaning. To save electricity, I had to clean the brass by the door in such conditions.

I used to hate cleaning the brass because of the smell of the cleaning liquid, and the mess it left on your hands. No matter how many times you washed your hands afterward, the smell was still there, which meant I couldn't pick my nose so often. The only thing I did enjoy cleaning was the lectern. It was taller than me, and shaped like an impressive eagle with its wings spread wide to hold the Bible, so it took some time to clean. I liked to save it for last, when no one was likely to come in and watch me. When the lectern was highly polished you couldn't help but look at it when you entered the church. It had been polished that often that it was easy to clean except that it took a long time. I took special attention to polish up the areas that would collect the polish that dried white. It would clog up in the grooves but, a little brush work took care of that. While I was in the choir during a Sunday service I would often see members of the congregation sitting opposite it looking hard at the lectern, and that would put a faint smile on my face.

So, I took off my jacket and rolled up my sleeves and sat cross-legged on the floor, ready to start cleaning everything else. I was really doing well until a woman carrying a big bunch of flowers came running into the church. She stood on the big mat, shaking the rain off herself and the flowers, then looked at me and said, "What an awful day it is." She stepped around me and went on up through the church. I looked at all the brass I had just cleaned, now splashed with rain water. I got a dry rag and wiped it all down again and carried on with my cleaning.

After awhile, I had cleaned all the moveable brass and placed it back in the correct position. I had been told-off for putting an item in the wrong place. I also put the altar cross in facing the wrong way, not knowing there was a right and wrong way for the cross. I didn't make that mistake again, because I definitely didn't want to upset my friend J. C.

It was now time for me to clean the lectern. Everyone who had come into the church had finally gone, leaving me all alone, or so I thought. It used to take me about an hour to clean the lectern. I really buffed and polished it very hard because it stood right in front of the people who sat in the first row. After I finished, I sat in the front row, exhausted, and stared at my work. I was really proud of the job I had done. The storm was still upon the church and the thunder was quite deafening. I was a little bit frightened, but as dark as it was, I could still see my reflection in the lectern and was staring at it with a proud little smile, when all of a sudden I saw another reflection appear. I swung my head around and found a young man wearing a vicar's collar smiling at me.

"I'm sorry, did I make you jump? I couldn't help noticing you staring at the lectern," he said in a friendly voice.

"Well," I said, "I just finished cleaning it and was, well...inspecting it."

He thrust his hand out to give me a damp, floppy handshake, and said, "My name is Reverend Peter Williams. I'm what you would call a traveling priest, and I'm attending this parish for about a month." Still holding my hand, the priest said, "And your name is?"

"Erm, it's Les Morris," I stuttered.

"And why are you in this church on a cold and miserable Saturday?" he asked as he sat down next to me.

"Well, my foster father is the verger here, and he tells me to come and clean the brass for the Sunday service," I replied.

The priest turned toward me and said, "What happened? Why do you have a foster father?"

"I don't know why. You see, I lived in an orphanage and..."

The priest interrupted. "You were an orphan?" Then he placed his hand on my thigh and looked at me and said, "If I can help you in any way, or if you get frightened by the storm," he said, "I will be in the vestry, all right?" And with that, there was a very loud clap of thunder. We both stood up at the same time, and he could see I was a bit nervous, so he hugged me.

"Remember," he said pointing again, "I'll be in the vestry," and then he disappeared into the darkness.

After cleaning up the mess around the side door of the church, I swung the big door shut and as the sound echoed through the church, a tremendous bolt of lightning lit up the inside for a few seconds. It was followed by an almighty clash of thunder, and then the power went off, because I saw the light go out in the choir-boys' room. That was where the cleaning cupboard was, which was where I was heading. Now that there was no light at all, it made the church seem very creepy.

The storm was getting louder and the church was even darker now and the thunder seemed to really echo inside the church. I was walking up the main aisle and looked up to see J. C., but I couldn't see him. It was that dark. After another loud crash of thunder, I heard a voice call out my name, and immediately looked up in J. C.'s direction, thinking it was him. But no, it was the traveling priest, who was holding a candle in the doorway of the vestry. He called for me to come and join him, so I changed my direction and headed toward him.

"Come in here until the storm blows over," he said.

As I walked past him, I noticed that there were three candles burning, which made the room quite bright. He pointed to a large chair and told me to sit down, then unscrewed the top off a thermos and asked if I would like some hot tea. That sounded like a good idea, so I got up and went over to him and he passed me some tea in a small china cup. There was more loud thunder. Then the priest sat in a large armchair and told me to join him. I went over to sit on the arm of the chair, but he pulled on my coat and told me to sit on his lap. I thought it was a bit odd, but because I was a little frightened by the storm, I felt more at ease doing that.

By then the whole church was vibrating with the storm, and the priest put his arm around me and said, "You will be all right now." We both drank our tea, which warmed us up a little, and then the priest started asking me questions. He asked if I liked it in the orphanage, and I told him I was happier there than I was with my foster parents.

"Was it because you had all those other boys to play with?" he asked with a smile.

"No," I started to explain, but he interrupted me and started saying strange things like, "Did you like playing with the boys? What sort of things did you do to each other? I hear there's a lot of that going on in the orphanages."

With a puzzled look on my face, I asked, "What things do you mean?"

"You know, boys playing with each other's private parts."

I again had a puzzled look on my face and said, "What are your private parts?"

He gave a big smile and put his tea cup down and took mine from me. Then placed his hand on my crotch and slowly rubbed his hand around saying, "This is your private part. Look, I have one too." And with that, he took my hand and placed it on his crotch and told me to gently rub it like he was rubbing mine. I went bright-red in the face and couldn't look him in the eye.

He could see that I was embarrassed, so he said in a soft voice, with his hand still lying on my now-erect penis, "Now don't be afraid. This is a perfectly normal thing for a young man to do. And remember, just because we get older, we still like to play now and then."

I kept thinking that he was a priest, and therefore the sort of man to trust, but I didn't know what to do. Then he got up and went over to lock the vestry door, and as he walked back to me, the lightning lit up the whole room. The priest hugged me and told me I was in safe hands. His hand went straight back to my private part, and he said, "I see you like this," and started undoing my fly buttons so he could get it out to rub it.

I really didn't know what to do; I mean, it felt good, but should I run out and shout? He kept talking about how it was a natural thing to do, and while he was talking to me he got his own private part out and placed it in my hand. My eyes opened wide at the sight of the thing, but he kept insisting it was fine to do it.

By then, he had undone my trousers and was caressing my bum while rubbing my thing. I told him I wasn't very good at that, but he told me I was doing fine.

"Now remember," he said, "this is our little secret. Don't tell anyone, because they will get jealous and wonder why I don't do it with them. I nodded and he repeated; "Now you understand – not a word?"

I answered yes, and he continued playing with my thing. I quickly told him that I was about to come and it went all over the place. He then told me to rub his harder, and it wasn't long before he did the same.

The storm had finally passed over and it was time for me to head on home. The priest saw me out of the church and said, "that it was a pleasure meeting you, and don't forget our secret." I smiled and headed to my foster parents.

The priest interfered with me one more time in the boiler room, and tried another time but he was unable to do anything because my brother Doug showed up. When I looked at him during the services while in the choir, he would never look at me and if he did happen to catch my eye, he quickly looked the other way. In due time, he left St. John's church never to be seen again.

All the way home, I kept thinking about the priest, but every time I thought of that incident, I kept saying, well he's a priest, and he should know right from wrong if anybody does.

Chapter Twelve

A Talk with J. C.

I was late coming out of school one day, and as I was running home met Smugger, who asked why I was running. I told him that I would get a good hiding because I was late, and he said, "You will still get the same hiding if you're ten minutes late or half an hour late."

As I thought about it, I realized he was dead right, and as I was already ten minutes late, I thought I might just as well walk back with him, so that's what I did.

When I saw Mrs. Green standing on the front doorstep with her arms folded I knew that this one was going to hurt. As soon as Smugger saw her, he walked over to the other side of the road saying, "I bruise easy; I'll see you."

I swallowed hard as I approached her. She simply stood to one side as I cautiously walked past. Then she slammed the door very hard and went into one of her fits.

That time I was really bruised and aching all over. But I suddenly retaliated and shouted that I was going to run away, and she stopped in her tracks. She paused for a moment, and still fuming shouted at the top of her lungs, "Well, go on then!" She pointed to the door, and then made a hasty move to open it. "Well, go on!" she said, holding the door wide open. I made a couple of side steps toward it when she shouted, "Come on, I'm not going to stand and hold this door open all night. If you want to run away, go. I know one person that will be glad to see the back of you."

I cautiously walked towards the door and stuttered, "I'm going to run…"

"Well, go. What will you live on? Where will you sleep? Come on, if you're going just bugger off right now."

Now that really did upset me. I had no intention of running away; I only said that in temper. Without hesitating, I ran past her, flinching because I thought I was going to get a thick ear as well. As soon as I was out of the door, it slammed shut behind me.

I stood in the gateway in disbelief thinking, they really didn't want me there or she wouldn't have made so easy for me to just walk out. The front room window curtain moved back, and I could see that she was still shouting and waving her arms. Although I couldn't hear her, I knew exactly what she was saying. I waited for a minute thinking that she would call me back, but no, she was still foaming at the mouth waving her arms around like a windmill.

Crossing over to the other side of the road, I just stood there and noticed several houses with their curtains to one side watching the dramatic performance. I still thought she would call me back, and all of a sudden the front door swung open and Teeth shouted as loud as she could, "Bugger Off, You're Not Wanted Here Anymore" And once again the front door slammed shut.

I started running up Manor Road with no idea where I was going, but I stopped a little way up the road to see if they were calling me back. But no. There was not a soul to be seen. I continued running until I was well out of sight. Then I slowed to a walk, with my head hung down, wondering what on earth I was going to do. I was hungry, and it was starting to get dark. It had just dawned on me what a fool I was, fancy running away before a meal. I suddenly started running again. "I know, I'll go and see Lonely," I thought. "He might have some food and I can stay in the warm boiler room with him."

Puffing and panting, I ran straight around to the boiler room, only to find it shut up tightly with the padlock firmly in position. I was very, very depressed and had no idea what I was going to do. I sat on the top of a tombstone with my head in my hands, wondering what to do next. I was hoping to be with Lonely who would take care of me.

After a while I started to feel cold. I went around to the main entrance of the church and swung the big doors wide open, went inside, flicking on the entrance light. It was so quiet that every step I took seemed to echo through the whole of the church. I felt like shouting just to make sure I was on my own.

As I slowly walked up the main aisle, I wondered if I had done the right thing. It was very nearly dark inside. Each footstep sounded louder as I made my way toward the first pew. I kept looking around me, and feebly said aloud, "Lonely, are you here?" But only my voice went around the church. I sat down half-way and again wondered what to do.

I sat there for a while, with just a shaft of light filtering its way through. I was beginning to feel a little frightened; not so much by the darkness, but by the silence, interrupted every now and then by a cracking sound from the timbers as they settled with the drop in temperature outside. The sound was coming from all directions, and I jumped a little at each one. I also kept looking around, thinking I heard or saw a movement.

Eventually I looked upward, and saw that there was a faint reflection of light from the crucifix, which made me leave my seat and make my way to the far end of the church. I looked at the statue of Jesus the whole time I walked, and listened to the sound of my footsteps. When I reached the end of the pews and stood near the pulpit, I sat down on the very first seat, almost directly under the crucifix. After I had wiped my nose and eyes, I looked up and said in a whisper, "Um, you haven't, um, seen Lonely, have you?"

Even my whisper seemed to take a long time to go around the church. I sat there some more and looked around in the steadily decreasing light. I saw the altar with the big candlesticks, the slight reflection of the brass cross that I had polished several times, the choir stalls, and the big organ with its towering pipes and the rear-view mirror that the organist used to watch us through.

Then I looked at the impressive lectern, which glittered with my heavy polishing, and finally to the pulpit, which stood high above so the vicar could see who was listening and who was asleep. I looked up again at the wonderfully carved figure of Jesus and said, "I've just run away from home, sir."

And in a bit louder voice, continued, "And I was, well, I was wondering if I could stop here for the night." As I said that, there was cracking and unexplained bumps around the church. I looked around in all directions before going on.

"I'm frightened to go home because my foster mother will beat me again."

More noises, but I ignored them this time. "And if Lonely was here, well, I would have stayed with him, and I could have left you in peace." I wiped my eyes and nose again, then suddenly went cold with fear. I could hear loud footsteps walking up the main aisle toward me. The footsteps got louder and louder and a shadow caught my attention, and I knew then it was someone big and tall. My eyes were wide open, but I couldn't move for fear. Beads of sweat started to roll down my face. Nearer and nearer the heavy footsteps came, but as much as I wanted to turn to see what or who it was, I couldn't move.

I glanced to my left at the shadow of the man who was nearly upon me. I tried to look up at the figure of Jesus, but I was numb and shaking, and all of a sudden the footsteps stopped. And then it happened.

I felt a hand gently touch my left shoulder. I spun around to look, and there was a man dressed all in black looking at me. I immediately screamed and leapt to my feet.

"It's all right, my child, it's all right. I am the vicar," the man said, and I involuntarily threw myself into his arms and cried. It was mostly relief at knowing that it wasn't who I thought it was, my foster father.

"Come and sit down," he said with a friendly smile. He sat next to me and told me to wipe my eyes, and calmed me down by saying that there was nothing to fear now, because he would help me if he could. I got my breath back while the vicar explained that he saw the entrance light on and that was the reason he was there. Then he asked what was the matter and who was I talking to?

I told him as I was blowing my nose that I had run away and that I was talking, well, I hesitated to say who I was talking to, because I thought he would think I was a bit of a fool, but I slowly looked up at the crucifix and his eyes followed mine.

"I was, um, talking to Him," I confessed, pointing upwards.

"I know," said the vicar kindly. "I was standing at the rear of the church listening to you. Do you know who that is?"

"Yes," I said, now full of confidence, "He's my friend. He's the only one I can talk to, and his name is Jesus, but I call him J. C."

The vicar frowned at that and asked, "Why do you call him J. C.?"

"Well," I said, "a friend of mine who came to help me clean the church once, by the way, his name is Smugger Smith and my foster parents have told me not to see him because he is poor. Anyway, he told me Jesus Christ is known as J. C."

I could see that the vicar was quite touched by what I had told him. Then he asked if I was happy living with my foster parents. I swiftly turned to face him and looked right into his eyes and said sharply, "No. I want to go back to the orphanage, where my happiness was taken from me. I want to be happy again."

He then gave me a friendly talk and ended up by suggesting that I go home, saying he was sure that if I told them I was very sorry, they would be compassionate.

Like a fool, I took his advice. I wished I'd hadn't, because when I got home I got the hiding of my life from both of them. First Mr. Green struck me with his belt, then Mrs. Green went into her windmill arm job, and then he gave me a final swipe with his belt. I ended up on the floor, once again bruised and aching. I remember wondering what the vicar would say if he could see me then.

And, believe it or not, all of that happened to clash with bath night. Now, bath night there was vastly different from bath night at the home. There was no shiny white enamel bath; in fact, the bath was a large galvanized metal thing that hung by a large nail on the wall outside near the toilet, and it was quite an ordeal to prepare.

You see, in order to have a bath, you first had to fill the stone boiler which was lead-lined, and underneath the boiler was a small fireplace to heat the water.

First you had to get buckets of water to fill the boiler, and then you had to light a fire underneath it. These two steps were very time consuming and they were done early in the morning so that the bath water was ready by tea time. Then you had to drag tub inside, and with the aid of a bucket, transfer the water from the boiler tap to the bath. And if you were the last to have a bath, as I was on that occasion, and all the other occasions, you had to sit in the water that everyone else had used.

On that night, I looked in the bath and there was a layer of scum floating on top of the water. I was hesitant to get in, but my foster mother poked her head around the door and shouted, "Get in that bath and then go right to bed, out of my sight." As soon as she slammed the door, I stuck my tongue out as far as I could in her direction. With my aching body, it was no joke getting in the bath, let alone getting out. Someone had left the big bar of carbolic soap in the bath so trying to pick it up was like trying to get hold of a lump of jelly.

The last one out of the bath (me) had to ladle all the water from it and carry it in a bucket outside to the drain. I apparently made too much of a mess when I tipped it down the sink. That isn't surprising, as it was a long way for a little chap to lift that big bucket of water, and it would have been much easier with the help of an adult.

Having removed the water, I then had to drag the bath outside and hang it up. Then I had to wipe out the inside of the boiler, and clean out the ashes from the fire.

I often wondered why I was always last to have a bath after doing all the cleaning up, I was ready for another bath.

Chapter Thirteen

A Shopping Spree

One memory I have from 51 Manor Road, was when my foster mother took my brother shopping when my foster father was at work. She liked to take Doug shopping and leave me behind. Why? Because he was her favorite.

Unfortunately, the last time they went shopping, I got bored and started chasing the black cat around the house. The cat jumped up on the sideboard and knocked over a vase which was supposed to be quite valuable. It looked like a cheap fair-ground vase to me. But anyway, I got a real beating for that, and that day was the first shopping day since that incident.

Remembering the cat chasing incident, my foster mother came up to me, put her face right up to mine, and told me to get to my room. She followed me up the stairs, shouting that I could not be trusted to stay in the house on my own, and that she certainly didn't want to be seen with me in the shops. When I got to my room, she dragged in a large wooden packing box. I looked at the box, wondering what it could possibly be for. Then she pointed to the box and ordered me to get in.

Dumbfounded, I looked at her and Doug, and said, "Get...in it? What for?"

"Because you can't be trusted to roam this house alone, so you have to be caged like the animal you are. Now get in the box!"

By then she was dragging me by my shirt, so I got one leg in and said in a frightened voice, "But I don't want to get in. Please don't lock me in the box."

But she grabbed my other leg and lifted it up and I fell into the box. I tried to get out, but she used all her weight to push me down. Then she got the heavy wooden lid and threw it on top, hitting me on the head. I could hear her asking Doug to hand her stuff to place on top to keep me in. I kept begging her not to keep me in the box, but within minutes I heard the front door slam. And then it was silent. My foster mother and Doug had gone shopping.

I was all cramped up in that dark, foul-smelling box. I tried to get into a different position but was unable to move. At the bottom corner of the box was a large knothole, about two inches around, and that was my only source of light and air for about three hours. All I could do was shut my eyes and think about the orphanage at Ashdon, wondering what Mrs. Woodley was doing.

Eventually, the cat discovered me, and was poking his claws through the knothole, so I struggled into a position where I could poke my finger through to play with him. He immediately clawed me and drew blood. I shouted bad things at the cat and ended up with my finger in my mouth.

I needed to go to the toilet and sat for some time trying to hold it. I tried to lift the lid off, but although I might have been able to, I was in such a cramped position that I couldn't move it. For a while I put up with the cramps and a bursting bladder, but I finally just peed myself, and what a relief that was! But the smell in the box soon became rank.

About ten minutes after that, I heard movement downstairs, and then the voice of my brother saying, "Shall I let Les out of the box, Mum?"

Yes, he called her Mum, which I hated him doing.

"No," she answered. "Leave him there until we put everything away."

Doug came into my room and asked, "Are you all right, mate?"

"No! Let me out of here!" I demanded.

"She told me you have to stay in a little longer, mate," and I could hear her shouting for him to come downstairs to help her.

Finally they both came to my room to let me out of the box. As soon as she walked in, she said in her angry voice, "That creature has peed in my packing box!" and then I could hear them removing objects from the lid. The lid came off and the light made me squint. "Get out of there you disgusting creature!" she commanded while hitting me on my head.

I tried to move but couldn't because my knee joints were locked in position. So she grabbed hold of my shirt and tried to pull me out that way, calling me all sorts of names all the while. Finally she used her foot to push the box over on its side. I half fell out, but still couldn't unlock my knees. She bent over me and started hitting me some more, and I was crying and begging her to stop, but she was in one of her crazy moods where she would only stop when she got tired. At last she stopped hitting me, but kept calling me all sorts of names and saying that I was in the orphanage because I was a reject and an unwanted, horrible child, and that they were fools to take me into their home.

For the grand finale, she shrieked, "We ought to put you in that packing box and ship you back to the orphanage with a label saying "Unwanted Creature." Now what do you say about that?"

I shouted. "Oh yes please, send me back to Ashdon."

Before she left the room, she hollered, "Get those stinky clothes off and into a cold bath."

I sat there sobbing, and Doug put his arm around me and said, "I'll help get the bath for you mate." I thanked him, but as soon as I hobbled down the stairs, my foster mother said in a sarcastic tone, "Douglas, that brother of yours is quite capable of getting his own bath." What with the weather being so cold, it turned out to be the worst bath of my life.

Chapter Fourteen

Early Nights

The school at Chelmsford was large compared with the village school at Ashdon, and as I said earlier, I created quite a scene when I first started. Once I settled in, I was fine, as long as I made it home on time.

Well, one day at school the whole class got held after school because we didn't complete our short test papers, so everyone went home late. But do you think my foster teeth, mother would listen to me? Of course not. As soon as I walked in the back door, she grabbed hold of me and started her windmill hitting job. The more I tried to convince her, the more she hit me. Then came the bit I really didn't like, when she grabbed my right arm and bit it as hard as she could. That time I think the whole street must have heard me scream.

When she finally let go, I looked at my arm and saw that she had drawn blood. She stood there shaking with that evil stare and pointed to the stairs, telling me to go, "and wait for your father to get home." I again made the mistake of saying the worst thing I could have said under those conditions, which was, "He's not my father, he's a FOSTER..."

Another cuff around the ears caught me off balance and down I went. The windmill started all over again. I was trying to protect my bleeding arm and finally managed to escape to the stairs, with my nose bleeding now as well. I crawled on my hands and knees up to my room, with her shouting all sorts of abuses at me.

I waited in my room for the dreaded sound of my foster father coming home, and when I heard him I started to tremble. I looked around the room to see where I could hide, but that wouldn't have worked anyway, so I stood in the corner until I heard the heavy footsteps coming up the stairs.

The door burst open and in he came, removing his belt as he walked toward me. I could see his lips moving and heard the noise of him shouting at me, but was too afraid to understand a word. He flicked his belt up at my face and the left side of my face went numb. Then he grabbed my shirt collar and threw me across the bed and started beating me with his belt, being sure the brass buckle struck my body just about everywhere. The final blow came as my foster mother stood in the doorway, arms folded, watching in glee as the belt buckle struck the back of my head. I let out the loudest scream I had ever done, as I was in very great pain.

The abuse probably would have continued, but I was saved by someone knocking on the back door. It turned out to be Ted from next door; he wanted to know what all the noise was about. My foster parents told Ted that every time I got a little slap I would get very dramatic and scream the place down.

"You just have to raise your hand to him, and he screams," said my foster mother. Ted was standing at the bottom of the stairs, and as he turned to walk out the door, he got a look at me as I almost fell down the stairs. He paused and looked hard at me and frowned and said,

"Are you all right, Les?"

I was about to answer when Teeth, I mean my foster mother, ushered Ted out saying, "Oh, he's all right, he's just looking for a bit of sympathy…erm thanks for checking, but, yes he's all right…" Then Ted left. As soon as he had gone my foster mother in a quiet stern voice said, "Where are you going? You came down for sympathy; well you won't get any from me."

I hesitated and said, "I want to go to the toilet." My foster mother stood to one side and I hesitated to walk past her because she raised her hand as if to strike me but changed her mind when she heard Ted talking to somebody outside.

When I came back from the toilet, she was still standing at the front door listening to the conversation outside through the letter box.

I was instructed to stay in my room until morning. I felt numb all over, and I had blood in my hair and on my arm and the top of my leg. I guess I eventually fell asleep, because the next thing I knew, Doug was shaking me to get up for school. He helped me to the bathroom and I had a quick wash, which was extremely painful.

Although I was aching all over, I was still more interested in getting some food. When I got downstairs, my foster mother looked me up and down and said, "Just look at you. How can you think you are worthy of a good home?" I gave her a look that she didn't like, because she grabbed hold of me and dragged me over to the kitchen sink while I shouted,

"No, please don't hit me again."

She immediately turned on the cold tap and pushed my head under the water and started to rub the blood off. It hurt and I started to shout, but she slapped me across the ear and demanded that I stand still. She washed most of the blood from my hair with a wet rag, but my head was still seeping blood. Then she dabbed some iodine on my wound, and I broke two of my nails clinging onto the draining board trying not to scream.

"If anyone asks you what happened, you tell them that you fell down," she ordered. I didn't answer, so she snapped, "Did you hear what I said?"

I stuttered "Yes" before limping off to school. When some of the children at school asked me what happened I simply told them that I fell over. One teacher commented by saying during class,

"Well, it looks like Morris has been in the wars again." and that caused the class to laugh. Back in those days, people didn't take steps to find out what happened to children if they had cuts and bruises. It was a regular occurrence and people were used to seeing children in that state. Reporting child abuse was unheard of.

My foster father worked at the Marconi factory, which made radios. It was in Chelmsford and involved shifts of either days or nights.

Whenever he left for work, he followed a certain ritual, which was going to the toilet after breakfast, putting on his jacket or top coat, and waiting for my foster mother to hand him his lunch – all neatly wrapped and placed in a work bag – then kissing her goodbye. After that, we were told to go to the door to see him off, and once he was out the gate, we were told to go outside and wave goodbye.

That always puzzled me because he never once looked back to see if we were waving, which I never did. In fact, he never said goodbye to either Doug or me. I think the whole thing was for the benefit of the neighbors, to show them what a happy family we were. Well, the immediate neighbors certainly knew differently. How could they explain all the screaming and shouting?

Whenever Mr. Green worked the night shift, it became what I called my "early night" times. Around 6:30 or seven, I would be sent up to bed while Doug stayed down in the living room with her until…whenever.

Of course I didn't like the idea of that, but what could I do about it? Absolutely nothing, so off to bed I went at whatever time she demanded.

One night I was sent to bed early, which I didn't mind because I didn't feel well. I asked if I could have a hot-water bottle because it was bitter cold and the only heat we had in the house was from the coal fire in the living room. She reluctantly gave me a stone hot-water bottle, which was only just warm and would turn ice cold soon enough. I was afraid I would attract abusive remarks by asking for it to be warmer, so I went up to bed and fell asleep cuddled up with the bottle.

I woke up a little later because my covers had slipped off the bed and my hot-water bottle was no longer warm. Shaking with cold, I got out of bed and took the bottle downstairs to see if my foster mother could put some hot water in it. I also had a splitting headache. When I got downstairs, everything was dark except for a faint flickering of light coming from the lounge door, which was ajar. Clutching the bottle, I went toward the door and stood, hesitating for a moment as I tried to decide if I should enter. But I was so cold that I slowly pushed the door open and walked in.

The couch was facing the nice roaring fire, and my brother and foster mother were sitting together soaking up its rays with the radio faintly playing in the background. They sat with their backs to me, so they had no idea I was in the room. I stood there for a while, shivering with the cold and the fear of waiting for them to look in my direction. Something was going on, but I couldn't tell what, because I could only see the backs of their heads and shoulders. And then it happened.

I coughed, involuntarily.

Both their heads swung around at the same time, and if looks could kill, I was a goner. My foster mother leapt to her feet and came screaming towards me. I quickly turned and ran for the stairs, but dropped the hot water bottle.

My foster mother picked up the bottle and started accusing me of spying on her. Then she threw the bottle at me as I was halfway up the stairs. It hit me on the left side of my back and knocked the wind out of me. I collapsed on the top stair, and as soon as I got my breath, begged her not to hit me.

She didn't hit me, but she did give me a couple of kicks, then bent down and grabbed me by the collar and dragged me into my bedroom, shouting what a horrible creature I was and continuing to accuse me of spying on her and Doug. Before she left my room, she waved her finger at me and shouted the usual,

"Wait until your father gets home. We'll see what he has to say about this incident." Then slam went the door.

I didn't have the energy to tell her he wasn't my father. I pulled myself onto my bed and felt really ill, but just lay there for a while, holding my side, which hurt with any movement.

I couldn't understand why she was so paranoid about me wanting some more hot water for my hot-water bottle. Normally, she would just shout abuse or throw something at me. It wasn't until later in life that my brother Doug confessed what was really going on when I had walked in. Apparently, that night when my foster father was on the night shift, Doug and my foster mother were sitting in front of the fire listening to the radio when Doug spotted her looking at his crotch. She gave him a puzzled look and demanded to know what he had in his trouser pocket.

"Nothing," said Doug, pulling his handkerchief out of his right pocket.

"No, no, this pocket," she said while squeezing the lump in his pocket. She pulled her hand away quickly when she realized that she had grabbed hold of his penis. My brother Doug was sitting with Teeth and he had a stiffy (erection). She then wanted to know and asked him, "What on earth is going on down there?"

By then, Doug was blushing and gave her a sheepish look. "I don't know," he said, "it just came up on its own."

"I don't believe you – get it out," she snapped.

"What? Get my thing out?" Doug asked.

"Yes. That surely isn't your thing, is it?"

By now, Doug's face was a scarlet red and he had an enormous stiffy, which he had a job getting out of his fly buttons. When he got it half out, he said, "There," and started to put it back in.

"No, no, no, I want to have a look at that. I can't believe that it's that big," she said, as she pulled the whole thing out.

Doug didn't know which way to look, as he was very embarrassed. "I had better go now," he said, and tried to get up, but my foster mother would not let go of it. She kept stroking it up and down and making comments like, "I had no idea it was so big. My you have grown up all of a sudden. Do you like what I'm doing?"

"Well, er, yes, but you know it will make a mess soon." Doug said, not knowing where to look.

"You mean you will come soon?"

Doug simply nodded.

"Then you had better get that handkerchief out again," she said.

Doug stiffened up by stretching out his legs towards the fire and said in a hurried murmur, "I'm coming," and the stuff went flying everywhere while my foster mother was rubbing his penis faster and telling him what a good big boy he was. She had a broad smile on her face, and I'm sure she was showing her happy teeth, and as she got up, she said,

"I have got most of it in your handkerchief."

She clutched the hankie in her hand, bent down and kissed Doug on the forehead, and said, "I'm just going to the toilet. Clean your-self up; I'll be back in a minute." And off she went, carrying Doug's handkerchief as if it was a treasured item.

My foster mother was in the toilet for some time, and when she returned she sat next to Douglas and with a big smile told him, "What we did tonight is going to be our little secret."

And so it was most nights when my foster father was on the night shift. But Doug was not allowed to touch her. After she had rubbed him, she would simply go to the toilet and spend 15-20 minutes in there. That was the ritual.

So when I walked in on them looking for some hot water, you can see why she reacted the way she did... DAGNABBITT!

Chapter Fifteen

On the Move

Having settled, however precariously, into school and that odd way of life, we were about to be unsettled again, because we were on the move. My foster parents moved to a place called Norbury on Croydon in the south London area, and dragged us along on February 25, 1952. The journey to Norbury was by a large Pickford's removal lorry. Once everything was loaded, Douglas and I, plus a helper had to travel in the back of the lorry with the bottom ramp hooked open, its chains allowing us to stand and look out the back to see where we had been. My foster parents sat in the front with the driver and that pesky cat. The journey was long and tiring, and I could taste and smell that terrible exhaust fumes for some time after we had arrived.

Although we had a fine big house and a better environment there, it meant that we had to settle into yet another school, and I didn't like that at all. I loved Miss Janie, and wished she could have come to teach me at my new school.

As we were in the process of re-settling down, for some unknown reason my foster father lost his job. I think it was the alcohol that did it, but because the house went with the job, guess what? We were on the move yet again. That time it wasn't to a better house, but we had to share a house in a village called Dodinghurst. The family, who lived there, was related to my foster mother. The house was a bit cramped. What with two more adults and two additional children, both boys, and only three bedrooms, places to sleep were scarce. Doug and I had to sleep on a sofa or an armchair, that's if the dog allowed us to. Very often at bedtime, if the dog was sleeping on the chair, we were not allowed to make the dog get off. It was his bed, they pointed out, and because he was getting old, he had first dibs. But if you could manage to get on it before he settled down, he'd let you share it.

So, it became a race each night as to who would sleep with the dog. If you didn't win the race, you had to sleep on the floor or sit at the table and put your head down in your arms.

After a month of friction between the two families, we were told to move. The term I heard was something like, "Get out, the lot of you." Here we were again, on the move. Would I get my own bed, as I was hoping for? Yes, I did get my own bed, but it was not a nice comfortable house. That move was to the worst place imaginable. We moved into a one room caravan, or trailer, right in the middle of a field. The four of us were crammed into that tiny space, and were constantly getting on each other's nerves. I hated it.

There was no privacy, no electricity, and the toilet was a bucket outside in a rickety wooden shed. In the middle of the night, when you wanted to go, it meant getting dressed when it was wet, and it rained just about all the time we were there. Plus you couldn't help but disturb everyone else on the way, so you also got told off and shouted at all the time. One night our foster mother cut a fart that you could photograph. I mean it was so bad Doug and I scrambled to get out of that tin can to suck in some fresh air, while we leaned against the wooden outhouse that now didn't smell so bad.

Doug said, "Are you all right, mate?"

I replied by nodding my head and muttering. "I think she singed the hairs in my nostrils."

Well, I soon got over that problem. I slept on the top bunk, where there was a small window, so if I wanted fresh air to go for a pee, I simply opened the window and did it straight outside. Living in such conditions made our lives even more miserable.

We traveled seven miles to our new school by bus. It was a terrible place, but just as I was getting settled, it happened again.

The Society heard about us, and came and inspected our living conditions, and without hesitation, took both of us back to Ashdon, our very first orphanage where we had been very happy at one time.

Well, I for one was very excited. The first person to welcome us back was dear old Mrs. Woodley. I sank into her arms with relief, and was very happy that I was now home and I could slowly feel a long lost smile growing on my face once again.

But things never turn out the way you think they will, and before we knew it, Doug and I were back with Mr. and Mrs. Teeth, our foster parents. That time we lived at 99 North Avenue in Chelmsford, Essex, and when we arrived, I was sick as a parrot.

I had honestly thought I had seen the last of them, but it was even harder to settle down. And of course, it meant yet another school. To make things worse, there was no church that I could run to in times of trouble, and there was plenty of that.

My age at that time was 12. I longed for a day when I could seek happiness, a time when I could feel comfortable with someone, and most of all, feel wanted. When I heard what other children did and what the future held for them, I often used to wonder what would become of me. I would see parents greeting their children from school, giving them a good hug and laughing and joking with them, and sometimes used to wish that child could be me. But, no, I had to beat the clock to get home to Teeth on time, or face the inevitable punishment.

The biggest problem with being dragged from school to school was that I lost a lot of education, so I constantly had to try to catch up. Invariably, whenever I just about caught up, it was off to another school to start all over again.

Now, did the Society know what was going on? Well, I doubt if they did. You see, they used to send a welfare person around to my foster parents now and then, to see how things were going. I was never allowed to talk to that person; my foster parents did all the talking. I was always told to sit still and look happy. I think they knew what I might say if I was allowed to have a conversation with the welfare person.

I remember one Saturday, I was told to clean myself up after break-fast because a welfare man from the Society was coming to see me. I was given the usual instructions to sit and say nothing or get my ears boxed after.

Sure enough, there was a firm knock on the front door, and before my foster mother went to the door, she gave me a frowning stare and waved her finger at me, indicating I was not to say a word. I sat on a chair in the living room while my foster father sat at the dining table reading a newspaper. In came my foster mother, saying to my foster father in a surprised tone, "Why, it's the welfare man coming to visit."

After the general introductions, the welfare man sat where my fos-ter mother pointed, smiled at me, and said "Hello."

I just looked at him and nodded.

My foster mother snapped, "Where are your manners, young man? Say good morning to the gentleman," so I immediately said,

"Good morning."

The welfare man started looking around for my brother. "Now, you are Les," he said, looking at me, "so where is Douglas?" My brother Douglas was helping a Milkman do his morning deliveries and was getting good money for it, so she told him not to rush home just to see him.

And as I had been warned not to talk, I simply looked over at her.

"Oh he's out getting some stuff from the shop," said my foster mother. My foster father, after getting a look from her, agreed.

"Yes, he's, erm, at the shop." Then he looked at her and waited for his next cue.

But the welfare officer stepped in by saying firmly, "You are aware that I am supposed to see *both* of the children on my visits?" There was a deathly hush for a few moments. The welfare officer fidgeted with his briefcase, then simply looked at my foster mother and said, "Do you know how long he will be?"

"Oh," said my foster mother, wiping her hands on her apron.

Then she took the apron off, folded it up, tucked it under her arm, and asked, with the faintest smile, "Would you like a nice cup of tea?"

"Oh, thank you, Mrs..." He obviously did not remember her name, so he simply smiled as she left the room.

The welfare officer cleared his throat and turned to me, saying, "Well, what I mean is, how is..." His eyes kept flicking over toward my foster father, thinking that he was going to answer while she was in the kitchen, although we all knew that she was the one that did all the talking.

Right on cue she burst into the room, having heard every word, and said, "Oh the lad's fine, and he's doing very well at school."

I gave her one of my looks, which she spotted, and I knew I would suffer for it later. She paused with the kitchen door half open and with her false smile said to the welfare officer, "Do you take milk and sugar in your tea?"

"Just milk thank you."

The officer was just about to ask a question when there was a loud knock at the door. Mr. Green sat up in his chair with a puzzled expression on his face. The welfare officer said, looking at me, "Maybe that's your brother Douglas," and gave me a big smile.

We could hear my foster mother answer the front door and telling whoever it was to wait there. She quickly beckoned my foster father to come to the door, and as he walked out, she gave the welfare chap another false smile and said, "We won't be long," and went out of the room.

The welfare officer didn't waste any time because that was the first time he had been able to talk directly to me. He leaned toward me and whispered, "Are you happy here?"

I leaned toward him and said in a loud whisper, "No! I want to go back to the orphanage."

He raised his hand to indicate not to say another word and again whispered, "I'll see what I can do." Then he winked and gave me a warm smile, which perked me up a bit.

Without warning, my foster mother burst into the room, looking at both of us with one of her frowning stares, and said, "What...did I miss anything? Has he..." and pointed her finger at me.

The welfare chap interrupted and said, "No, he never said a word. You're a quiet lad, aren't you?" I simply smiled at him. Then the welfare officer got up from his seat and tucked his papers in his briefcase and looked at Mrs. Green and said, "Well, I must be off."

My foster mother had a bigger frown on her face that time. "But you haven't interviewed us or the children, and I have your tea in the kitchen."

"You are aware that both children have to be present for my visit, and I cannot sit around waiting indefinitely for Douglas to show up." He paused to secure his briefcase in his hand, and continued. "I have other families to visit, so I will have to schedule another visit when you have both children at home." He pushed past her and entered the hall.

Mr. Green was still talking, or should I say arguing, with the gentleman at the front door. Mrs. Green, with her projected voice, said, "Excuse me, please," and both men stood to one side.

Mrs. Green was full of apologies to the welfare man, who continued walking toward the gate with her close to his heels. The two men continued their discussion, and when the welfare chap finally escaped, my foster mother came back bursting into the room. I had just stood up to stretch my legs when she pushed me back into my seat, finger waving, face not far from mine, and shouting, "What did you say to that welfare officer? Come on, I want to know. Did he say anything to you?"

"Nothing," I said cowering from her and staring at those teeth and getting the odd whiff of her breath. She grabbed me by the hair and looked me in the eye and demanded,

"WHAT DID HE SAY TO YOU?"

"Nothing, he never said a word," I said, flinching. She finally let go of my hair when we were joined by my foster father. She looked at him and mumbled,

"I know he's lying. See if you can get anything out of him," then stormed out of the room. My foster father was already in a bad mood from talking to the person at the front door, so he immediately started shouting at me, demanding to know what I said to the welfare officer. He was taking off his belt as I shook my head and lied again,

"I never said a word to him."

Without warning, my foster father swung his hand across my face and made me shout aloud, "Why are you doing this to me? I haven't done anything!"

Then the living room door burst open again, and my foster mother came in a panic. "Leave him, the welfare man is coming back."

My foster father quickly started threading his belt back on, telling me to stand there and don't move. I was holding the side of my face because it was throbbing. After a loud knock on the front door, my foster mother opened it and you could hear her saying in a surprised tone, "Oh, you're back so soon! Did you want that cup of tea I made?"

"No, thank you. I seem to have left my leather gloves behind," he replied, and pushed his way past her.

"I will get them for you," she said, trying to beat him through the living room door. But he beat her to it, saying,

"I know exactly where I put them."

My foster father was standing in front of me when the welfare chap walked in.

The welfare chap went straight to the chair where he had been sitting and said, "Ah, there they are." As he bent down to pick up his gloves, he turned his head to look at me.

I was still nursing my face, but quickly pulled my hand down to reveal a bright-red hand mark. The welfare chap frowned when he saw my face, then, continued to reach for his gloves. "Well, sorry to trouble you again so soon, but this time I'm really going because I'm late." He tried to say goodbye to me, but my foster father wouldn't move, so he put his head around to one side and said, "Goodbye, Master Morris," waved his gloves, and hastily made his exit.

And that was the last I ever saw of that welfare chap. But my foster parents never did find out what I said in their absence.

They got away with having us for about four years, until one day another welfare officer came and took Doug and myself away. When he arrived, my thoughts went back to the welfare officer that allowed me to tell him what I wanted.

I found out much later that while I was still at Chelmsford, Mrs. Woodley came all the way from Ashdon by bus to see Doug and me. but Mr. and Mrs. Green Teeth sent her away without even letting her into the house. I wonder why? Were they trying to hide the fact that they had two very sad children in their care? Or were they frightened that she might report her findings to the Society, and they would lose out financially?

I have since learned that the Greens had always indulged in drink, and that Mr. Green's favorite pastime was betting on the horses. When I think about that, I ask myself, "When was he doing all that?" Who was cleaning his church? What a good cover-up it must have been, being a church verger.

At last, the Society stepped in and shipped us off to another orphanage, but unfortunately for us, it could only be described as HELL.

Chapter Sixteen

Buckhurst Hell

On February 26, 1953, Douglas and I were delivered to a large orphanage called Buckhurst Home, which was on the London Road in the city of Leicester. When we arrived, we were in great spirits. Well I was, but Doug had mixed feelings. I mean, he was the one my foster parents had wanted, but the Society wouldn't separate us, so he had to tag along. I was feeling great because I knew that it was going to be the end of all those beatings. How wrong I was.

As soon as we walked into the orphanage and were introduced to the master and matron, I had a horrible feeling that the home wasn't what it appeared to be. My high spirits dwindled to an uncertain tremble. We had arrived just in time for tea. The assistant matron showed us to the dormitory, where we were told to quickly dispose of our things and get washed and come down for tea.

As I sat and had my tea, which was a watery plate of baked beans and a piece of badly smeared margarine bread, I couldn't get over how deathly quiet it was in the dining room. There were 23 boys and three staff members in that room, and the only sounds were the scraping of knives and forks across plates, and the occasional cough. I scanned the room without turning my head, and would sometimes catch another child looking at me. Whenever that happened, I would give a faint smile, but got nothing in return.

Everything was so clean and tidy that it seemed unnatural for a houseful of children. There wasn't a smile on anyone's face, and that certainly went for the master and matron, who dominated the large table at the far end of the room. As I looked over in their direction, the matron's eyes met mine and I gave her a shy smile. She returned a look that would stun a Doberman at 50 yards.

The matron was not only big, she was massive. I think the best way to describe her was to say that she looked like an unpopular all-in mud wrestler. She had sunken eyes, puffed-out cheeks, tight lips, and several chins. She wore the traditional white starched headpiece that made her look like she was ready to hang glide, and what little hair was showing looked as though someone had just placed it on her head and let it dangle there looking like a well used mop-head.

And oh, those hands! I reckon they could do anything that a monkey wrench could; they were about the size of dinner plates. I noticed when she was eating that her fork would scoop up food, and without her eyes ever looking down, bring it up to her mouth, where she shoveled it in at great speed.

The master was completely the opposite. He was about as tall as she was, but much thinner and very stern looking, with wiry features. In fact, he was very similar in appearance to Mr. Green. His eyes were like the matron's, however, they continuously scanned the room, in wait for some child to do wrong.

I then turned my eyes toward the assistant matron. She reminded me slightly of Mrs. Woodley, though no one could ever take the place of Mrs. Woodley. She was a little smaller than Mrs. Woodley, and didn't have that warm smile or that friendliness about her, but she definitely looked more human than the master and matron.

After tea, the matron stood up and all heads turned in her direction. She gave a little cough, and then said in a loud voice, "As you can see, we have two new boys who arrived today. They are brothers called Morris. Now we will go about our duties and the Morris children will remain in the dining room. Right, you're all dismissed."

All the children got up quietly and most of them left the room. Two of the lads started clearing the tables. Meanwhile, the master and matron and the assistant matron remained standing behind the staff table. The matron beckoned Doug and me over to them.

"As you may have noticed, I am the matron of this home and you refer to me as Matron, and this is my husband who will be referred to as Master." Then pointing to the other person, she said, "And here we have Miss Willis who you will call the Assistant Matron or Miss." After a short pause she gave us both a hard stare and she continued. "Do either of you suffer from any ailments or disabilities?" I looked at Doug and he looked at me because neither of us knew what those big words meant. "Well answer me," she snapped.

We both shook our heads saying, "No Matron."

The master, with his hands on his hips, took over by saying, "We run a strict home and will not tolerate any nonsense from anyone. We have rules that will be obeyed and each child is responsible for allocated jobs." The master then folded his arms and looked at the Mud Wrestler, sorry I mean matron, who then pointed to the assistant matron saying. "The assistant matron will show you to your dormitories."

After lunch the next day, the master and matron gave us a tour. The large house was set back off the main road with a well-kept garden in the front. It had all sorts of nicely placed shrubs and trees, and the long drive that ran up the side of the house eventually disappeared around the rear into a large, open tarmac area. Beyond that was a well laid-out walled garden with a large brick building that ran the length of the grounds. Beyond that was a paddock with a small orchard.

I looked at Doug and softly said, "It would be great to have that penny-farthing bike here." The matron and master both swung around at the same time and she said, "What are you two talking about…are you talking about us?"

We both froze. "No…No…" said Doug "We were talking about how big and spacious this home is compared with Ashdon." The matron gave a gruff and a grumble and we moved on, but Doug and I both looked at each other but dared not say another word.

Back inside the house, the very first thing you notice is the magnificent grand stairway. Its beautiful, highly polished wooden banister curved its way from the top landing down to the bottom step. It looked perfect for sliding on, but the master was quick to point out that the staircase was, "Out of bounds to all children, unless they are on duty cleaning it." He sort of shouted it, which made me jump. "If I suspect any child of even *thinking* of sliding down that banister," he continued, looking directly at me, "He'll get the biggest hiding of his life."

He must have been reading my thoughts. Then he pointed across the hallway to his study. "Now this room is private and you do not enter, is that clear?" he said in a sharp tone, looking at Doug and me both in turn. "When you do have to report to my study, you knock once and wait. You do *not* keep knocking on the door. Do you understand?"

We both nodded at the same time and said a feeble yes.

That was my first impression of the place, and I did not like it one little bit. My first experience at the orphanage was – would you believe it? Bath Night. It happened to be the second night we were there.

Now, the system in Leicester worked like this: If you were a teenager, you took your baths unsupervised downstairs, but if you happened to be under the age of 13, as I was, then you had your bath under supervision upstairs, and what an embarrassing situation that was. The drill was that you stood single file in your underwear with your towel around your neck outside the bathroom, which was upstairs between the dormitories. There were always six or seven children waiting, and in the winter you would be shivering with the cold, hoping that when it was your turn you would at least have warm water. It was never hot.

I was the last in line. When it was my turn to have a bath, I walked into the bathroom and was surprised to find the assistant matron inside, testing the water with her elbow.

"Ah, Master Morris, now take off your underpants and get in the bath." She promptly sat down on a chair at the foot of the bath. I honestly didn't know what to do or think or even where to look.

"Come on," she snapped, "we haven't got all night."

As I was very shy, I turned my back on her as I slid down my pants, and then lifted a leg to get into the bath.

"Come over to me, will you? I want to examine you," she said before I could get my foot near the water.

I froze. I was in no position to face anyone at that moment, as I think you know what I mean. You see, it wasn't all that long before that I had learned the art of masturbation, and well, I just stood there with a very red face.

"Will you come here at once or do I have to fetch the master?" she snapped again.

At the word "master," I quickly turned toward her and stood in front of her erect, if you'll excuse the expression.

"That's better," she said. Her eyes dropped down to my embarrassment.

"Hold out your hands," she said in a softer tone, and proceeded to check my fingernails. Then I had to lift one foot up at a time so she could check my toenails, which she trimmed with the clippers that were neatly laid out nearby. Then she stood up and ran her fingers through my hair, asking me if I did a lot of scratching. I assumed she was looking for bugs. Having completed that little task, she told me to get into the bath. As we each sat down in our positions, she quietly said, "You're quite a big boy for your age, aren't you, Master Morris?"

Well, I didn't know how to answer that. In fact, I wasn't too sure what she was referring to, so I just sat there.

"Right," she said, sitting back in her chair with her legs crossed. "There is a procedure on how to have a bath here, and I will tell you how it is done so on future bath nights you will know exactly what to do."

She paused and pointed to the shampoo. "We start with the hair. First, you wet it thoroughly. Then you put a little shampoo on your head," she said. "Well, get on with it."

So, I splashed a lot of water on my hair and did as she instructed. I rubbed in the shampoo, but not hard enough, so she got up and leaned over the bath and dug her nails into my scalp to give my hair a thorough wash.

"There. Now rinse all that soap off. The reason we do the hair first is because the water is nice and clean, so you start from the top of your body and work your way down."

I suddenly had a horrible thought. Although my eyes were filled with soap, I forced one open to scan the bathroom as the image of the dd white-enamel jug flashed through my mind. But my fears were unfounded. Here you had to rinse off most of the soap with the bath water. Then the assistant matron used a small jug to rinse the remaining soap away, so that was nicely done.

I washed my face and the top half of my body, but then things became very embarrassing.

"Right, now I want you to stand up and wash the rest of your body."

I thought something like that might happen, and I was dreading it. You see, I was still in an awkward position. I just sat there and made out like I didn't hear her.

"Now come on, Master Morris, surely you're not shy, are you? Stand up."

Well, I slowly got up, holding the flannel so it hung down the front of me. I saw her look down in that direction and I'm sure she had a faint smile on her face when she said, "Now, I want you to put plenty of soap on your flannel and wash between your legs, and then all around your private parts."

My face must have been as red as the soap I was using. I did as she instructed, but when I went to wash my private parts, I started to turn away.

"There's no need to turn away; I have to make sure that you keep yourself nice and clean. Now wash it thoroughly."

As I put soap around it, you can guess what happened.

Miss, that's what we were supposed to call her, sprang to her feet, saying, "No, no, no, not like that," and then took over.

"Now Master Morris, there is no need to be embarrassed," she said sternly. "I have seen more of these than you ever will, and if anyone should be embarrassed, it should be me." She gripped her hand around my penis and pulled back the foreskin and rubbed plenty of soap around it. "It is very important that you do this regularly as germs and bacteria can form under that area." She then told me to do it to make sure I knew what to do.

"Now it's most important that you keep this part of your body clean at all times. You will, perhaps, appreciate my advice when you get older." And she was dead right, you know. She kept on washing my private parts, and when she had finished, I was in a worse state than when she had started.

After I rinsed off, she told me to get out and dry myself. As she gently helped me dry my back, she said, "Now there's no need to get yourself all embarrassed over that," pointing to my private part. "It's a perfectly normal thing to happen to a child of your age, so on future bath nights, don't worry about it. Right?"

"Thank you, Miss," I said as she left the room.

After that, I seemed to get on with the assistant matron very well. Then again, she was the only member of the staff that anyone could get on with.

Our daily routine in Leicester went something like this: Morning call was at 6:30. After washing, we would dress in our work clothes and do our house jobs. The orphanage did not employ cleaners. We children did the cleaning. In fact, any job to be done around the house was done by us. We scrubbed floors, washed dishes, dusted, polished, and cleaned shoes, along with hundreds of other little tasks. The worst one of all was the job of looking after the boiler. That was normally given to someone who was on punishment, and the same went for cleaning all the shoes. But more about those jobs later.

Once we were done, each job had to be inspected by either the master or the matron. If the job was not done right, you could very well miss your breakfast, and to make matters worse, you could be late for school. If you were late for school, you were in extra trouble because the master had told the school that if any boy from the home was late, it was his own fault and he should be caned. And that's exactly what would happen. And you were caned when you got back to the orphanage for being caned at school.

After our morning chores, we had breakfast and went to school. We had lunch while we were at school, but instead of playing outside afterwards with the other children, we had to report back to the home to do more chores, then rush back to school for the afternoon.

After school, we again had to run back to the home, change into our work clothes, do more jobs, and then wash for tea. After tea, we were sent to bed. Life was as exciting as that. There wasn't a lot of play time at the home. Actually there was no time for play there.

My first face-to-face encounter with the matron was on Saturday morning the second week I was there. My job was to get on my hands and knees and scrub the long stone corridor and steps that led to the rear of the house. Believe me; it took a long time to do the lot. When I had almost worked my way to the steps, sweat rolling down my face, the matron appeared at the far end of the hall. I spotted her and was suddenly struck with fear, so I looked down and started scrubbing faster. Although I wasn't looking at her, I could feel her standing there, staring at me with her arms folded.

Then she started walking toward me. I raised my eyes as far as they would go without lifting my head and continued scrubbing. I could tell by the way she was scanning every inch of the floor with her several chins and double neck wobbling with every movement that knew I was in trouble.

When she came up next to me, I stopped scrubbing and moved to one side so she could pass. As I knelt there with my right hand over the scrubbing brush, she loomed over me by placing her foot across my hand and put her full weight on it. I let out a scream.

"MASTER MORRIS!" she bellowed, "I thought your job was to scrub this floor CLEAN." She leaned forward to put even more pressure on my hand, which was turning blue, while I screamed, I told her I was doing the best I could. Then she released her foot, picked up the bucket of water, and threw the whole lot down the corridor. I can still hear the sound the bucket made as it bounced on the stone floor, water gushing everywhere.

"Do it over again you horrible thing, and report to me when you have," she growled. Then she wobbled off; no doubt to see who else she could terrorize.

I sat on the wet floor holding my throbbing hand, which had swollen right up, when all of a sudden I heard her voice rolling down the hall.

"I thought I told you to scrub that floor! Get on with it, you sniveling wretch." Then she disappeared.

I retrieved the bucket, got more water and started all over again. That time I had to scrub with my left hand, as I couldn't do anything with my right, and it took a lot longer to do. When I had finished, I wiped my wet hands on my trousers and stood there for a few minutes trying to pluck up the courage to report to the matron.

After knocking just once on the master's study door, I stood outside and waited, clutching my injured hand. I waited. And waited. I was staring at the highly polished banister thinking, "One day, I will slide down..." when the door opened, which made me jump. There she was, the dreadful matron in all her glory standing before me, obviously in her element in her outsize blue outfit and that big starched hat thing made her look like someone from the circus.

"Go stand in your corridor and wait for me to come and inspect it," she snapped. "And woe betides you if it's not clean this time!" She went back into the study, slamming the door behind her.

Giving another quick glance at the banister, I again threatened that I would one day slide down it. It really was so tempting.

I went back to the corridor and did a final check myself. It looked all right to me. It was still a little wet, but it was clean, so I stood there waiting. Suddenly the back door opened. In came the assistant matron. As she made her way over to me, I made sure that she noticed me clutching my swollen hand.

"What on earth have you done to that?" she asked, pointing to my hand.

Hoping for a bit of sympathy, I told her all. I had just finished when we heard the master's study door slam, so she hurriedly said, "I'll look at that later," and left.

I gave a quick final glance down the corridor, and to my horror saw a leaf lying in the middle of the floor. It must have been stuck to the assistant matron's shoe. Clutching my hand, I ran down to retrieve it. Then I heard the matron yell, "Do you call this corridor clean?"

I froze in stooping position, squinted at her, and wondered what she was going to do next.

"What is *that?*" she asked, pointing at the leaf.

"Um, the wind must have blown it in, Matron," I said, not wanting anyone else to get into trouble.

"Well," she said, pausing to think for a moment. "We can't have these leaves blowing in the house now can we?"

"Er, no, Matron," I answered, as I watched her jawbone moving up and down, which I was to learn was not a good sign. She grabbed hold of my hair and dragged me to the cleaning cupboard to show me the big bass broom used for sweeping outdoors.

"Master Morris, so that we don't have any more leaves lying around on our nice clean floors, you will now go outside and spend the rest of the day sweeping up the leaves from the drive and around the back. I'll have you sweeping the whole of Leicester. Report to me when you have finished. Now get out of my sight."

After she left, I stood in the cupboard with disbelief. I couldn't believe that I now had to sweep outside. There was a fine rain and it was a little windy and I couldn't use my right hand. When I let my hand hang down, it felt like a dead weight.

I sat down, with tears in my eyes thinking of Ashdon and Mrs. Woodley. The pain in my hand was awful and the thought of what I had to do, made it worse. Then a figure appeared in the doorway. Startled, I looked up, but sighed with relief when I saw it was Doug.

"What's the matter?" he asked, and then spotted my hand. "How did you do that?" As soon as he touched my hand I let out a scream, as it was very painful to the touch. Sobbing my heart out, I told him what had happened and what the matron had told me to do.

"But it's raining and you can't work with..." he suddenly stopped talking, for now the matron literally filled the doorway, with both hands intertwined cracking her knuckles.

"What is going on in here? I thought I gave you a job to do, Master Morris." She growled like a bull dog.

When the ripples of her chins had settled, I said, "I was just going to..." but Doug interrupted,

"Matron, my brother can't sweep up the leaves because of his hand. He can't even use it. Can I do it for him?"

The look she gave him was enough to turn both of us into pillars of stone, and it set her jaw working even faster than it had before. I stood up, trembling with fear.

She suddenly slapped Doug's face hard and yelled, "How dare you interfere with my judgment?"

Then she pushed past him and commanded me to show her my hand. She grabbed it, twisting it roughly in all directions as if to examine it. I screamed my head off. She threw my hand back at me and shouted at Doug, "If you're so keen to work, then you can take everything out of this room and scrub it from top to bottom. I will inspect it before you put everything back. And don't you *ever* question my judgment like that again or you'll be in big trouble." And away she went.

We looked at each other and pulled our pointed tongues back into our mouths. "I'm sorry," Doug said, "it will be lunchtime soon, and she might change her mind." With that thought, I dragged the big broom outside to start my job, which I had no idea how to tackle. After trying several ways to push the broom with my left hand, I found that the best way to do the job was to bend down and pick the leaves up, as the majority of them were wet and sticking to the ground. Although it was agony and the rain was dripping off me, I was getting on quite well. When I heard one of the lads shout,

"They're all going in for lunch," I ran to the house to wash my face and hands, but upon entering I was confronted by – yes – the matron.

"Morris! You horrible untidy creature! You don't just leave a box and a broom lying around the driveway. Just where do you think you are? Go and fetch them now," she hollered into my ear.

Having picked up the offending items, I washed my left hand, the right one was too painful to touch, let alone wash, and joined the queue for inspection, which was being conducted by the assistant matron. When she saw my hand again, she whispered, "I'll attend to that later," and waved me in.

Just like all the meals at the home, it was silent during lunch, with the exception of one or two lads who were crying as quietly as they could. The matron had obviously had a good morning going around upsetting all the younger children.

I glanced over and watched her eating. It made me feel bitter to see her, unconcerned as you like, shoveling food down with so many unhappy children around her.

One of the lads at my table whispered to me, "How did you hurt your hand?"

I immediately looked across at the matron, who gave me an evil stare, so I took that as a warning and signed to the other lad with my eyes. The subject, of course, was dropped.

After lunch, I could have screamed when I got back to my job. There were just as many leaves on the area I had cleaned as there was when I started, even though I had only been gone a short time. I looked at the house and saw the matron standing at the window, watching me. That meant I must get on with it, so with a big sigh I started all over again.

Around four o'clock, it was getting dark and cold, so just to get warm, I went into the house to go to the toilet. On my way back out, guess who was standing there with arms folded?

"What do you think you're doing? You haven't finished your job yet, have you?" she said, moving right up on me.

"I've just come to use the toilet, Matron, and it's getting dark out there."

"Well, Master Morris, we will put a stop to that, won't we?" she said sarcastically, walking briskly over to a light switch. And with sheer elegance, as if she enjoyed the very movement, she flicked the switch on and turned to me with a false smile. "There, Master Morris. You have all the light you need. Now get outside." She looked as if she was going to belt me one around the ear, so I quickly ran outside, only to find that it was raining even harder. It was also a lot colder.

I had been collecting leaves and getting soaked for some time when I noticed that everything had gone quiet. I stood for a moment wondering why when it suddenly dawned on me.

"Oh no!" I shouted to myself. "Its tea time, and I bet I have missed it!"

I ran into the house and then froze. I didn't know what to do. You see, I was told that if you were late for a meal, you missed it and there was no use going in, but I was that hungry. I threw my coat off and quickly wiped my face and went to the dining-room door. I trembled and gave a big sigh and thought, "Here goes," then slowly opened the door.

The usual silence went even quieter. As I stood in the doorway, all eyes focused on me. I had forgotten to wipe my hair, which was dripping wet, so water was rolling down my face in different directions.

The silence was broken by the sound of the matron's chair scraping the floor. With her mouth full of food, she rose to her feet and shouted, "WHAT DO YOU WANT?"

"Um, I've come for..."

"If it's tea you want, Master Morris, you're too late. NOW GET OUT OF HERE!"

I slowly turned and went out of the room, but the wind caught the door and slammed it hard behind me. Within seconds, the door was flung open and the matron appeared so she could slap my face and then hit my swollen hand with all her might. I screamed the place down, as I was in agony.

"Don't slam doors behind you when you have been spoken to!"

I looked at her in amazement. "I never slammed the..."

She threw another blow at my face and shouted, "And don't you back-chat me!" As soon as she said that, the wind slammed the door behind her even harder than before, and she gave me a ferocious stare, as much as to say, "Don't you dare say a word." Which I would have done, but I had had enough beatings for one day. I just stood there with a blank expression.

The matron went back into the dining room as fast as she had come out, leaving me wondering what to do. I was starving, but at the same time felt very sick, so I went and sat on a chair in the bathroom and nursed my hand.

With my head in my hands, shivering with cold, I was feeling really fed up with life and started chewing over the thought of running away. But I had no idea where to go. All I really wanted was some food and to be able to curl up in my bed.

My thoughts were intruded on by the presence of two people. I got to my feet, which was an effort, and had to rub my eyes dry because they were full of tears. When I could focus, I saw that it was the master and matron. My heart skipped a couple of beats and I backed away.

"What a pathetic sight," snarled the matron as she stood with her arms folded. But now it was the master's turn to have a go at me.

"Matron tells me that she inspected the driveway you were supposed to sweep but you apparently haven't done it yet. What have you got to say to that, Master Morris?"

Well, I was struck dumb again. It was then that I truly wished that I was dead. If there was anywhere I could have run to, I would have gone that very minute.

"Well?" snapped the master.

"Sir, I have..."

The matron interrupted. "It looks as if he hasn't picked up one leaf. I think he ought to be taught a lesson."

"Right," said the master. "As of Monday evening, you will be on punishment with the job of cleaning shoes, and I will make sure that you do them properly."

I think the matron was thrilled at the outcome of that; it seemed to perk her up a bit, if you know what I mean. Before she left the room, she instructed me to take off my wet clothes, place them on the hanger nearby, and go upstairs to wait for the assistant matron to do the baths.

As I waited for the bathing to start, I sat on my bed, shivering in an undersized hand-me-down dressing gown. When it was time, Miss made sure that I was the first to go. She was very concerned about my hand, saying she would find a dressing for it after my bath.

Sliding into a hot bath did wonders for me. I more or less felt better instantly. Miss washed my hair for me, and as I was having difficulties, ended up washing me all over. When it came to washing my private areas, she asked if I could manage to do it. I said, "I think so," but she stopped me, and said,

"It's all right, I'll do it."

When I stood up, she looked down below and said with a smile, "I see you're not embarrassed tonight." Well, my face went red straightaway, as I hadn't even thought about it until she mentioned it, and now look what she had done. She washed my private parts with such care that things started to happen.

"I see I spoke too soon." There was that nice smile again. That smile did a lot for me while I was there, but she wasn't like that to all the children. When I think about it now, if you fitted in with the staff, you were all right. But I obviously didn't fit in with the master and matron.

Anyway, Miss put a dressing on my hand and said she would look at it again in the morning. I told her that I would go down and wait for supper, but she told me that you did not get supper when you were on punishment.

I stood there with my mouth wide open. "But Miss, I'm starving!"

"You must be. I will try to bring you a couple of biscuits (cookie) later." All supper was that day was one biscuit and a watery cup of cocoa anyway. I gave a big sigh and thanked her, then went and climbed into my bed.

I must have gone to sleep as soon as my head hit the pillow, because the next thing I knew, I was awake early in the morning, with a pain in my hand.

I turned over and felt some crumbs on my bed. I frantically felt around. There were two biscuits tucked under my pillow. I smiled to myself and ate them in record time. Then I went back to sleep.

That was my first taste of the treatment to come at the Leicester orphanage and oh yes, it does get worse.

Chapter Seventeen

A False Front

One really disconcerting thing about the master and matron was that they were such nice people to anyone outside the home. I'll give you a couple of examples.

One day, three officials from the Society came to spend most of the day at the orphanage. We children were unaware of the visit until we came home from school, for there on the back doorstep was the master with two of the guests, welcoming us into the house.

"Hello, Master Morris. Did you have a nice day at school?" he asked in a friendly tone. Well, I was completely taken back when he said that, and looked around to see if he really was referring to me. And by golly he was.

"Yes, thank you, Master," I replied cautiously, waiting for the catch, but there didn't seem to be one.

"Don't bother to change young man; just wash your face and hands and get ready for tea." I stood there with a stunned look on my face because I just couldn't believe what I was hearing. Neither could the other lads.

While we waited for tea, the matron was going around with the other visitor handing out big bars of chocolate, which we had never seen before. Wow! She handed a bar to each one of us with the falsest smile I ever did see. Attached to it were the immortal words, "Now don't eat this until after tea, will you?"

The "will you" was more of a threat than a request, but for the first time since I was there, morale shot right up. When tea was dished out, there was even more excitement, which I think embarrassed the master and matron, who were giving one or two of us their powerful looks.

That was the very first time that I heard all the children talking whilst having a meal. Normally not a word was spoken, so that meal was very unusual. The tea itself was far better than what we normally had, and there was plenty of it as well. We were even asked if we wanted seconds. Now that was too was highly unusual, and of course everyone put up their hands for more. We had the biggest plateful of baked beans on toast, and lovely fat sausages instead of the skinny ones we normally had, and the biggest selection of cakes I have ever seen. And there was not a crumb left.

That's what the three visitors saw, with big smiles all around. The master and matron told us to remain in our seats while they saw the Society men off the premises, and as soon as the visitors were gone, things abruptly got back to normal.

When the master and matron returned to the dining room, it was obvious that they were back in charge. They promptly informed us that they were disgusted with our behavior. The matron used that as the excuse to go around and collect all the bars of chocolate, inspecting each bar to see that it was still intact.

One little lad had attacked his, and mine was missing four squares as well.

With a cuff around the ear, the other lad was sent to wait outside the master's study, and I was soon standing beside him, holding my ear and awaiting our punishment, which would come very soon. For out came the matron, clutching a large pile of chocolate. She brought it into the study, either to eat it herself or to put it into a box marked "For Special Occasions."

The master came from the dining room after dismissing the rest of the children and telling them to do their jobs, which would have normally been done by now. He was in a foul mood.

He threw open the study door and reached above it. At that, the other lad and I both swallowed hard, for we knew what he was reaching for – the cane. After the master gave us a thrashing with his tongue, the matron gave us a thrashing with hers, but really she was just there to see the torture. The master stood in front of us, bending the cane in all directions. He then told the other boy, who was much younger than I, to hold out his hand, which he did, though he had a job holding it still. Then there was an almighty swipe, and I screwed my eyes up as the lad got three swipes on each hand and screamed the house down. He was then told that his punishment was to wash up all of the tea stuff. Off he went, crying his eyes out.

I stood there with sweat rolling down my face as the matron looked at me with glee in her eyes.

"Hold your hand out, Morris," the master commanded. I uncurled my sweaty left hand and slowly held it out, shaking as much as the other lad had. I'm sure the matron was smiling. Then there was the swish of the stick. A severe pain ran through my hand, up my arm, and right through my body. I quickly shoved my hand under my arm.

"Again!" shouted the matron.

I slowly put my hand out again.

The master was standing on his toes to get his full weight behind the next swipe. It came down hard, and that time I couldn't help but let out a scream. The tears started. He did that six times to my left hand, which was now as painful as the right one, which was still bandaged up.

Doubled up with pain, I had a job just standing, but now had to wait for him to tell me which punishment I was on. And then the worst happened.

"Hold out your other hand."

I stood upright, mouth wide open, trying to focus on my tormentors through eyes full of tears.

"Hold out your right hand. Are you bloody deaf?"

I felt very sick. Then I heard the voice of the assistant matron, who had entered the room dressed in her hat and coat. When she heard the master's request, she said, "Surely you're not going to..."

"I do believe you're off duty Assistant Matron, aren't you?" the master said in a surprised but firm voice. I think he had assumed she had already gone out. The assistant matron reluctantly walked away. I looked toward her for sympathy, but she had already gone.

"Now hold out your hand," the master shouted, grabbing hold of my swollen hand and putting it in the upright position. I shouted as the pain ran through my entire body. I slid down the wall and writhed on the floor and felt as if I were going to die.

Although they were now both shouting at me, I never heard a word, and could only see their lips moving. They got me to my feet. Gasping for breath, I pleaded with them, but suddenly felt another sharp pain on my badly swollen hand. I let out an almighty scream and collapsed on the floor as things went black.

I woke up early the next morning to find I was lying on top of my bed with a blanket over me. My body ached all over and I felt very weak, but oh, my hands! They both felt as if they had been burned.

That morning everyone acted as if nothing had happened. The master put me on shoe cleaning for two weeks as punishment. I will come back to the shoe cleaning later.

Another classic case of their falseness was at Harvest Festival time. Various churches and organizations would bring their produce to the home to help feed us little lads. If only they knew what the master used to do with all that food, they would have had quite a shock. Whenever someone brought food to the home, the master would meet them at the front door and politely tell them, "How much the children will enjoy all this wonderful fresh food!" Then he would get several of us to take it through the house to the back door, where a large garden trolley was waiting. We were told to load all the fruit and vegetables into the trolley and await the master.

Once he had got rid of the visitors, the master would instruct us to dump the food into the long, deep trenches we had to dig for the occasion. That was another punishment job; digging out the trenches. We were all very tempted to pick out, say, a nice, ripe, juicy pear to eat, but we dared not as that was a punishable offense.

One time a lad took an orange out of the trolley just before it was tipped out. The master picked him up and literally threw him down into the trench. When he landed, his face hit a pumpkin, which broke his nose. When the doctor came, the master said the boy had been playing on the wall in the garden and fell off onto his face.

Now you may well be thinking that perhaps the home had more food than it could handle. But we certainly could have done with more on our plates, and it angered us to think that there was some extra fruit and vegetables to eat. But no, they simply buried it. They could have sent it to the local hospital if we weren't allowed to have it.

I know who I would like to have buried instead of the fruit.

Another example was the day the matron decided that I ought to be in long trousers, and told me to try a pair on. They were far too tight for me, but she knew different and said they were all right. When I sat down at school the next day, my pants split wide open at the rear seam. Naturally, the children at school thought it was highly amusing, but I was humiliated and feared the matron's reaction when I got back to the home.

As predicted, she went up the wall when she saw them. I, of course, was given a hiding and put on punishment simply because the pants were too tight.

So I was back in short trousers and the lads at school took the Mickey again as they always seem to be doing, just because we were from the home.

Chapter Eighteen

Cleaning Shoes

When Doug reached the age of 15, he could leave school and leave the home, which didn't please me one little bit. The day he left, I stood hugging him in the hallway. Although we weren't extremely close, he was a great support to me. What was I going to do without him? He slipped me a piece of paper with his address on it.

"If you want me at any time, that's where I will be," he told me. "Well, I had better go now."

On came my tears, which were increased by the master grabbing me by the collar and pushing me down the hall.

"Get on with your work," he ordered.

Then the front door slammed and I was alone. I think I cried the rest of the day.

Not long after losing my brother, I was sent away myself. I was given no warning, but was simply picked up in a car one day. The date was June 18, 1954 to be exact. I was driven to a special home in Leighton Buzzard.

That particular home was special in that you could do anything you wanted there. If you wanted to smash a window, you could do it and not get told off. If you wanted to hit someone, also no problem. The reason for all that was they wanted to study you and see what sort of person you were.

The normal stay there was for three weeks, but after only one week they sent me back to Leicester. No, I didn't do anything wrong – they sent me back because they thought I was a nice little lad. Well, I was really, but only when I was in the right environment. When I got back to Leicester, I hated it even more than I did before, especially now that my brother wasn't there.

After I returned, I went to bed and had a dream that I was with some other children in a town somewhere. I don't know what town it was, but the bit I do remember was that I wanted to go to the toilet very badly. I desperately ran around the town looking for somewhere to go. At the end of one street, I saw a sign for "Toilets," so I ran until I got inside, and was so relieved. You must know the feeling.

Unfortunately, when I awoke the next morning, I had wet the bed. I just couldn't believe it, I had never wet the bed before, but there was no doubt about it. And that day just happened to be the day that sheets were changed, but to make matters worse, the matron was on duty. It was normally the assistant matron's job, but she was away.

Now, during sheet change you had to stand by your bed. As the matron came around with clean sheets, you had to hold up your dirty ones for inspection. I was the last one to be done. When the matron got to me, I had already thrown my sheets on the pile in the middle of the room. She went berserk and frantically went through the pile, then held up my soaking-wet sheet. I started trembling.

"Just as I thought, carry your mattress downstairs to be washed and dried, NOW!" she shouted as she cuffed my ear. Having cleaned the mattress and put it to dry while everyone else was having breakfast, I was then dragged to the master's study, where I had six strokes of the cane and was told I would have to clean shoes for the next week.

Then came the most humiliating part. I had seen other children who had wet their beds go through the treatment, but I never thought I would be one of them. For that part of the punishment, which they made into sort of a ritual, I was escorted outside as the other children were encouraged to participate by mocking me and calling me names.

I was told to stand over a drain in the middle of the open area behind the house, where they ceremoniously placed the offending sheet on my head and made me stand there for the rest of the morning. To make sure you stayed, the master or matron came out periodically to give you a glass of Epsom salts to drink. Then you were called all sorts of names to humiliate you. In the afternoon, you had to do the dirtiest job they could think of.

The day I had to stand there, another lad was being punished because the matron had heard him make remarks about her size. No one could get away with that. His punishment was to stand in the yard not far from me and hold two house bricks up in the air. That was a regular bit of their treatment, but that poor lad collapsed, and as he fell, a brick he was holding hit him on the head. He was sent to hospital, where the master told them that the boy was fooling around in the orchard climbing trees and fell onto a rock. Of course the master threatened the lad if he said any differently.

After that, they stopped that form of punishment, but that poor lad had eight stitches in his head as proof of their barbaric treatment.

Now remember, as part of my punishment, I was on shoe cleaning for two weeks. Apart from being a time-consuming job, it was hard work, especially when the weather was wet because everyone took delight in running through puddles and collecting plenty of mud.

The shoe room was in the cellar. All around the room were large shelves, which contained the 23 or so pairs of shoes. But one pair stood alone. That pair was the master's, and you were expected to bring his shoes to a brilliant shine. So, after running all the way back from school and quickly changing into my work clothes, I was stuck cleaning shoes. I had the shock of my life when I saw all those muddy shoes waiting for me to transform them.

With a big sigh, I started to wash them before attempting to polish them. Then it was time for tea, so after a quick wash and some tea, back down to the cellar I went to start the polishing. There was nothing to sit on, so my legs soon started to ache on the hard concrete floor. The only light I had to work with was a small one, but I did my very best.

While the other children were having supper and going off to bed, I still had to finish my job. After some time, I finished the last pair and was absolutely tired out, but it was time now to report to the master for inspection. I knocked on his door and waited. And waited. Finally, he emerged and said, "Yes?"

"I've finished cleaning the shoes, Master," I said, wishing he would get a move on. "Go to the shoe room and wait for me," he snapped, and slammed the door.

I returned to the shoe room and stood there for ages before he finally decided to show up. He had a suspicious look in his eye, which gave me great concern. He casually walked up to the shelves of shoes, then plucked up a pair and brought it under the light to give it a thorough inspection. The shoes had a nice shine on them, but when he looked underneath, he spotted a trace of mud. His face went red as he pointed to the spot and said, "What is *that*?"

There was no point in saying anything, so I just stood there looking at the shoe he was referring to. I could barely see the mud. If there had been better lighting, I could have done a better job.

The master threw the shoes to the other side of the room and picked up another pair without saying anything. He threw them aside as well, and then another pair, and then he lost his temper. His arms went wild as he started clearing off all the shelves, and shoes were literally flying in all directions.

I tried to shelter myself against the wall, but it turned out that I was the target of fire. He ended up throwing all the shoes at me and calling me all the names he could think of, including some I had never heard before. I now know what he called me, and I would call him worse than that!

As that was going on, the matron appeared at the top of the stairs. Perhaps she got bored listening to the radio and thought, "Let's go have a bit of sport in the shoe room." While the master was giving me a verbal telling-off, the matron went around the shelves, clearing off any shoe that remained and kicking any that happened to be near her foot. The master eventually made his way to the steps with the matron close behind him. Then he pointed his finger and said, "Now get that lot cleaned up and report to me again!" and disappeared.

The matron, who always liked to have the last word, added, "Leave him down here to rot," and slammed the heavy door shut.

I went over to the bottom step and sat down with my head in my hands. Although my eyes were filled with tears, I was too stunned to cry. I just sat and looked between my fingers at the state of the room. Eventually my eyes were attracted to the shelves. All the shoes were gone, except the pair on the very end – the master's.

I rose to my feet and went straight over to them. With a faint smile on my face, I picked the shoes up and imitated the master by inspecting them.

"These shoes are disgusting, Morris," Then an evil glint came to my eye, I held the masters shoes in front of me got out my very clean penis and took great delight in peeing in the master's shoes. Then I threw them as hard as I could across the room. That made me feel a much better, but I still had the task of cleaning them. The worst part of all that was sorting the lot into the right pairs.

I had a job just keeping my eyes open because I was very tired, but I eventually went back to the master's study and gave a loud knock on the door. I waited, but there was not a sound to be heard anywhere. As I stood there for what seemed like an eternity, my eyes trying to close up for the night, I wondered if I dare knock again, but thought better of it.

I ended up leaning against the wall with my eyes closed, but the sound of my name being shouted startled them open again. The master was coming down the main staircase, wrapping his dressing-gown cord around his waist.

Everyone had gone to bed. I could have been in the shoe room all night for all he cared.

"Well," snapped the master as he reached the bottom of the stairs. He just stood there looking at me.

"Er...I have finished the shoes, Master."

"And it's about time. Now get to bed and out of my sight," he snarled, and went back up the stairs.

I went up to the welcome sight of my bed.

Now, getting that kind of treatment every night was affecting me at school, and I was caught sleeping during a math lesson because I was so tired. I was brought to the front of the class and given four strokes of the cane, two on each hand. The incident was reported to the home, and during tea that evening, I was subjected to the same treatment in front of all the other lads, although the master gave me six strokes.

Cleaning shoes that night was a very painful job. The only thing that eased the pain was that the master had visitors, so the assistant matron inspected the shoes, and she merely went through the motions of checking them.

The next morning, when I got in line for inspection for school, the master gave me a crack across my ear. Holding my ear, I looked at him with a questioning stare, as much as to say, "What the hell was that for?"

"I have just seen a pair of shoes go out of this door with mud on them, Master Morris. What have you got to say about that?"

Because he had missed out on having a go at me the previous night, he intended to make up for it that day. I told him I had cleaned the shoes as best I could.

"Well, your good enough isn't good enough for me, so tonight when you clean underneath each shoe, you will also polish them. Now get out of my sight!"

What he really was trying to do was make me late for school, but I ran like a scalded cat across the park and made it in the nick of time, which brought a victory smile to my face.

After lunch, as usual, I came back to the home to do jobs. My job was to sweep out the shoe room, which I did in record time. But when I emerged from the basement, I noticed all the other lads had gone, so I ran down the corridor in a panic, lost my footing, and bowled over into a heap on the floor, hurting my knee and left arm. I scrambled to my feet and was limping toward the back door when the master and matron appeared.

"What do you think you're playing at, Morris?"

I froze and told them that I had tripped.

"LOOK!" shouted the matron, pointing to the long skid marks that I had made on the floor with my shoes.

"Get it cleaned up," snapped the master.

"But I'll be late for school," I pleaded, but the matron loomed over me and with nostrils flaring screamed,

"GET IT SCRUBBED UP NOW!"

Well, you can't argue with that, can you? So I limped around to the cleaning cupboard, and with bucket and scrubber removed the marks. I was then allowed to go back to school. They knew I was in trouble as they stood and watched me hobble down the drive.

When I reached the park, I stopped and looked around to see if any other school children were around. I didn't know exactly how late I was, but I did know I was very late, so I stood behind a large tree wondering what to do. If I went to school, I would get the cane, all because of that horrible master and matron.

"I know," I thought, "I'll stay away from school; they won't know." So I decided not to go. But what could I do all afternoon? I had nowhere to go. As I slowly walked around, I fumbled through my pockets for the bit of paper that Doug had given me with his address. I found it and saw in big letters, London Road, which was the same road the home was on, and just opposite from where I was standing. I limped as fast as I could to the address.

Doug had gotten a job at a small hotel as a trainee chef, and when I knocked hard on the rear door, a man half-opened the door and brusquely said, "Yes?"

"I'm looking for my brother," I said.

"Who's your brother?" he snapped.

"Douglas Morris," I told him quickly.

"He's busy," the man said, and went to shut the door.

"But I must see him," I begged.

After giving me a hard look, he said, "Wait here," and shut the door.

While I was waiting, I wondered what I should tell Doug. Without any real thought, I decided that I was going to run away, and at that moment, the door opened.

"What are you doing here?" my brother asked with a smile.

I mumbled some jumbled-up sentences and finally ended up saying that I was fed up and was going to run away.

"Run away? But where will you go?" he asked, frowning.

"I don't know, but I'm going."

"What about money? Have you got any money?"

He had a point. I hadn't a penny to my name, and there I was going out into big, wide world with nowhere to go and nothing in my pockets. I looked at him pleadingly, and he felt into his pocket and produced half a crown.

A voice shouted his name, so he said, "Look, I have to go. Take this, it's all I have, and the best of luck." He smiled and waved and that was the last I saw of my brother for many, many years.

I stood on the pavement wondering what on earth to do. Now I had money – not a lot – but to me it was a fortune. All I wanted was a place to go, and the only place I could think of was the home that I had spent a week at recently. I had no idea where it was, except that it was in London.

Before I knew it, I was heading for the railway station. All the way there, I was rehearsing what to say to the ticket man, as I knew I didn't have enough money to go all that way. While I stood waiting to ask about a ticket, I started to get worried, and was deep in thought when the ticket man spoke to me.

"I've just come from my Auntie's and I have lost all my money, except this," I blurted. I held up the half crown.

"Where do you want to go?" asked the ticket man.

"London," I said nervously, looking around at all the people who were standing behind me.

"Ah, well, you won't get very far on half a crown young man. You had better go to that window over there and tell them all about it," he said, and then started talking with the next person in line.

I went to the window he told me to go to, which had a big sign saying "Inquiries." I told the woman the sad story about losing my money, and she seemed to have a sympathetic ear. She came from behind the counter and took my hand, saying, "We had better get this sorted out. Come with me."

We briskly strode away, weaving in and out of people and objects until we came to a door, which was half open. Letting go of my hand, she stood to one side and said, "In you go," but as I started to walk in, I saw the sign on the door, which sent shivers down my spine. "POLICE," it read, and as if by instinct, I turned and ran.

I had no idea where I was running to; I just kept going in and out and around people and objects, although my knee hurt, I seemed to be doing all right. I hoped I was getting closer to the way out. I took a turn and ended up on the ramp to one of the platforms. Then I heard the cry from behind: "Stop him!"

People stopped and stared and one person tried to grab me but failed. I gave a quick look over my shoulder and saw three police-men running after me blowing their whistles and shouting, "Stop!" It stopped everyone except me. Two old people made an attempt to grab me as I went past them. One of them fell, and I glanced over my shoulder to see if he was all right.

Then it happened. I bumped into an old lady who fell to the ground; I lost my balance and wanted to help the old lady. But a heroic railway porter thrust his hand trolley in front of me and I stumbled over it, ending up in a heap on the platform with a multi-tude of people staring down at me. The three policemen took charge and helped me to my feet. I was in agony and the tears started build-ing up. I had failed and was now dreading the consequences. As the police escorted me back to their office – one on each side and one in front of me – they cleared all the people away who wanted to have a look at what they had caught.

I pulled my handkerchief out of my pocket, and the piece of paper that had my brother's address on it fluttered to the floor. When I tried to tell them what had just happened, they ignored me. Apart from the half crown he had given me, that bit of paper was all I had to remind me of my brother.

As I stood in the police office, the woman who had brought me there was giving her reasons for thinking I was a suspicious character. If only she had known, I thought. The policemen thanked her and she left.

"What's your name, son?" asked the policeman behind the desk.

I just stood there, tight-lipped.

"Where do you live?" asked another, who also got only silence. "Someone give him a cup of tea and a chair."

I rubbed my legs because they were hurting me and sat down. The officer who gave me a cup of tea said in a friendly voice, "Here, drink this, and then tell us why you ran away from this office."

I was about to say thank you for the tea, but suddenly there was a barrage of questions coming at me from all directions. Finally the policeman behind the desk said, "Look through his pockets and see if there are any clues in there."

I stood up, and a constable went through all my pockets and placed each item on the desk, naming it as he went: "One handkerchief. One pencil. One fountain pen. And one half crown. That's it, sir."

They all looked at the items for a moment. Then the desk officer commented, "Well, there's not much to go on, is there?" More questions, but I kept my silence.

The constables were at the stage where they were going to start getting annoyed when one of them, who hadn't said much before, said in a deep, casual voice,

"I've got an idea that he's from that orphanage on the London Road, sir."

At that, my head spun around in his direction, which caused me to drop my cup and saucer.

The constable behind the desk said, "You may be right there," and looked in a little book on his desk. "Ah, here we are. I'll give them a ring; they may be able to help us," and promptly dialed the number.

Not a sound could be heard except the faint ringing tone from the telephone. I began to tremble, as I suddenly realized what was going to happen to me. Then the officer spoke.

"Is this the master I am speaking to? Ah, good. This is the police station at Leicester railway station. We have in our custody a young man whom one of our constables thinks is from the orphanage," he said, and went on to describe me and the fact that everything I was wearing was gray, it was easy for the master to claim me as one of his.

My hands were sweaty and I couldn't stop shaking. Everyone was looking at me, and I got the odd smile off one or two of the policemen. I looked over my shoulder toward the door, but a policeman looked at me and shook his head. Yes, I was thinking of running again, but I don't think I would have gotten very far; I ached that much.

The officer on the phone continued, "That's no problem, sir. We'll send a car for you immediately." As he put down the phone, he instructed the policeman who had suggested the idea to go and pick up the master.

"Well, young man, have you still nothing to say?" he asked.

I just looked at him and squinted, wondering what to tell him but knowing it wouldn't do any good anyway. I had so much fear built up that I quite honestly felt sick.

It didn't take long for the policeman to return with the master. I sat there fidgeting with my hands, which were wringing wet, sweat rolling down my face. The master stood in the doorway with a big grin on his face.

"Well, well, Master Morris, what on earth are you doing down here at the railway station, apart from causing these policemen all this trouble?"

I couldn't get over how nice he was being. He came over and placed his hand on my shoulder. I looked up at him with suspicion.

"Yes officer," he said, "this is one of my lads. I just can't imagine what has gotten into him, but he will be all right when I get him home."

That was the bit that was worrying me.

After a lot of talk, the master looked at me and said, "Now, Master Morris, before we leave I want you to apologize to these officers for causing all this trouble."

I lifted my head and said,

"I'm sorry."

"That's all right, son. Let's just hope that whatever has upset you, the master can sort it out," said the officer in charge.

I bet you know what I was thinking.

"Oh, by the way," said the officer at the desk, pointing to the items on the table, "I believe these are yours, son."

The master picked them up, and with an inquisitive look handed me everything, except the half crown, which he kept in his hand. After being offered a lift, the master said, "No, it's all right officer, we'll take the bus. It will give me a chance to talk to him on the way home." Then he bid everyone goodbye and we left. Even then I thought about running off, but, my body told me no.

We walked out of the station to the nearest bus stop and waited for a bus without the master saying one word. When the bus arrived, he sat on a side seat at the rear downstairs and I sat opposite. He told the conductor where we were going and passed him my half crown, then slipped the change into his jacket pocket.

I sat with my head hung low and glanced up at him. He had his very mean expression on his face, and I knew I was really going to get it when we got to the home. I even thought of jumping off the bus, knowing that I could run faster than he could. The more I thought about it, the more I wanted to do it, but it was too late, we were there. He still hadn't spoke, not one word.

We got off the bus, crossed the road, walked up the drive, and went in the back door. That's when it all started.

The matron charged straight up to me like a bull and put her full weight behind a blow to my face. I felt my head shudder and thought my teeth were going to fly out. The master ripped his jacket off and threw it on the floor, but the matron was still swinging at me and shouting abuse.

"Leave him to me," shouted the master.

I started to run down the corridor, but not quickly enough. The master grabbed me and gave me a blow to the chest, which knocked the wind out of me. As I doubled over in pain, he brought his knee up and caught me in the face. I screamed and started shouting, but it seemed to only encourage them. While the matron kicked my leg, the master struck me on the nose with his fist. The blood came gushing down. I shouted that I was sorry.

"I'll bloody well make sure you don't ever think of running the hell away from my home again," he screamed, and hit me in the jaw.

That was it; I couldn't take anymore. I sank to the ground, but they hadn't finished with me yet. The master, still raging and swearing, dragged me to my feet and threw me against the wall in the corner. The matron was still having a turn and thumped me in the ribs. As I screamed and cried, she shouted, "Go on, shout as loud as you like. There's no one here that cares about you," and gave me another crack across the face.

I slid down the corner onto the floor, blood streaming from my nose and tears mingling with the blood. It was making a right mess of my clothes and the floor. I curled up into a ball and was begging them to stop when the master said,

"Where did you steal that half crown from?"

It was difficult to talk because my lips were swollen, but every time I told him that my brother had given it to me, he replied, "I don't like little boys who steal."

I just wanted to die. It was difficult to breathe because of my nose, and I couldn't focus on what was going on. Everything was going blurry and it was hard to concentrate. The matron was saying something to the master in a muffled tone.

"The other children will be home soon. Leave him there in the corner as an example to any would-be runaways." He agreed that this was a good idea, so they grabbed me and propped me up in the corner. When I tried to wipe my nose, they told me to leave it alone and not move a muscle. I dropped my head and there was an outcry, "Lift your ugly head up and keep it there."

I could hear them talking, but I couldn't see where they were because my eyes were stinging so badly. I wanted to wipe my eyes and blow my nose but every time I moved, one of them pounced on me. My knees were trembling, and I felt like I was going to collapse. The blood was clogging up around my nose, which meant I had to breathe through my mouth, so blood was also getting in there. I must have looked as bad as I felt.

As the other children came in the back door from school, the master pointed me out and told them that this would be the treatment they would receive if they had any ideas about running away.

After what seemed like an eternity, the master stood in front of me and said in a sarcastic tone, "We are all going for tea now, Master Morris, and while we are in there, you will go and get changed and clean yourself up. And once you have done that, you will clean all the shoes, and I will inspect them thoroughly. And once you have done that, you will then do the boiler."

I gave a big sigh.

"Yes, you may well sigh, but by the time I've finished with you, you'll wish you had never been born. So your punishment duties are cleaning shoes and stoking the boiler, FOR THE ENTIRE MONTH," he shouted. Then he disappeared, muttering to himself.

Given the way it felt when I tried to move, I was sure every bone in my body was broken. I eventually got going and made straight for the toilet. I put my head down the toilet pan and was sick for some time. When I tried to get to the sink, I fell back on the floor. I pulled myself up and thought I was going to be sick again. Then I saw my reflection in the mirror. What a sight that was! I looked harder into the mirror and was squinting trying to identify myself.

"Is that really me?"

My face was distorted with the swelling, and my school clothes were covered in blood. I threw them in a pile on the floor and put on my work clothes. I could not stop my nose from bleeding, and when I looked down at the floor there were trails of blood everywhere, so I had to get some water and mop it up or be in even more trouble. For awhile, I just sat in the shoe room with my head back, holding my hankie over my nose.

Eventually the bleeding stopped, so I started cleaning the shoes and thinking about the events of the day. If I had only gone to school, I would have just gotten the cane there, and then gotten it again when I came home, instead of all that. Or I could have taken a bus and not tried the railway, but where would I be now if I had gone on a bus?

All those thoughts went through my mind as I plowed my way through the shoes. It was agony. Every movement I made seemed to have an ache associated with it. And yes, I did have the energy to pee in the masters shoes again. And after a very long time, I staggered to the master's study, gave a trembling knock on the door, and waited.

The assistant matron came out of the dining room, and seeing me, froze in her tracks. She stared at me for awhile, then gave a frown and walked away, shaking her head. Then the study door opened. The master stood before me and sharply said, "Go to the shoe room and wait there," and went back into his study.

I went to the shoe room to wait and wait and wait and yes, wait. When the master finally arrived for inspection, I was very surprised because he said the shoes were all right. "Not good enough, but they will do," was his comment. "Now get to the boiler room," he commanded.

I might have guessed there was something worse in store, for there in the boiler room was the biggest, messiest pile of coke I had ever seen. It had just been delivered through a hole in the roof. You see, to deliver the coke, they would lift a manhole cover up and tip large bags of the stuff into the hole, so it falls and rolls and goes everywhere. The master followed me into the room and said, "Right. Your first job is to shovel all that coke to the wall. Then you sweep the floor clean and then make the boiler up for the night. When you have done all that, I want to inspect it." And so he made his exit.

With that, I sat down with my head in my hands. I didn't know whether to scream or to cry. So I did both, and not a soul came into the boiler room to see if I was all right. After what seemed like hours of shoveling coke and sweeping up the dust, the sweat was rolling off me, and I was covered with fine black grit. And oh, how my body ached. But I still had to set about stoking the boiler.

First I had to rake the bottom with a long iron rod to get rid of the ash. Then I had to fish out any lumps of clinker. Having done that, the next job was a bit awkward. To actually load the boiler, which was too high for me, I had to stand on a box to shovel in the coke. It was a work of art to get each shovelful in, and in my condition it was a very painful task. After a great struggle, I somehow managed to fill the thing. I then pushed in the damper that allowed the boiler to burn slowly. And that was that. I had finished my jobs.

It was only then that the hunger pains let me know that I was missing something. I wiped the sweat from my face, as it was time to report to the master. I knew it was very late because everything was very quiet. I hobbled over to the stone steps leading from the cellar, and as I started climbing them, the master suddenly appeared at the top.

"Where are you going?" he asked as he walked down the steps.

"I ...I was just...coming to...report."

He went straight over to the boiler, looking all around the room as he went. "Have you made this up?" he snapped, lifting the lid up and peering in.

"Yes, Master," I nervously replied.

"Right, get yourself scrubbed all over and go straight to bed," he said as he allowed the lid of the boiler to slam shut, which made me jump.

It was wonderful to climb into a tub of hot water and rest my weary body, but I was anxious to get to bed. I quickly cleaned myself following the routine the assistant matron had taught me. In fact, I still do to a certain degree. You see, since I had turned 13, I was allowed to bathe myself.

It wasn't until I stood up that I noticed that my body was bruised all over, and when I looked at the color of the water, I knew my nose was dripping again. I just stood there watching the bright-red blobs of blood hitting the still water. It was the only sound I could hear.

Realizing that I was alone, I started to get frightened. I hurriedly got out, dried, and held a cold wet flannel over my nose as I crept into the dormitory. With only a dim nightlight, I was able to get to bed without disturbing anyone. Oh, it was heaven to slip between the sheets, but then I felt something by my shoulder. Would you believe it? Some kind soul had left me two biscuits, which were very welcome.

I had just dropped off to sleep when I discovered that my whole body was moving up and down. My eyes flew wide open. All I could see was the face of the master, so I screamed. I thought I was having a nightmare, but it really was the master.

"Go and light that boiler; it's out," he said in a loud whisper, and pulled off my bedclothes.

I sat up and in a soft voice said, "The boiler is out? It shouldn't be. I pushed the damper in." I was full of thought as I got dressed, but as I was putting on my shoes, one of the lads quietly said, "It was the Master who pulled the damper out. He very often does that when you are on punishment." With that, my informant turned over to settle down again.

Well, I didn't know what time it was, but it was still dark and sure enough, when I got to the boiler room, the damper had been pulled out. When I looked inside the boiler, there was nothing but ashes and a lot of clinkers.

Teeth

Chapter Nineteen

A Little Bit of Luck

I went through hell during that month of punishment, doing the boiler and cleaning shoes. There were times when the master would not only throw the shoes around the cellar, but me as well. I couldn't concentrate at school and would drop off to sleep. What with the brutal treatment at the home and the caning at school, I was in a right state.

My hatred for the master and matron got stronger, growing to such an extent that I swore that when I was 15 and able to leave the home I would have my revenge. I know it wasn't a nice thing to think, but that's how I felt. Unbeknownst to me, a dramatic change was ahead.

One morning I got up and went through the usual routine: I scrubbed the corridor, ate breakfast, changed for school, and stood in line for inspection. But when it was my turn to stand in front of the master, he just looked at me and pushed me to one side, saying, "You stand over there," then carried on inspecting the other lads. I stood against the wall with a large question mark over my head, wondering what on earth I had done now. I ran through all the possibilities but couldn't think of what might have upset him or the matron.

When everyone else had gone off to school, the master instructed me to stand in the corner. Now the last time I was in that corner, he was knocking the life out of me. I swallowed hard. He stood in front of me, giving me one of those stares, and finally said, "You will stand in this corner until I tell you to move."

I just nodded, still swallowing hard, and he disappeared.

"What about school?" I thought aloud, scratching my head. I desperately tried to work out what was going on, but after several hours I gave up and just stood and waited for whatever was going to happen next.

With the exception of two or three minutes, when I was excused to go to the toilet, I stood in that corner for five hours. And then it happened.

The master and matron both appeared. The master was holding a suitcase, which I fixed my eyes on, wondering what and where and why. How I wished someone would just tell me what was going on!

They stood there in silence until the master finally sneered, "Well, Master Morris, this is a happy day for the Matron and me." He looked over at her, then back at me. "You're no longer wanted here, so you are being sent away."

He threw the suitcase at my feet.

"Now show me your play locker."

I followed him to the playroom, but it was a waste of time because I had nothing in there. When did I ever have time to even go in that room? But at least it was an excuse to move.

When he discovered I had nothing in my locker, the master sent me back to the corner to wait some more. Eventually I heard a car pull up. I didn't know whether to be happy or sad, but surely there couldn't be any place as horrible as that one. Or could there? I was instructed to use the bathroom, which I gladly did and went back to my position in the corner.

I heard a lot of talking in the entrance hall before I was summoned to appear. I was then introduced to Mr. George Luck, who seemed like a very nice man, and told to go and sit in the car. As I walked past the grand staircase, I looked up at the banister that I never had a chance to slide down. The assistant matron was standing at the top of the stairs and gave me a wave. I waved back and shouted, "Goodbye Miss and thank you!"

The master swung his head around to see who I was shouting at and graced me with one of his famous stares. I, in return, gave him a cheeky grin; then ran to the car, where I found a lad from a different home – Patrick Ayres – who was going to the same place as I, wherever that was.

At last, Mr. Luck climbed into the car. I still couldn't believe that I was actually leaving the place, so I immediately asked the gentleman if I would be coming back.

"I should very much doubt it," he replied. "Why do you ask?"

"I just hope I never see those people again," I said with relief.

As the car drove off, I didn't even look back to see whether the master and matron were standing on the front step crying because of me leaving.

Chapter Twenty

Hello, Hunstanton

On the long journey to East Anglia, where Mr. Luck said he was taking us, we talked nonstop, mainly because he asked Patrick and me all sorts of questions about the homes we had just left. I gladly told him everything about the wicked place I had been, and as Patrick had just come from Leighton Bussard, where I had stayed for a week, we had something in common.

Before we knew it, we were there. It was our new orphanage – St. Christopher's Home, Hunstanton, Norfolk, which was a seaside resort. I had only seen the sea once before, long ago on that week-long holiday from Ashdon.

Although I was very excited about coming to the new home, and anywhere had to be better than Leicester. Mr. Luck told us that we would like the place. I had to ask him what the master and matron were like. He told us that they were his favorites out of all the homes he visited.

"So here we are," he announced as he drove through a side gate that led to a small tarmac playground. The playground had a large set of steel swings, which looked like they got a lot of use, and a very long wooden shed.

The home itself was made of red brick and had a metal fire escape, which gave me a quick flashback of Ashdon, although the Ashdon fire escape was much more dramatic.

Mr. Luck opened the car door for us and led us into the house. I was very nervous about meeting the master and matron. It didn't matter what the environment was like; the master and matron were the main factor. Once we were introduced to them, I felt as if a huge burden had been lifted from my body. I could already tell that they were caring and loving people.

The master was a big, well-built man who could produce a large, friendly smile that showed all his teeth. The matron was the complete opposite in size, but had an equally welcoming smile and was very motherly looking.

As I shook their hands, I politely said, "Hello, it's nice to meet you, Master and Matron," but I was immediately corrected.

"No, we don't use those terms – master and matron – here," the master said with a big smile on his face. "You call me Uncle, and my wife, Auntie."

He then pointed to a little red-faced woman who was standing shyly to one side, saying, "And this is the assistant matron, whom you call Miss Jones. Now what I want you both to do, is come with me to the bathroom, have a quick bath, and change those clothes. Then I'll show you around the house after that."

Although it seemed a little strange that we should have a bath immediately upon arrival, there was logic in his method. You see, if you have something delivered to your house, you first examine the goods to see if they are all right, and note down any defects before signing for them. It was a bit like signing for a Federal Express package. It was, I assumed, the reason for the bath.

While Patrick and I had a bath, the master – sorry – Uncle, checked us both over. When he saw all the bruises on my body, he called Mr. Luck in to have a look. I was asked to stand up, and when I did, Uncle started pointing to each mark on my body. When I turned around to face them in the full Monty position, Uncle gasped. No, not at how big I was.

"How did you get these bruises?"

I just stood there with my head hung low, afraid to tell him.

"Now come, Les, you can tell me." My eyes lit up at the sound of my new master calling me by my first name. I hadn't been called by my first name for so long that it made me feel great. I told him all.

He patted me on the head and said that he would get Auntie to come and see if I needed any medical treatment. As he went out, I heard him talking to Mr. Luck.

"Well, that's exactly what he told me in the car coming here," said Mr. Luck as they left the bathroom.

Uncle said to Mr. Luck "I'll go and get my camera and get some evidence to send to head office."

After they left, Patrick, who was in the next bath, popped his head over the top of the partition and said, "Let's have a look at all those bruises."

I stood up again and showed him, pointing to them all.

"Cor, no wonder you ran away." He quickly got back in his bath because Auntie had come in with her assistant to check me over.

After telling me to stand up again, which I promptly did, they both gasped – no, not at my private parts. After making some comments to Miss Jones, Auntie asked her to treat my open wounds, and mentioned that there were two severe bruises that they would have to keep an eye on.

We were then rejoined by Uncle and Mr. Luck.

Auntie said to Uncle, "What sort of person would strike a nice young man like this?" Uncle was now taking more photographs of my bruised body.

When they all left the bathroom, I heard Uncle saying that he was going to send the pictures to the Society's head office in London.

St. Christopher's Home was situated on a corner and was shaped like a Y. The longest part was on the main road that went to Old Hunstanton and the coast line. The smaller section went down a side street. It seemed much bigger than the Leicester home, but it didn't have the large grounds to go with it.

As Patrick and I were shown around, we got a friendly, lived-in feeling about the place. We actually heard music playing on a radio in the dining room. It was wonderful to think that it was my new home, and when Uncle took us outside, he showed us the bike shed. Pointing to one bicycle, he said to me, "Now this bike belonged to a lad that has just left the home, so you can have this one." Turning to Patrick, he smiled and pointed to another bike and told him he could have the use of that one.

Needless to say, I was thrilled to bits. It was like someone giving me a car today. I was that excited. There was only one problem. I had no idea how to ride that type of bike, but with my early days on the green bike, it didn't take me long to get the hang of it.

As we walked away, Uncle turned to us and said, "I take it you can both ride a bike?"

Patrick replied that he could, and I said that I had never ridden one like that before, but I could ride a penny-farthing bike.

Uncle swung around to me and said, "Were you ever at the Ashdon, Essex home?"

I beamed at the very sound of the place, and told him that I was.

"So you're the young man that went down the hill on the penny-farthing bike in Ashdon? You wait until I see Auntie and tell her!"

We continued our tour of the home. When we went around to the front of the house, Uncle had great delight in showing off his aviary full of budgerigars, which he used to breed and would periodically take to shows, hoping to get a winner. It was his hobby. Because I took an interest in the birds by asking all sorts of questions, Uncle told me that when I got settled in, he would let me look after them.

I just couldn't believe all that was happening. I immediately felt that at last I was in a place that I could take pride in calling home.

As we went through the front door, I looked up at the statue carved above it.

"That's a statue of St. Christopher, whom the home is named after," Uncle explained as we entered the front hall. Then he pointed to a small room to the left, which was a sitting room. It had an array of comfortable chairs and an upright piano, which caught my attention.

I raised my hand.

Uncle told me that it wasn't necessary to raise my hand unless asked to do so. "Did you have a question?" he asked.

"Er, yes. Can anyone...." I hesitated and looked at him. He was smiling, so I knew it was safe to ask, and continued, "Play that piano?"

"Yes, by all means! It's a wonder that it still plays, what with all the pounding that it gets from the children."

Next to the sitting room was a study.

"This room is a private room for me and Auntie, unless, of course, we invite you in," said Uncle.

Opposite was a long staircase leading up to the dormitories, which we visited next. There were two large rooms, one for the smaller children and one for the bigger children, with Uncle and Auntie's bedroom in the middle. At the end of the room for the bigger children was another small room, which had four beds.

"That room is for the older boys," Uncle explained. "You and Patrick will be moving in there when two of the older lads leave, which won't be long."

So we started out in the large dormitory. Our beds were opposite each other, right next to the big boys' room.

The beds here were like those in the other orphanages, low metal with noisy springs. There were lockers by each bed to put stuff in, so I put my bits in the locker and on top of the bed to show that the bed was occupied. You see, if a bed is known to be empty, other children will automatically jump on it and mess it up.

Then we went downstairs to visit the playroom. It was directly under our dormitory, so it was a big room. At the far end were some large play lockers, where each child had his own space. In one of the corners was another piano. I pointed to it, and Uncle immediately went over and lifted the lid, saying, "I think there are two or three notes that still play on this one."

I asked Uncle how many children were at St. Christopher's. He said that it catered to 24, which was the total right when we moved in.

We walked through the large dining room, which was laid out similarly to those in the other homes, and went into the large kitchen, were we found Auntie and her assistant having a nice cup of tea with Mr. Luck. We joined them, and Uncle and Auntie went over all the rules and regulations with us, which was sort of standard stuff.

At one point, Uncle interrupted by saying to Auntie, "Remember the story of the little lad who went down the hill on a penny-farthing bike in Ashdon?" He pointed his finger at me and continued. "*This* is the young man who was responsible for that!"

Just about everyone in the room had heard the story, and they were all amazed, except for Patrick, who had no idea what we were talking about. I told him I would tell him the details later.

Someone looked at the clock, and the staff said that we would finish the topic another time. The children were about to come home from school, and as they put it, "The peace is over for a while." Uncle told us to keep looking around in the meantime.

The kitchen had a big Aga cooker that had to be stoked up with coke – one of the big boys' jobs, no doubt. We continued on through the pantry and the storage room into the boiler room. The boiler wasn't as big as the last one I had to deal with, but it was still another big-boy job.

The boiler room also contained an aviary of canaries, which made a lot of noise. There were two large galvanized dustbins nearby with some kind of thick liquid inside. I had just put my head down to try and guess what was in there when a voice from behind me said, "Eggs."

We were surprised to look up and see a young chap, who promptly stuck out his hand and introduced himself. "My name is Roger. Uncle told me to show you the rest of the home. And I see you are looking at our mysterious bins. I hate this job," he continued, walking toward them. "You see, you have to put your hand in this funny-looking water stuff, which is all slimy and nasty, to retrieve the eggs that are stored in there. Apparently it preserves them."

Roger then took us outside to see a large wooden hut, telling us its history along the way. "This used to be the old Hunstanton Scout Hut. It was donated to St. Christopher's when the Scouts got the use of the church hut. The trouble is that it took away a lot of our play yard."

He opened the door to the hut and revealed another aviary full of canaries. "It's more of a junk place at the moment. Uncle keeps saying that we're all going to come in here one day and clean the place up, but that was two years ago, so who knows? You may have the privilege, because I'll be leaving soon."

Pat and I fit right into life at St. Christopher's, adjusting easily to the new environment with its kind Uncle and Auntie. One of the earliest things I remember about my stay there was the day we had the privilege of watching television for the very first time. No, the home didn't have a television; a local person loaned us a set for a very special broadcast by the BBC. We were all going to watch the coronation of Queen Elizabeth II. Not only was it a historic day, but we were going to witness it as it happened live at Westminster Abbey in London. I had never heard of Westminster Abbey.

That may not seem so surprising to you, but we didn't even know what a television was. And what, exactly, was a coronation? It was a tremendous landmark in English history. Or, to put it as Pat did, "Princess Elizabeth is going to be presented with a gold hat and that will make her a queen."

Well I suppose he was right, but I was more fascinated by the television itself and kept looking around the back of it. Eventually I was told to take my seat. All the tables in the dining room were pushed to one side with all the chairs in a semicircle. The little chaps sat in front, with the taller ones to the back. Uncle stood in front of us and explained how we were about to witness history in the making. He also told us who had loaned us the television and what a television was.

I stuck my hand up and asked, "How does the picture get into the house and appear on that screen?"

Uncle smiled and answered by saying, "Good question. The picture comes from a signal to an aerial, which we have stuck out the window, so if all goes well the picture will come in via the window." He smiled at me and commented that it was all new to him too, so he didn't know much more about it than we did.

I got up and went outside to where the wire was hanging out the window, waiting for pictures to come in from London. It wasn't long before Pat came out to see what I was up to.

"What are you looking for?" he asked.

I wasn't really sure myself, so I pointed to the wire sticking up in the air and said, "How does a picture come out of the air through to this wire?"

Pat simply shook his head and said, "They're just saying that because they have no idea."

There was a loud tap on the window and a hand beckoning, so we walked back inside, still trying to work out what Uncle had been talking about.

It took a long time to sit and watch the coronation, even though it was something that most of us didn't know anything about. At school we had big debates, which were interesting and all made sense, but I was very confused as to how the coronation got into St. Christopher's Home.

Chapter Twenty-One
A Rose with Thorns

Moving to St. Christopher's meant that once again I had to start over in another school. It was vastly different from any other school I had been to. You see, the main school was in the town, but the population had grown and the school hadn't. About a mile away from the main school was a large hut that for some reason was known as the Hoarser Hut. How on earth it got that name, I have no idea. The hut was where all the older pupils went, and where I was sent for my studies, along with Pat and two other lads from the home.

The Hut was one big room outfitted only with the bare necessities, but we seemed to manage. It stood on the side of a busy, dusty road that had a continuous stream of trucks and machinery charging up and down it. That was because they were building the new Hunstanton High School just across the way. The new school was quite a modern-looking building. In fact it looked like a very, very large greenhouse. So the hut was only a temporary measure. Thank goodness for that!

My teacher there was a young man named Mr. Williams. He had the job of teaching just about all the subjects, but the class only had 12 students.

One of the chaps in the class, Tim, stood out above the rest of us, for he was already nearly six feet tall. His father was a doctor who had a lovely old MG motorcar, which he would run his son to school in each day. We Home Boys had to walk about a mile to school, but whenever the doctor saw us, he would stop and tell us to pile in. It was great fun.

I decided to make a fresh start at the school and try to catch up on a lot of subjects. I also took great pride in my writing, and kept most of my books tidy, that is, until a certain young girl named Rose sat in front of me.

Rose became a nightmare to me. You see, we all had a large wooden desk with a hole at the top right hand corner for our inkwells. Rose had long blonde hair, and just about every time I went to dip my pen into the inkwell, I first had to clear her hair away. I politely asked her several times to keep her hair away from my ink, telling her that she should be more careful or put it up out of the way.

Pat, who sat next to me, once shouted at her about the matter. Well, she didn't like that and complained to Mr. Williams, who sided with her. It seemed to make her do it even more. Being a gentleman, I sort of put up with it until the day the end of her hair got soaked with ink and she swung her head around, causing a great smear of black ink to splatter across the book that I was writing in.

I was hopping mad, but she thought it was very amusing and got the giggles. The teacher wanted to know what was so funny, so I showed him what she had done to my book. He still took sides with her, saying she couldn't help it. With that, she turned around and stuck her tongue out at me. So I swore revenge.

After the lunch break, Pat called me over to the ditch he was standing in. When I got to him, he pointed to a very large toad and said with a big smile, "Are you thinking what I'm thinking?"

"What a good idea," I said, and with that, he picked up the toad and hid it in his jacket. We got back into the classroom first, so I quickly lifted the lid of Rose's desk while Pat threw in the toad. I shut the lid as quickly as I had opened it, and then sat waiting at my desk like the innocent lad that I was. Pat did the same.

We sat there patiently with big grins on our faces; then watched Rose's every movement as she came into the classroom. She was talking nonstop to some other girls, but eventually made her way over to her desk. She was still yapping as she sat down, and without looking at what she was doing, opened her desk and slid her hand in.

Well, I think she must have touched the toad straightaway, because she suddenly thrust the lid up high and then screamed and yelled and threw herself away from her desk, crashing into my desk.

The toad must have thought that Rose was his mother, because he jumped right onto her lap. There was another hysterical scream as Rose stood up and started shouting at everyone who tried to help her.

Pat crawled under her desk and picked up the toad, which was now lying on its back with its feet over its ears. He quickly got rid of the evidence.

The whole classroom was rolling about with laughter, including myself. Mr. Williams tried to bring everyone back to normal, whatever that was. Rose, with a bright-red face and black-streaked hair, tried to tell him what she had found in her desk.

Alas, the smile was taken off my face when I was hauled in front of the room to have six strokes of the cane; three on each hand. Although it was painful, it was well worth it.

The next day, Rose did exactly the same thing she always did. I had spent the previous evening copying out what she had messed up in my book and that long blonde hair of hers messed it all up again. That time I was not only mad; I was furious.

I stuck up my hand and told the teacher. He snapped at me, saying, "Morris, just get on with your work. I'm going to write a report to the orphanage about your behavior."

Rose turned around and stuck her tongue out at me as far as she could, then swung her head so the ink went everywhere. I was gritting my teeth, wondering what to do, when Pat caught my attention by miming scissors. I winked at him and got a pair of scissors out of my desk. Then I grabbed hold of her hair and hacked off a large lump. She started screaming and pulling away from me.

Needless to say, I was in trouble again. Not only did I get the cane and have to write out 100 times, "I must concentrate on my work," I was also in trouble back at the home.

Although Uncle never punished me for that, he did give me a good telling-off. But when the teacher telephoned him, Uncle simply told him to move either her or me away from each other. Unfortunately, Rose's father was furious and came to the orphanage to complain about me. But Uncle apparently took care of everything.

The outcome of all it was that the teacher finally did move her out of everyone's way. I was still able to sit next to my best friend, which was fun until the teacher separated us because of too much giggling.

Pat was a true sport. Although he only had one lung, it didn't seem to bother him much, except when he got overly excited. Sometimes when we laughed too hard, like after the toad episode, he had to stop and calm down for a while.

When the teacher saw Pat looking funny, I had to explain to him that he was all right but just needed to relax for a bit. Of course, all the class got to know about Pat's problem, and some of the children were mean to him about him being a disabled Home Boy. Sparks flew when that sort of thing happened. I always stuck up for him, but he also did a good job of sorting people out. Pat was like my brother.

Chapter Twenty-Two

Best Friends

Most of the children who had been at the home for some time could swim, and if you couldn't, Uncle would make certain that you learned. Having learned, you would then be allowed to go to the beach on your own. The home had a beach hut at Old Hunstanton, and often during the summer we would march down there in twos with large boxes of food and all sorts of things to keep us occupied. I think the main purpose of that was to tire us out so we would go straight to sleep at bedtime.

We older boys with bikes were allowed out on our own as well, so Pat and I used to ride all around town and have some fun. You see, we both had a good sense of humor.

One day, we went to a fish & chips shop. While we stood in line, Pat started laughing. I asked him what he was laughing at, but he just kept on laughing louder and louder, until all the people in the shop were looking at us. I ended up laughing with him, but still hadn't a clue about what was so funny. Then the other people in the shop started laughing. As for Pat, he was now sliding down the tiled wall, just crying with laughter.

The shopkeeper next door was wiping his hands on his apron and looking over at us until even he started laughing.

So, if you will, picture two young lads sitting on the floor in a fish & chips shop full of people, tears rolling down their cheeks and holding their sides as some laughed and others just smiled.

"What are you laughing at?" I asked him again.

Between bouts of laughter, Pat finally cried out, "Cod!" That one word was all that was necessary to set him off again. I couldn't do a thing with him the rest of the day.

Pat and I used to go through life looking for the funny things, but it sometimes got us into a lot of trouble. One of those occasions was when we both got thrown out of the choir. I think it was a tradition that the older boys at the home joined the church choir. It wasn't for our voices. I'm sure it was just to fill the choir stalls.

One Sunday evening, Pat and I crawled into the orchard next to the church and got a few juicy apples to eat during the service. He sat at the end of the pew opposite me, even though they always tried to keep us separated if they could, and indicated that he wanted an apple because he had given all of his away. So I carefully fumbled around in my pocket so no one would notice, and waited until we all had to kneel.

With great skill, I rolled an apple across the steps in front of the altar and he retrieved it. But he wanted more. I successfully rolled another. It was the third one that caused all the trouble. The problem was I didn't realize that the apple had an awkward shape. As it rolled along, it suddenly turned and rolled down the steps leading to the main aisle.

As soon as the members of the congregation caught sight of the mysterious apple, heads turned and faces pulled expressions of amazement. My heart didn't go up into my mouth until I saw that the vicar had caught sight of the apple as it slowly rocked to a standstill. As the vicar was giving all of us choir boys a very hard stare over the top of his glasses, I carefully turned my head to see if the choirmaster had seen what had happened. He had. He was staring into the rear-view mirror on top of the organ, and his expression was worse than the vicar's.

I then looked at Pat, who was crying with laughter. "Oh no," I thought. It wasn't long before I started laughing too and not much longer after that before half the choir was giggling. Because Pat and I had been warned several times previously about our behavior, we were dismissed from the choir that night.

Another group we were thrown out of was the scouts. The scout hut was next to the vicarage. How we got involved in the scouts, I have no idea. We used to participate in all the activities, but not with the proper attitude. For example, the scoutmaster once asked Pat,

"Can you light a fire with two bits of wood?"

To which he replied, "Yes, as long as one bit is a match."

Similarly, I was asked when we were studying first aid, "What do you do when you break your leg?"

My reply was, "You limp." With a shout of laughter, Pat set me off laughing as well. By that point, the scoutmaster had had enough of us, so he sent us outside until we could stop that silly giggling and take things seriously.

Near the scout hut was a cherry tree that belonged to the vicar. Now Pat and I had been told off on many occasions about helping ourselves to these cherries. The vicar just didn't like the idea of us children stealing them. While we were "cooling off" outside, we just happened to end up in the cherry tree, eating large quantities of fruit. Guess who just happened to walk around that way? Yes, the vicar.

It was his shouting at us to come down that caused the scoutmaster to come running from the hut, followed by a large pack of children, all wondering what was going on. We sheepishly climbed down the tree, pockets filled with cherries. The vicar gave us a stern telling-off and then gave us our marching orders. All the scouts witnessed the scoutmaster pointing us away from the premises and telling us never to return, while the vicar shouted that he was going to report us to the orphanage.

By the time we got back to the home, Uncle had already heard what we had been up to, and after another telling-off, put us both on punishment. But it was nothing like the punishment I had had at the Leicester orphanage. We continued to perform our usual daily jobs, but on Saturday morning we would have to do the punishment job as well. As soon as we finished it, we could then do what we would normally do.

Chapter Twenty-Three
A Different Kind of Christmas

One thing the Hunstanton home did was introduce me to a very different kind of Christmas. The Christmases there wouldn't have been possible without the aid of the American Air Force base not far away called Sculthorpe. The tradition was that the Air Force would take over the house while we were all at school one day, decorating it with all kinds of Christmas finery. There would be a large tree, heavily decorated, and great big balloons with a half-crown coin in them, and colored lights all over the place, and snowflakes sprayed around the edges of all the downstairs windows.

When I came home from school the first year, I was completely amazed and wandered aimlessly from room to room, just gazing at the splendor of it all. The outstanding feature was of course, the Christmas tree, and the number of presents around it. I had never seen such a sight.

I looked around to see if anyone was watching, and bent over to see if my name was on any of the presents. As much as I tried, I couldn't find any. Then I thought that perhaps there was one big one at the bottom of the pile with my name on it. If that wasn't wishful thinking, I don't know what was.

The goodwill of the townspeople always peaked at Christmas. They would arrive at the home with donations of all sorts; some brought food, others toys. And even neatly dressed carol singers would come in the evening to sing in exchange for Auntie's mince pies that she was famous for making.

As with the other homes I had been at, the children with relations tended to get lots of presents, while the rest of us just got cast-offs. One thing Uncle made sure of was that one of the children who had very little would win the best-decorated play-locker contest, which was held every year. Each child would decorate his locker in the chosen theme. Sometimes it would be a nursery-rhyme theme, but that particular Christmas it was Charles Dickens's *A Christmas Carol*.

I spent a lot of time decorating my locker, which included a picture of a four-poster bed, a fireplace, and a window with cotton wool at the bottom to indicate snow. I had a picture of Scrooge sitting in a chair, and in the crack between my locker and the next lad's, I had a ghost coming through the wall. But the lad next to me kept pulling the ghost onto his side. When I confronted him, he got mad and twisted up my ghost. So I had to keep making new ghosts.

Well, I did win for my display, and Uncle and Auntie presented me with a big box of chocolates. I almost ate the lot and remember feeling quite sick afterward.

Another highlight of the Christmas holiday was a visit to the air base itself, where we had the time of our lives and ate all sorts of things. That was where I got my taste for cashew nuts, and sometimes when I eat them now, I think about those days. We would be driven to and from the base in an old patrol motor coach, which I loved to ride in. On that occasion, they had to halt the journey on the way back so a number of us could keel over and be sick.

That old motor coach also used to take us from our school hut to a place called Brancaster where we had our woodworking classes. Although we all enjoyed getting out of the regular classroom, the woodworking teacher was not very kind to us innocent young men. His policy was "Absolutely no larking around in the workshop," and

I suppose he was right, as there could have been some serious accidents if he hadn't kept us in control. If we did cause trouble, out would come his two-foot steel ruler, and without any hesitation, he would whack you across the bum several times. Boy did that smart too, but it was when he caught your arm or hand that it really hurt!

One day, we put a stop to him using the ruler by nailing it down to his bench. When two of the lads started fooling around, he went over to the ruler to pick it up and found it wouldn't move. What made it worse was he ripped off one of his nails trying to pick it up. So he got the biggest piece of wood he could lay his hands on, and oh, there were some sore bums that night.

We didn't have many trips to Brancaster because the new high school was completed and ready for us to move in. The first day was chaotic, but things settled down and – would you believe it – I was made a school prefect. I think the headmaster gave me the position to encourage me to study harder, but the only subjects I really took an interest in were art and biology. I did very well at them.

Now that I had become a prefect, I had to take on certain duties. One of them was to make sure that everyone got their half pint of milk, and to make sure that they put their empty bottle in the milk crate. Then you made sure that everyone went outside to play. At playtime all children were to be outside the building, unless of course it was raining.

So, the perks of the prefect job also gained me new friends who I would let inside when it was very cold out. One of these friends was a girl I very much liked named Allison. I used to write her notes because I found it difficult to talk to her. You see, there weren't any girls at the orphanage, and I'd never had a chance to socialize with them.

If one of the Home Boys were invited to a birthday party, he would not be allowed to go. The orphanage policy was that lots of children get invited to various events, but many do not, and it was considered unfair for some children to go out to parties etc, while others don't. So logically, no one got to go. So, that's one reason it was so difficult for us to mix in with the opposite sex.

One day, I sent Allison a note via Patrick. On that particular note, I asked her to meet me in the cloakroom for a talk at a certain time. All morning I rehearsed what I was going to say. What I didn't take into account was that I had told Pat I was going to kiss her if I could pluck up the courage. I had told the wrong person, because he spent the morning scheming up a little plan.

After lunch, I ran along to the meeting place, making sure my hair was right and that my tie was straight. There was Allison, sitting in the cloakroom. Our eyes met and I came to a grinding halt. She rose to her feet as I approached her and she started fiddling with the note I had sent her. I just stood there and returned her smile while undoing and redoing the button on my jacket, which was a nervous habit of mine.

"What did you want to see me about?" she asked, in a low cautious voice, as I undid my jacket button again.

I looked around and could see nothing but rows and rows of jackets and coats. I decided we couldn't be seen, so I did my jacket up again, and stuttered, "Well, I just...wanted to see...you on your own."

With that, she came right up close to me and puckered her lips and closed her eyes as if she were waiting for a kiss. After wondering how she knew that I wanted to give her a kiss, I quickly looked around, undid my jacket, and puckered my lips as well, hoping that our lips would somehow collide on their own, and make contact. Then it happened.

"Come on, give her a kiss, we haven't got all day you know," someone said in a loud whisper. As my eyes sprang open, seven lads came out from behind the coats. The ring leader was Pat, of course.

I looked at Allison as she stood there with a big grin on her face saying, "I'm still waiting."

I did my jacket up again and said to all of them as I stormed off, "I suppose you think this is very funny."

For some time after that, whenever one of the seven saw me, they would pucker up their lips and making a loud kissing sound followed by all sorts of crude remarks.

Chapter Twenty-Four

Earning My Keep

Each Saturday morning after we all did our jobs and Uncle inspected them, he would gather us into the dining room and pay us our
pocket money. The money wasn't a lot, but at least we got paid, and
were free to do what we liked with it. Most of the young lads would
run around to the shop next door, buying as many sweets as they
could. But I and a lot of the older boys saved our money until we
went into town. Since Hunstanton was a seaside resort, there was
always plenty to do with the few coppers you had.

We were also encouraged to earn money in other ways as well. In
fact, the eldest boy at the home worked at the local cinema as an
assistant projectionist on weekends and holidays, while another did
a paper route and a third was a delivery boy for a greengrocer shop
that provided deliveries of fruit and vegetables to the community.

It was the little greengrocer shop that I had the pleasure of working at for two weekends because Simon, the lad who usually helped
out there, was sick. The owner was a wonderful man named George
Raines. He used to spend a lot of his time at the orphanage entertaining us children and helping out during various events.

Customers would call their orders into Mr. Raines's shop, and then
the delivery boy would take the fruit and vegetables to their homes.
That would all be done with the help of a big black bicycle that had

a large metal carrier on it. You'd put the boxes of orders on the carrier and off you would go.

The very first time I did it, I started by showing off. Mr. George Raines kept asking me, "Will you be all right? Now you be careful with my produce, I want them to arrive in one piece." I assured him that I knew what I was doing and threw myself onto the bike, not realizing how heavy the thing was. Down I went, with apples and oranges rolling around with potatoes. I kept apologizing, but he insisted it was all right as long as I ran down the apples that were rolling down the hill, heading for the beach.

"Hurry, hurry," he said, pointing in the direction they were rolling. I retrieved all the produce, and after Mr. Raines carefully examined everything, he said, "You're not mounting a horse, you know. You have to get on the bike with a lot more care. You have precious cargo on board."

I got on that second time much more carefully, and set off to deliver three boxes to three houses within a mile radius. Sometimes the customers would pay me for the goods and even slip me a shilling or two as a tip. That made the low paying job much more worthwhile.

When I got back, there were more boxes waiting to be delivered, and so off I would go again. Mr. Raines was always very thankful and rewarded me well.

When Simon was well again, he told me he wanted his job back, so I had to step down. But it was fun for the two weekends I did it.

Back at the orphanage one Saturday morning, I was working in the aviary with Uncle's birds when I saw a Bentley pull up outside the home. A very smartly dressed couple got out of the car, but instead of going to the front door, they came directly into the aviary. I thought that they wanted to buy a bird, because Uncle used to sell them now and then, so I just kept on working. They spent some time talking about the birds; then asked me if the master of the home was in. I directed them to the front door and told them to ring the bell and someone would attend to them, as it was awkward for me to get out of the aviary.

About half an hour later, I was sent for by Uncle and told to get my best clothes on, as these visitors wanted to take me out for tea. I thought that was very nice of them and changed in record time. The next thing I knew, I was sitting in the back of the luxurious Bentley, with all the lads looking on with envy as we glided away toward town. After visiting some shops, they took me to an exclusive hotel for afternoon tea. They allowed me to have whatever I wanted, but just some nice cakes and tea did it for me. We ended with a drive around town, with me pointing out various places of interest and answering questions.

It turned out to be a lovely day, and these people came several times to see me. They tried to spoil me by buying me this and that.

One day when they came, Uncle sent for me to join them in his study.

When I went in, everyone rose from their seats, and I felt quite honored that they would do that for me. After they greeted me, I was instructed to sit down, and then they revealed why I was there. Uncle broke the ice by saying, "Mr. and Mrs. Williams have taken a liking to you, and now that they have gotten to know you, and you obviously like them, I want you to tell me what you really think of these people."

I sat for a moment, thinking now that was an unusual question. Then I answered, "I like them very much," and they both smiled.

Uncle continued. "Now do you like them enough to live with them? You see, Mr. and Mrs. Williams are looking for a child to adopt, and they would very much like to adopt you."

I started to speak but was interrupted by Uncle. "Now I know you have been through a bad spell with fostering, but I can assure you that home life with these good people would be far better than you have experienced. So don't give us your answer just yet. Think about it first."

I had already thought about it, so I rose to my feet, saying, "Uncle, I do like these people very much, but I would much rather stay here. I'm happy here and all my friends are here."

The smiles disappeared from all the faces. Mr. Williams stood up and said that he realized all of that, but would I please think about it, as they had done for some time.

The thought of Chelmsford flashed through my mind, and as I was actually being given a choice, I quite firmly said, "I'm sorry, sir, but this is my home and I don't want to be taken away again." I looked down and listened to the sudden silence.

Mr. Williams took my hand and shook it firmly, saying, "It has been a pleasure to have shared your company, and although my wife and I are disappointed, we understand and hope you will continue to be happy."

So we said goodbye, and Uncle dismissed me. I couldn't get out of that room fast enough. I stood outside the door and gave a big sigh. Then Pat came along and asked what was going on. I told him as we walked off,

"Do you know that those people wanted to take me away?"

Pat stopped in his tracks and looked at me, saying, "What, those people with that big posh car? No wonder they were taking you out for tea and all that. What did you tell them?"

"I told them that I was quite happy here."

Pat put his hand on my shoulder and said to me that he was glad, as he didn't want to lose a friend, and that made me feel much better. Then off we went on our bikes to the beach.

Chapter Twenty-Five

At the Cinema

Uncle was a well-known character in the town, and quite respected for everything he did, not only for the home, but for the town itself. You see, each year Hunstanton put on its own Pantomime, and Uncle always had the leading roll as the Dame. If he detected acting talent in any of the lads, he would encourage them to take part in the show. Another lad and I were asked to join.

We had great fun doing the show, and during one Saturday matinee, I was asked to take over a part that involved a lot of script, because the person whose part it was couldn't get time off work. As I knew his part, I went on stage with no fear and got on well – or so I thought – until the prompter was frantically waving his hand trying to attract my attention.

Uncle, with all of his experience, indicated that someone was at the door and sent me off to find out who it was. It was then that I discovered that I had skipped three pages. When I got back on stage, Uncle asked me who was at the door. I told him "It was the invisible man."

And uncle replied, "Tell him I can't see him." which caused a great deal of laughter – especially from Uncle – who later complimented me on how I handled that incident, and so the show continued.

Overall, the Pantomime went very well, and I enjoyed it very much. So, you see, Uncle was a great support to all of us. We still got into trouble and were punished for it, but we all considered him and Auntie as our true guardians. I know they both helped me a lot in life. First he gave me the job of looking after his aviary, and then he let me join the Pantomime each year.

One day, Uncle sent for me. I thought that I was in trouble and tried to think of what I had done wrong. When I arrived in his study, he greeted me with a smile, which meant that I could relax a little. He then told me that one of the older chaps was leaving the home that weekend and wanted to know if I would like to take over his job at the cinema.

"Wow!" I shouted. "Yes, I would love to!" I felt like jumping into his arms.

"Well, you had better get on your bike and go see the manager now; I told her you would be coming." Not another word was said. I flew out of the room and ran through the house like a mad thing, leaving a cloud of dust as I sped off on my bike, arriving at the cinema in record time. I soon found myself knocking on the door marked "Manager." When I entered, a woman was standing behind a very large desk.

"Are you from the home?" she asked sternly.

"Yes," I replied, still very excited.

She pointed me to a chair; then sat behind her desk. My chair was one of those that make a noise whenever you move, so I apologized every time it squeaked. After she told me what she expected of me and the hours I would be required to work, which was on weekends and during school holidays, she told me that I would get three pounds for working a full week.

I couldn't wait to start.

She then told me to go and meet the head projectionist, who would instruct me on my duties.

"Do you know where to go?" she asked.

I assumed I did, because I knew where the door was that led to the projection area was, so I told her, "Yes, I do." But it wasn't as easy to find as I thought.

I made my way through all the seats in the cinema to reach the door where I had once seen the other lad go when I was there to watch a film.

When I went through the door, I found myself in a very small room full of electrical things with another door at the far end. I boldly walked up to the door and gave it a firm knock, but there was no reply. I gave it an even harder knock and coughed a few times, hoping that someone would hear. I could hear talking, so I knew someone was in there, so I knocked harder and coughed some more.

Finally I heard a faint voice shout, "Come in!"

I turned the handle and opened the door and walked through, but my eyes sprang out of my head when I saw the number of people standing around, all staring at me and wearing broad grins.

You see, I had found the outside exit. And I was now standing at a bus stop right outside the door, with a crowd of people standing there waiting for the bus. With a very red face, I quickly shut the door and looked around for another option. Seeing a steel ladder that connected to a spiral staircase, I proceeded to climb it. Half-way up, I came across another door. I gave it a knock. There was no reply. After giving it another firm knock, I slowly opened the door and was confronted by a cleaning woman with a bewildered look on her face.

"Yes love, who are you looking for?" she asked.

I looked around and realized that I had done it again. That time I was in the balcony foyer.

"I'm looking for the projection room," I said, as I watched her going through the motions of dusting. As she pointed upward, a large bit of her cigarette ash fell onto the thick carpet, and she instantly rubbed it in with her foot.

"Keep going up and you'll find it."

I thanked her, and as I left she started laughing, saying, "You don't have to knock to come in here, love." I just gave her my best fake smile and continued my journey to the top.

At the top of the stairs a very tall man with a rugged complexion, gray hair, and great big feet was there to greet me. He thrust out his hand which was the size of a dinner plate to greet me and said, "I'm Bob Large, and…you are?"

I was staring up at him and replied. "Urm, Les Morris."

He told me that he wouldn't need me until Saturday morning, but he might as well show me around while I was there. The first room he showed me was the rewinding room, which was also where the films were stored. It had a large bench of slim lockers that contained all the reels of the film that were being shown that week. Each locker was numbered to keep the reels in order.

Then he showed me the big room, which had the projectors in it. It also had a twin-deck turntable for playing the music and little windows that the film was shown through. It was all fascinating.

Mr. Large took great delight in showing me how the projectors worked. Then he took me downstairs to show me how to open the curtains. You had to go through the cinema and onto the stage for that job. After explaining it all, he said, "I will see you on Saturday morning."

When I got back to the home, I found out that someone had donated a new bike. New in the sense that it was nothing like English bikes. In fact, it was an American bike. Uncle was looking around for someone to give it to when he saw me.

"What on earth is that?" I said when I saw it. After telling me, he asked if I would like to try it.

"Yes, I would," I said, and away I went.

The bike was smaller than my bike, but it was also sturdier and had big thick tires and it certainly moved faster than mine did. As I headed toward town, I felt quite proud riding as fast as I could. But as you come into the main part of Hunstanton, there a steep hill to go down and boy was I moving. I wanted to turn left at the bottom of the hill, and I was going pretty fast, so I felt for the brake handles, but there were none.

"NO BRAKES," I shouted at the top of my lungs.

After just missing a car, I somehow managed to get the thing turned and follow the road to the left. I handled that all right, then I tried steering through a rough old car park in an effort to get it to stop. I had my feet on the ground and trails of dust belching out behind me when I realized I was heading straight for a café that had tables and chairs outside. Quick flashes of Ashdon and the green penny-farthing bike went through my mind. I glanced down at the new bike, and would you believe it, it was pale green.

Then it happened.

Tables and chairs flew all over the place in the wake of that bike tearing through the café at top speed. As I lay on the floor, rubbing my leg, the owner of the café came out and gave me hell. Luckily, nothing was broken, but you'll notice that whenever anything like that happens, there are always a lot of people about to witness the event. No doubt I made someone's day with that little exhibition.

Picking myself up and feeling a right fool, I apologized and walked all the way back to the home, pushing the bike. I was met by Uncle, who asked me why I was walking.

"Because there are no brakes on this thing!"

He laughed and said, "Oh, I forgot to tell you that on American bikes to apply the brakes, you have to pedal backwards." Although I was smiling too, I was really thinking that now was a fine time to tell me. So I put that bike away and went back to my old one.

I was by now coming up to the age of 15, and therefore was asked at school what I was going to do. After a little thought, I said that I wanted to stay in school for another term, because I had lost so much education over the years. The home and school all agreed, but it would mean that I would be the oldest boy in the school.

Because of that, the headmaster sent for me. He informed me that I was now promoted, if you like, to head prefect, and he presented me with a badge. I took great pride in putting it on my school blazer, making sure that it was in a position that everyone could see. I noticed a great difference in people's attitudes toward me, even the teachers. But I didn't let it go to my head. In fact, what it did was make me study harder.

Getting up on one particular Saturday morning was no problem. I was full of excitement, for that day I was to start my job at the cinema. After having breakfast and doing my morning job, I was on my bike heading down to the cinema. When I got to the projection room I was greeted by Mr. Large, who said, "My word you're keen, you're an hour and a half early!"

I just smiled and said that I was anxious to learn as quickly as possible. I spent most of that morning following him around and sometimes getting under those large feet of his. I stood very close to him, as I watched him thread the wide film through the machine and talk me through it. I was amazed at the amount of loops and bends and slips and sprockets the film had to go through before it was ready for action. Then he put in the new carbon rods that produced the bright arc light.

As it was time for the children's film to start, Mr. Large then told me to go and get ready to pull the curtains. He reminded me not to pull them until I saw the film hit the main curtain, and then to pull slowly. With that I went off.

As I walked through the cinema, I heard my name being shouted out by some of the children from the home and some of the lads from my school. The whole house was full of children of all ages, and the noise? Well, they were all as excited as I was, knowing that I was now part of the action. I know that when I used to sit there, I often wondered how showing a film was done, and now I knew…well nearly.

I got onto the stage from the rear and couldn't get over how dark it was. Although I knew where I had to go, it was very difficult to find my way to the edge of the curtain. I finally made it, and that was when I started to sweat and worry. For when I saw all the ropes, I couldn't remember which one I had to pull. After fumbling around, I selected the one I thought was it and waited. At last, the film reflected onto the curtain and I slowly pulled the rope.

All of a sudden, there was uproar. I looked at the curtain, and to my amazement found I was pulling the big safety curtain down. I frantically pulled it up again and grabbed another rope. Then there was a loud crash at the back of the stage. The manager came out and grabbed the correct rope, pulling the curtains open to thunderous applause. Then she pushed me to one side and told me off as she wrapped the rope around a large nail.

"This is where this rope should be," she said, and stormed off. I was to have gone back through the cinema, but I thought under the circumstances I would go around back to get in. The door there was locked, so I ended up back at the main entrance, where the door-man wouldn't let me in. I told him that I worked there, but as he had never seen me before, he thought I was telling stories until a young lady came to my rescue.

"This young man does work here with Mr. Large," she said to the doorman, and then gave me a smile that made my face go even red-der. She asked what my name was and I stuttered it out and she said that hers was Ruth.

"Come on, I'll show you the easiest way to the projection room." I asked her what she did at the cinema and she told me. "I go around during the interval selling ice creams and snacks and where you're going to work, one of your jobs is to shine the spotlight on me so the audience knows I'm there."

She led me up to the balcony foyer and through the door that took me to the spiral staircase. I thanked her and received another lovely smile, which made me feel good and funny.

Mr. Large, who used to get quite annoyed if things didn't go right, wasn't too distraught about my first incident, and so carried on with his instructions. I watched him change over from one projec-tor to another. He pointed out that when the film in one machine is coming to an end you have to watch the right-hand corner of the screen for a mark or spot to appear. When you see that, it means it's time to switch on the other projector and wait for a second mark to appear. When that one comes up, you open the shutter on the new reel. That will automatically shut down the other machine. (I bet you didn't know that. Just watch for the spot to appear on the right of the screen.)

It was my job to take out the reel of film that had been run and rewind it. Mr. Large emphasized that on no account should I rewind the reels too fast, as sparks can fly off them and that is a fire risk. I used to rewind them with extreme care until I got the hang of it, and I gave them some stick.

Another part of my job was to go down to the café with a large tea jug and get it filled for Mr. Large. I also had to bring back a large bag of sticky buns, but I was allowed to have a quick cup of tea while I was there. The café was also where we had lunch, because on Saturdays we worked all day.

After working until about 11 o'clock that night, I was quite pleased with my first day. At supper the next day with Uncle and Auntie, I sat in the kitchen and told them all about the events. They already knew about the curtain episode, because the lads took great delight in telling them about it.

After a couple of months working at the cinema, I got quite confident and thought I could do the job on my own. Then Mr. Large put me to the test. Unbeknownst to me, there was a changeover due to come up, and Bob, as he asked me to call him, said, "Do you think you could do this projector change?"

Without hesitation, I said, "Yes, I know I can."

"Right. It's all yours then; I am going for a cough, spit, and a draw." That was his way of saying that he was going for a smoke. As there was no smoking allowed in the projection room, he had to go downstairs.

I stood in position waiting for that little spot to appear on the screen, and when it came, I changed over the machines and was quite proud of myself. I then threaded the next reel of film through the projector. Once the job was completed, Bob walked in.

"Well done! I knew you could do it, and I must say I couldn't fault it." He was full of praise and that certainly encouraged me. It was also good for him, as he could now go off for a break without any worries, instead of standing watch at the back of the cinema.

Chapter Twenty-Six

Smoking in the Boiler Room

I looked forward to working at the cinema, but I still had to go to school and with homework on the weekends, things got a bit hectic. But I managed to survive.

The caretaker at the school was a friendly chap who lived on the school grounds in the caretaker's house. He learned that I had started smoking and allowed me to visit his house during lunch to have a smoke with a nice cup of tea.

One of my duties as head prefect required that I go to the boiler room each day and record the temperatures of each boiler. Because the school was new, they were very interested in sorting out the heating system, which apparently had given them a bit of trouble. It was down in the boiler room that I got into trouble. I was documenting all the temperatures with the caretaker when one of the teachers caught me having a cough, spit, and a draw behind the boiler. He went straight to the headmaster and reported me, and within minutes the headmaster sent for me.

I knocked on the headmaster's door and waited, adjusting my clothing and pushing my hair back and all that stuff you do when waiting outside the headmaster's office. Outside his office was a lighting system. If the red light was on, you had to wait; when the green light came on, it was okay to enter. I was thinking, the master of the Leicester orphanage would have loved that traffic light thing. He'd have one installed at the home for sure. Then I got back to worrying again. I was very nervous. I stood with my eyes glued to the lighting system and fiddled with my jacket button. My hands were getting very sweaty, but as the odd schoolmate walked past, I smiled and passed the time of day as if nothing was wrong. When one of the lads asked if I was in trouble, I said,

"No, no, I'm just waiting to see the headmaster about prefect stuff, you know," and made it sound as if it were routine.

When the green light came on and my expression changed. I was hesitant about entering, but the headmaster got angry if you didn't go in on green, so I walked into his study and saw him placing his pipe in a great big glass ashtray.

The headmaster was a very stern-looking man, and what made him look even sterner was that he wore a ruffled black cape and had a little mustache that made him look a bit like Hitler. He also would wet his fingers and smear his short black hair flat.

As I stood there waiting, he fiddled with his odd-shaped pipe, which was still issuing smoke, and gave me a hard stare complete with a frown. After a moment's silence, he said, "I'm surprised at you Morris. I thought you, of all people – especially from the home – could have been trusted."

After another pause, he stood up and came from behind his desk saying, "Now the fact that I made you head prefect does not mean that you can do just as you like, and that you're exempt from punishment." He reached for his cane, which was on top of a filing cabinet, and started bending it.

"Have you anything to say?" he asked.

I swallowed hard and said, "No, sir. I'm sorry to have disappointed you, sir, and it won't happen again."

"Right. Now hold out your hand; this is going to hurt me as much as it will you, Morris."

"You wouldn't like to bet on that, would you?" I thought, as the dreaded swish came, followed by the pain. Two strokes on each hand. And the pain was, well, painful.

As the headmaster went back behind his desk, he told me to take off my head prefect badge. Now, that was more painful than the cane. I fumbled around trying to get it off, but I had bent the pin to hold it in position because it kept falling off. With stinging fingers, the task of removing it was impossible.

The phone suddenly rang, so the headmaster instructed me to bring the pin back on Monday, as he had urgent business to attend to.

The rest of the day I went around pretending that nothing was wrong. Well, I didn't want the chaps to know that the head prefect had gotten the cane, did I?

I saw the headmaster before I left school that day; he often used to stand outside as we were dismissed to make sure all the buses did the right thing, and that everyone left in an orderly manner. When he spotted me, he beckoned me over. He stood there with his hands behind his back, flapping the black cape up and down behind him, which he often did when he was in a good mood. Then he looked down at me and said, "You know, I remembered that you are in fact 16 years old, and so if you want to smoke, that is entirely up to you." And after a short pause he said "But you don't smoke on the school premises." I do believe he smiled just a little bit as I thanked him.

Then he said, "Oh, by the way, you can keep your badge. But remember, no smoking at school. Now be off with you."

I thanked him again and ran off with a big smile on my face. "Phew, that was a relief," I thought to myself.

I caught up with a couple of lads from the home, who both looked at me and said, "Did you get into trouble with the headmaster today?"

"No, no. We just had a talk about prefect duties," I lied. "Who told you that I was in trouble?" I demanded, but they wouldn't say.

That Saturday morning was a sad day for me, for my great friend Pat had turned 15 and was leaving the home. After he said all his good-byes, I accompanied him to the railway station. On the way, we reminisced about our time together, and although it was a somber moment for both of us, we seemed to be doing what we did a lot of, which was laughing. As we passed the fish & chips shop, Pat pointed and said "Do you remember?"

"Cod," I replied. We had another great laugh, although brief, and then it turned to tears as he got on the train.

The old steam train gave a blast of its whistle and as it slowly pulled away, he shouted out to me. I had no idea what he shouted, but on my way to work, I realized it reminded me of when Doug left me at the Leicester orphanage, because Pat was certainly like a brother to me. I never saw or even heard from Patrick Ayers again. But I often wonder what the old bugger is up to?

The morning went very quickly at the cinema, and without any hitches. At lunch time, Bob said that he would stay in the projection room for the break as he had some important work to do, but asked if I would bring him back some food. I agreed and went down to the café. I was now well-known there and always had a welcome when I walked in. I liked to sit by the window so I could watch all the holiday people walk by.

That day's special was homemade steak & kidney pie, which was my favorite, and they had already loaded up my plate before I arrived.

After a few minutes, Ruth walked in. She spotted me and I colored up straightaway when she gave me one of her smiles.

"Can I join you, Les?" she asked.

With gravy dripping from my mouth, I stood up for her, as we were taught to do that at the home, and said, "Oh yes."

She smiled again, telling me that I had gravy down my chin. As I sat down, my tongue reached out as far as it could to retrieve it. And then I dropped my fork. As you can see, I was in a right state.

Ruth ordered the same lunch I had, and was eating it with more precision than I was mine. She asked how the job was going, and then asked a lot of personal questions, and in between my dropping things, we seemed to get along all right.

But it was now time for me to get Bob's lunch and return to the projection room. While the staff was getting his food ready, I just sat and looked at her. I had run out of to things to say. She had what you might call a country complexion, and long, flowing hair that stayed on her shoulders with a slight curl, and lips that sort of trembled as she spoke. I found out that she was 18 and lived in Heacham, the next village south of Hunstanton.

I was looking at her eyes, which were blue, and was drifting miles away when my name was called. I jumped up from the table, knocking most of the stuff off it, and said I must go.

"I may see you this evening, then," she said, as she poured the tea from her saucer back into her cup.

"Uh, er, yes. Goodbye," I stammered.

As I went to the counter, I accidentally hooked a man's arm just as he was putting a spoonful of red-hot soup to his lips, so the soup landed on him. I was so busy looking at him and apologizing that I didn't see the café cat sleeping on the floor, and I trod on it. The cat didn't like that one little bit, and let everyone know by screaming the place down as it flew out the door. After paying for Bob's food, I left the café like the trod-on cat.

Time seemed to fly by, for I soon found myself too old for school. I went around saying farewell to all my friends and teachers, and finally to the headmaster, who shook my hand firmly and wished me luck for the future. Although I was glad to leave school, it was still a sad occasion. That seemed to be my life, saying hello and goodbye.

But I didn't have to say goodbye at the home. I was not yet fixed up with lodgings, but the home had a spare room in the attic that I could move into temporarily for three pounds a week, which was very good of them.

Whenever a chap left the care of the home, Uncle and Auntie would take them to a tailor's shop in town and kit them out with a selection of clothes, so I looked quite a smart young man, apart from some horrible teenage spots.

As for a full-time job, I worked at the cinema and was now earning seven pounds a week, which made me feel good.

So, to sum up, my days at Hunstanton were the best of my days in the care of the Church of England Children Society, and although part of my early upbringing had scarred my memory, I put no blame on the Society. I owed them a lot, and Hunstanton certainly made up for the bad moments in my early life. And although I had technically left the Society, they came to my rescue later on, and I often wonder where or what I would be doing now if they hadn't.

Chapter Twenty-Seven

A Close Encounter

I had been working full-time at the cinema for about two months and things were going well. The film I was showing that week starred Elizabeth Taylor, of whom I was and still am a great fan. I got my scissors out in the rewinding room and cut out a frame of her to add to my collection of favorite stars, then rejoined the film. I had more frames of Liz than any other star. When I was in my room, I used to hold them up to the light and just gaze at them.

But that week, something new happened at the cinema. Cinemascope was introduced to our picture house, and the workmen were busy putting up the vast new screen, which took up the whole of the stage. We also had to have modifications to the projectors. The two main parts that had to be added were a plate and a large lens. The lens was fixed so that it could be swung up after moving the old lens down, as required.

It also meant that I had to learn a new procedure, which didn't take long. The entire staff was excited about the new project. I say that Cinemascope was new, but it had been out for some time, and was old to the world beyond Hunstanton.

That weekend, we showed our very first big-screen Cinemascope feature film and the whole town was excited. They thoroughly enjoyed it, and would you believe, I didn't make one mistake. At least not until the day I spoke to Ruth. After that, I just couldn't do anything right. That day during lunch, when I often used to see her, Ruth asked me to escort her home after we had finished work. She told me that she got frightened cycling to Heacham alone in the dark. I agreed, and then became very excited.

Mr. Large went for his usual cough, spit, and a draw and left me to do the changeover. Normally that was no problem, but that particular change was from a flat film to Cinemascope. I got the projector all loaded up and waited for the spots to appear, then waited for the other projector to shut down, and the change was done. So off I went to the rewinding room to rewind the film, all the time thinking about Ruth and what I would say to her.

In my haste, I forgot to put the clip on the spool, and so while turning the rewind handle as fast as I could, the reel suddenly flew off, trailing film everywhere.

I heard heavy footsteps on the spiral staircase, so quickly returned to the projection room. Then the telephone started ringing. I was just about to answer the phone when Mr. Large appeared with a wicked look on his face.

"What the bloody hell do you think you are playing at? Leave that phone and put some music on and dim the lights," he shouted. He went over to the projector I had just switched on and shut it down, then put it in reverse. After doing what he told me to do, I asked him cautiously what was wrong. He simply picked up part of the new modification, the plate, holding it up high.

"What about this? You obviously didn't check your work like I taught you. What the bloody hell is wrong with you today?" he shouted as he reached for the phone that was still ringing away.

"Yes, I know, it will only take a few minutes to rectify," he shouted at whoever was at the other end, and slammed the telephone down.

I wanted to get back to the rewinding room and gather up all the film before he saw it, but he told me to stay and watch what he was doing, then do the lights and stop the music. When I was finally able to go and clean up, the manager arrived, which she very rarely did. When she saw the film all over the floor, she went berserk. Then Mr. Large saw it and he did the same.

Before I was allowed to clean up the mess, which took some time, the manager told me in a few sharp words, "If you ever make a mistake like this again, you will have to look for another job, do you understand?"

I felt very uncomfortable after that, because Bob kept an eye on me the rest of the evening and kept going on and on about how I must check and double-check my work as I did it. After I apologized and said that it wouldn't happen again, he started to calm down.

The thought of seeing Ruth really bucked me up.

My last job each night was to pull the curtains, and then I was free to leave. As I waited, I checked my appearance and combed my hair. Then the moment came, and I pulled the curtains. It was then that I started to get nervous. As soon as the curtains joined together, I ran off the stage and down the steps and came to a grinding halt. Standing at the bottom of the steps was the manager, waiting to give me yet another telling-off. She went on and on, but as she was talking to me, all I could think about was Ruth. Would she wait for me? Finally the manager's mouth closed and so did the cinema; the building was virtually deserted as I ran through. Usually when I left, there were a lot of people outside, but tonight there was nobody. I started to panic and ran as fast as I could to the bike shed, my cycle clips clutched tightly in my hand. Although it was dark at the shed, I could just make out a figure standing there.

"Is that you, Ruth?" I shouted as I ran toward her.

"Yes. What happened to you?" she shouted back. Puffing and panting, I got very tongue-tied trying to tell her what had happened. She had thought it might have had something to do with the change-over, and she laughed at me getting things all mixed up.

We walked to the road and I put my cycle clips on under a street lamp. I soon realized that I had put them both on one leg, but left things as they were because I didn't want her to see what a clumsy fool I was.

Then we set off and Ruth suddenly stopped and said. "Les do you want to go the main road or along the bank that runs alongside the seashore?" I was quick to answer.

"Well, let's go along the seafront." She agreed and we set off. I told her that I had no idea that the embankment went all the way from Hunstanton to Heacham, It was a moonlit night and you could see very well. I had never been along there, so I agreed to follow her.

It was a nice warm night and the full moon flickered across the calm sea. On the horizon two ships were slowly making their way to heaven knows where. The track we were traveling on was dusty and full of dips and bumps, and some of the holes in the track were very deep. As I rode behind Ruth, I noticed that she must have known all the potholes, for she weaved in and out of them. I tried to follow, but I ended up hitting more than I missed. Every now and then I would get a whiff of her perfume, which was very pleasant.

As we rode, she talked to me, but I couldn't hear a word she was saying. All of a sudden, she shouted something, but as I was shouting back, "I can't hear what you're saying," I fell off my bike. I had hit a large pothole, which was what Ruth was trying to warn me about. I wasn't hurt, so I just brushed myself down, feeling a right fool. Then she suggested that we walk for a while, and so off we went again, pushing our bikes. Ruth did all the talking.

As we walked, I noticed that her left hand was hanging down by her side, waiting I supposed, for me to hold it. But I just hadn't the nerve to reach out for it. After walking for some time, looking at her hand and trying to pluck up courage to hold it, I stretched out my hand just as she took hers away to hold her bike steady.

"Let's have a rest here, shall we?" She said, dropping her bike down on the ground and running down the steep sandy bank to the beach. For a while we just sat there, watching the gentle waves rolling in and crashing in slow motion onto the beach. Everything was quiet and peaceful except for a bird in the distance, which was shouting its head off. I suppose the lovely fresh smell of the salt air and the seaweed made it quite a romantic evening.

Ruth broke the silence, saying, "Isn't this a lovely evening? I very often sit on the beach on my way home. It's so relaxing and oh, how peaceful." She turned to me and saw me running sand through my fingers like an egg timer.

"Don't you think it's peaceful, Les? And why are you sitting so far away?" she asked, as she moved herself right next to me. "Are you shy?" She tried to look at me, but I had my head down, looking at the sand that was now sticking to my sweaty hands.

"No, I'm not shy," I lied. I was not only shy, but very nervous as well. You see, that was the first time I had ever been really alone with a girl, and I wasn't quite sure what was going to happen. Let's face it, she was two years older than I was, and she had obviously been out with other lads before, while I on the other hand, was hopelessly inexperienced.

Ruth broke the silence again by asking me if I had been out with a girl before, and as I shook my head from side to side and sort of whispered no, she immediately grabbed my gritty hand and sort of laughingly said, "I don't believe you." I kept my head down and she continued. "Well, have you ever kissed a girl before?"

I had to think about that one. I knew that I had been near to doing it, but I just couldn't think of anyone. "I might have," I said, still not looking at her.

"Well are you going to kiss me?" she asked.

I propped myself up on my elbow and leaned towards her and gave her a quick kiss on her cheek and settled down again. "Is that it?" said Ruth. There was a glint in her eyes as she slowly pushed me down on the sand, and I swallowed hard as I saw her pouted lips heading for mine. I shut my eyes and grabbed a handful of sand in each hand and squeezed them tight. When her lips collided with mine, it was like static shock passing through me, which made me open my eyes. I had the biggest stiffy I think I have ever had, and no way of hiding it. As she moved her lips slowly across mine, she was making all sorts of sounds. My sweaty hands were now overloaded with sand. Finally she lifted her head and our lips lost contact. With her face only about an inch from mine she said,

"Now it's your turn to kiss me," and she promptly lay back on the sand.

Not only were my lips numb, but so was my whole body. Although I had enjoyed the kiss, I didn't know if I could manage to give her an equal one. I swallowed hard when she said, "You haven't had any experience, have you?"

I didn't know what to say, so I just lay there gazing into the sky, hoping somehow that something would come to me.

"Well, come on, you have to kiss me now." After rubbing my hands free of sand, I slowly raised myself up to face her. She was lying motionless, with her lips puckered and eyes closed, and my eyes were wide open as I gazed down at her. She looked radiant with the moonlight reflecting on her face.

Something inside me was telling me to get on with it, but another part of me was saying not to. My heart was pounding even harder and I was actually trembling as I got on my knees and looked around.

"There is nobody around. Come on, I'm waiting," she said with a smile. As I got another whiff of her perfume, I plucked up the courage to lean over her, and with puckered lips I went to kiss her on the cheek, but she swung her head around and our lips met. She clasped her hands at the back of my head and pulled me tight to her face. My shoes were digging hard into the sand and I thought I was going to ejaculate. I tried to pull myself away, but we were locked in that position for some time before she released me, saying, "Now, I bet you liked that, didn't you?" When I didn't answer, she said, "Are you going to do anything...or is...that it?" I was trying to stutter something when without warning Ruth climbed on top of me. My eyes popped out like chapel hat pegs as she wiggled her body down until her crotch connected with my stiffy.

In slow motion she moved her body up and down, and commented, "Well, at least something knows what to do." The problem was the rest of me just didn't know what to do. I had all the feelings, but that was a far as I could go. I just knew that my stiffy was enjoying it.

Ruth whispered in my ear in a sexy voice, "Would you like me to get him out for you?

And would you believe, I said, "NO."

"Are you going to get it out then?" she asked in a louder, much less sexy voice.

"Well…erm…I don't know." I stuttered.

And then it happened. She sat up and grabbed hold of my hand and placed it on one of her breasts.

Oh, what on earth do I do now? I froze up. And then she undid the buttons on her cardigan.

"What on earth is she doing?" I thought, and started looking around again. Then she grabbed my hand and uncurled it, because I had it tightly clenched, and then placed it on her BARE breast.

I could have died. I just didn't know what to do. My hand remained unmoving in the position she put it. Her breasts were very firm, but I had no idea what to do with them. I frantically looked around to see if there was anyone around.

"There is nobody around, Les. Now just relax," she said, holding my hand very tight. "Look at me, Les," she said softly, but I couldn't, and as much as I tried to pull my hand away, she held it even tighter.

Finally our eyes met, and with that smile of hers, she said, "Does that feel good? Does it do anything for you?" But I looked away from her again, as I just didn't know what to say or do.

Of course it did things for me, but I was so embarrassed and so confused that I had no idea how to answer her. She relaxed her hold and I quickly withdrew my hand, but was still frozen in the kneeling position. Without warning, she lifted up her bra and grabbed my hand again, but that time held it against her bare breast even harder than before. I just couldn't believe what was happening and beads of sweat started to roll down my face, which was by now glowing hot.

Oh, how I wished I knew what to do. I tried to look at where my hand was but couldn't. All the time she was talking to me, I never heard a word she said, as my mind was all a jumble. Then she again relaxed her hold.

I sprang to my feet and faced the sea, fiddling with my hands.

"Les, didn't the home ever talk to you about the birds and the bees?"

Unable to answer her, I just shook my head and watched her do her buttons up. The she got up and looking down at me, said in a very unromantic way, "Oh…you're hopeless…I'm going home."

All I could come out with was, "I had better get back to the home as well, or there will be..."

"I've made a right bloody fool of myself, haven't I?" she snapped, and started walking away.

"Well let me take..." I started to say.

"No, you stay there and think about what you have missed." I followed her up to the bikes and she didn't say another word. She got on her bike and rode off into the darkness with me calling her back to start again.

"Ruth, please don't go," I shouted several times, but there was only the rattle of her bike as she rode off. "RUTH," I shouted louder, and it echoed through the still night, but she continued without saying a word. So I just stood there, watching the red light of her bike fade into the darkness and whispering her name to myself. Within a few moments there was nothing; she had gone.

I slowly turned and kicked a stone down the bank before picking up my bike and getting on it. I sat there thinking for a few moments and managed to produce a faint smile when I thought that I had actually touched her breasts with my bare hands. With a final look around, I went to get on my bike, but still had a stiffy; I looked down at it, actually apologizing to him for letting him down. It was a long ride, and it took all that time for my stiffy to go down.

Chapter Twenty-Eight
Another Close Encounter

Uncle was a very kind and understanding man whom I really respected, despite the secret side of him which very few people knew about. He sometimes had sexual encounters with one or two of the older lads.

As Roger had told me the first day I arrived, the large wooden hut in the play yard was a very good place to store stuff, especially donated stuff that the home really didn't need. It was also where Uncle had an aviary of canaries, and it was because of the canaries, that he asked three of us older boys to help him one night with a problem there.

"There are mice getting into my aviary and eating the birds' food, but I have no idea how they are getting in," he explained in a low voice. He flicked on his torch and selected the correct key, then said softly, "What we need to do is surround the aviary and keep watch to see if we can spot the little devils." He smiled as we all made our way to the door.

Once inside, he pointed the torch beam to the position he wanted each one of us to stand. In a whisper, he said, "You can sit, kneel, or stand, whatever you feel comfortable with." He then turned on a faint sort of night light, and we all stood and watched the aviary. It was very quiet in there. From where I was standing, I could see the home with all the lights on, and the other children running from room to room having fun. And here I was, standing around waiting for a mouse. But low and behold, we heard a rustle in some paper. We each tried to say something, but Uncle went, "Shush, keep very quiet."

All of our attention was back on the aviary. Because the space was small, Uncle had to squeeze past us as he went around and around looking I supposed for mice. But then he fiddled around in his trouser pocket and said in a low voice, "Okay, whoever spots the mouse first, gets this half crown."

After that, we all looked much harder. I looked in the area of the rustling that we heard earlier, and whispered loudly, "Bingo! There he is!" We watched the little mouse freeze for a moment. Then it sniffed around and crawled through a small hole in the wire mesh.

Uncle pushed his way around to where the mouse had come through and said, "I don't believe it! How could a mouse get through that tiny hole?"

And then another mouse came along and did the same thing.

When Uncle moved past John, one of the lads paused and said, "What's that?" then put his hand between John's legs and said in a low voice, "Hey, John's got a stiffy." Then he asked him to get it out.

John was a bit reluctant, but he did, and then Uncle felt Peter and said, "Have you got a stiffy, Peter?"

"Well, sort of," Peter said with embarrassment, and Uncle told him to get his out too. So Uncle had one in each hand and was rubbing them both.

Then John asked, "Have you got yours out, Les?"

Well, seeing all that was going on, I did end up with a stiffy, and Uncle turned to me and said, "Get yours out, and I'll tell you what. We will have a little game." He felt around in his pocket again and produced another half crown.

By then, Uncle was rubbing my penis and getting his out and placing my hand around his. I was soon rubbing it, which was a complete surprise to me; I couldn't believe I was doing that. But because the other lads were doing it, I just went along with it, and very soon Uncle had us all in a tight circle rubbing each other.

Peter suddenly said, "Look at all the mice in the aviary!" and we all swung our heads to look, but Uncle said, "Oh forget the mice, I know where they come from now. All right, here's a half a crown for the first one to come, but before we all start, does everyone in here want to stay and do this? If not you can leave now," and he looked at each one of us in turn, and we all said it was fine. I think it must have been the half a crown was what did it, but to me it all seemed harmless and not like Uncle was forcing us to do something.

Then Uncle said, "All right, what I want you to do is hold the penis to your right and slowly rub it." So each of us got hold of one another, but I ended up holding Uncle's, which was not so long as it was fat.

"Okay, just rub slowly, not fast, and let's see who comes first. Let us know when you are coming," he said.

It was deathly quiet while all that was going on, though we heard the odd sound of the birds, which were obviously restless because of our presence. But it wasn't long before John announced that he was coming, and Uncle flashed the torch on him and we all watched him win the half a crown. That seemed to trigger everyone else, and suddenly Uncle announced he was coming, and we couldn't believe the amount that came from him.

Before leaving the hut, Uncle emphasized that we keep that little matter to ourselves, and mentioned that we could do it again if we wanted to. Because we three were the oldest boys in the home, we had the separate four person room at the end of the big dormitory. That night we lay in bed talking quietly about the episode in the hut. It appeared that we didn't hold a grudge against Uncle, but Peter wasn't sure if he would do it again, although he said he had enjoyed it.

John flicked his half a crown in the air and said to Peter, "I bet you would for half a crown." Peter just smiled and said goodnight.

The next day was Saturday, the day we get our pocket money, and when the three of us got our money, we found that Uncle had slipped in a ten-shilling note for each of us, and that made us feel all right.

After the hut episode, Uncle seemed to take to me even more than he did before. He gave me the job of looking after all of his birds, and sometimes he would leave cigarettes in the aviary to attract me over there. Often he would come into the aviary when I was feeding them and play around with me, and sometimes he got John to join us. As far as John and I were concerned, it meant we didn't get punished, and we ended up having fun. No other children were involved.

Chapter Twenty-Nine

Lodgings and Leavings

One morning, Uncle told me that he had some news for me. My ears pricked up when he told me that a Mrs. Williams on the next street had offered to put me up in lodgings. Although the thought of leaving the home upset me, the thought of having the freedom to do as I pleased, as well as having a bit more privacy was welcome. So after breakfast I went round to see her. I knocked on the door and Mrs. Williams appeared. When I introduced myself, I stood there with a smile on my face and my hand outstretched to shake hers, but she just stood there and looked me up and down.

"So you are the young man Uncle has sent round, are you?" she said in a loud voice.

"Yes," I replied, my smile fading. I was beginning to have my doubts about the place already.

"Well, I had better show you your room. Are your shoes clean?" she asked, looking down at them.

"Yes," I said, giving them a final hard wipe on the mat.

"I like to keep my house clean and tidy, and if you decide to stay here, then I would expect you to keep it that way," she said, as we reached the top of the stairs.

She opened the door to a small room and said, "This will be your room. You will notice how clean it is. I will expect it to always look like this."

I nodded and told her that I would make sure it was. Then she pushed past me to open another door. "This is the bathroom and toilet. You will keep all your cleaning stuff in your own room and not in here, and I don't want to see any black rings around my tub after you have bathed. You will clean it out, and the same goes for the sink."

I nodded again and moved out of her path as she pushed past. She gave me more rules of the house at the top of the landing. "These are the only rooms you will use, apart from the kitchen, where you will have your meals. If you are not in time for them, you go without."

Again I nodded, and said, "I understand."

"Now the master of the home said you finish work at around 11 o'clock at night. Is that correct?"

"Yes," I replied with a nod.

"Right. I want you in this house by 11:15 at the latest, and if you are not in by that time, the door will be locked. Now, when are you moving in?" she snapped.

I wanted to tell her that I wasn't, but I knew that Uncle wanted my room and that I couldn't stay at the home forever, so I said I would get my things over right away.

"All right then, and I will see you when you come back. You know that you pay a week in advance."

"Yes, all right, Mrs. Williams, I'll be back in half an hour."

I walked down the stairs and turned to thank her, but she was no longer in sight. So I went back to the home and gathered my things.

After collecting my few possessions, I went back to my new home if that was what you would call it, and went up to my room, which was just about big enough to swing a small cat in. There was a single bed, a table, a chair and a small cupboard for my clothes. The floor was linoleum and had a rug, which looked homemade, possibly by someone who had never made one before. It was that nice.

That room was where I would stare at the ceiling and four bare walls for hours and wonder about the future, and of course think about Ruth. The main thing I suffered from was loneliness, and I was determined to get over it. Some of the lads from the homes found it difficult to adapt to the outside world, and if they were spending their lives in the type of surroundings that I found myself in, I could now see why they committed suicide. I couldn't understand it before, but it was much closer to reality now.

Work wasn't going down too well either. As much as I tried to talk to Ruth, she just didn't want to talk to me. She even went as far as to bring her new boyfriend into the café one day while I was having lunch.

When I finished work in the mornings, I would wander around on the beach and have my lunch in another café, for the fear of bumping into Ruth. Although I didn't know what love was then, I now know that, in my own way, I was madly in love with her. It made things worse when she was on duty selling ice cream. To draw the attention of the audience to her, I had to follow her with the spotlight, and that was painful.

So I was downright miserable. The only person I could talk to was Uncle, but he was quite proud of me, so I felt I had to assure him that I was getting on very well, daring not telling him the truth.

What with dreading to go to my digs and not wanting to go to work, I was in a right state. One day I walked straight up to the manager's office of the cinema, and told her I wanted to give a week's notice, which made her sit upright in her chair. "Why?" she demanded, so I told her a white lie. "I'm not happy with working every night."

She told me that I was doing very well and that she was thinking of giving me a raise in wages, but I still declined. At the end of the next week, I would be out of a job.

It wasn't until that afternoon when I was walking aimlessly along the beach that I realized what I had done. I would have no job and wouldn't be able to pay for my lodging. After a lot of thought, I realized that I would have to use my savings, because I had a good sum put away.

That night after work, I lay on my bed thinking about various things I could do, but the thought of Ruth always came back to my mind. I would lie and think and think about that moonlight night and what she was doing to me and what I would have liked to have done to her. But, alas, it was not to be. I made up my mind to go and see Uncle the next day and have a chat with him.

I told Uncle my story, except the part about leaving the cinema because of Ruth, and he asked what I had intended to do for a job. After he made several suggestions, I agreed that I would join the Boys Army, which was called the Junior Leaders. The next week, I had completed all the necessary interviews and medical examinations and just had to wait to hear the results. On my last day at the cinema, I saw Ruth and gave her a longing look, and she opened her mouth as if to say something but must have changed her mind, for she turned and walked away and I never saw her again; only in my dreams.

When I came down for breakfast one morning, my landlady handed me a brown envelope. Stamped on the front of it were the words, "Her Majesty's Service" which I involuntarily shouted out, and as I ripped the envelope open, my landlady, not wanting to appear too nosy, said "What's there that you should get all excited about?" So I told her what I was going to do and a faint smile came to her face. I always thought that she didn't like the idea of having a lodger, but no doubt she thought she should help the home.

"Well, I wish you well, but don't forget to pay me your rent before you go, will you?" She forced a smile as she put my breakfast in front of me, but it didn't take me long to get it down, and I then went straight around to Uncle to tell him the good news.

And so came the day that I left Hunstanton. I said all my farewells and paid the landlady for my lodgings, and with all my worldly goods packed in my suitcase, I was at the Hunstanton railway station boarding the train for the beginning of my new life. I had decided to make the military life my career.

As the steam train slowly huffed and puffed its way out of the station, I stood at the open window having a final look at my memorable home town and who should I see, but Ruth. I went to shout her name but changed my mind but I do believe she got a glimpse of me before I left the station.

After changing trains in London, I found myself on a train heading for a place called Newton Abbott, in Devon. The entire way I had mixed thoughts, all of which came wandering back to Ruth.

Chapter Thirty

An Unexpected Development

Joining the Junior Leaders as a boy soldier was the start of a new life for me. Although I was a little nervous, I was still quite excited about it all, and before long I arrived in Newton Abbot. As instructed, I boarded an army lorry that would transport me and one or two other lads to our new home – The Junior Leaders Army Barracks.

After getting my uniforms and going into my assigned barracks, I couldn't help but think that the place was a little like the orphanage. I reached down and touched the metal bed frame and found that it was just like the heavy iron ones I'd left behind at Hunstanton.

About 15 of us new recruits had arrived at the same time, and the first thing we did was put all our kit in the tiny lockers by our beds. That meant folding each item into the size of your handkerchief; that was the only way you could get it all in.

The next job was to make your bed with the sheets and blankets that were issued. Now in the military, there is one right way of doing everything, and you don't make a bed the way you and I would normally do it.

As I was getting ready to make my bed, a young lad named Tom came over and introduced himself. Then he told me, "You know, there is a right way and wrong way to make a bed in the army."

I stopped what I was doing and asked, "What do you mean?"

"Well, you have to make envelope corners on your bed or you'll be in trouble." He paused, then, added, "If you give me half a crown, I will show you how to do it." I smiled at him and said that I already know how to do it, and promptly showed him.

"How did you know that?" he asked, but before I could tell him, he was off to try his ploy on another new chap. So, that saved me half a crown.

Our first day of basic training consisted of all sorts of drills, which I loved. There was, for example, marching and swinging your arms shoulder high with the instructor shouting in your face, and the rifle drill, which required throwing a heavy gun up and down and then leaning it on your shoulder. There was so much to learn that at the end of the day we were all exhausted.

At supper each night, my new friends and I would sit and chat about all sorts of stuff. The subject often turned to girlfriends. One day, one of the lads said, "Les, how come we don't hear about your girlfriend? I mean, we've shared all our stories, but we haven't heard about the girls in your life. Do you have a girlfriend?"

Everyone was staring at me, and I blushed. I didn't know what to say until I remembered the cinema. "Yes," I said quickly. "Her name is Ruth."

"Well, do you have a picture of her?" asked one of the chaps.

"Er, no, I haven't got one."

Fortunately, Tom changed the conversation to talk about the drill instructor, so I escaped any more quizzing on the subject of girlfriend.

After nearly six months in the Junior Leaders, I was very happy and doing quite well. I got along with all the lads and was taking extra classes to help me catch up on the schooling I had missed. Proving yourself as a Junior Leader helped when you were ready to join the "Man's Army," as they called it, because you were already tuned up for the real thing. More than ever, I was going to make the army my life and career.

One day I was outside cutting the grass with one of those push-type lawn mowers when one of the officers approached and called out my name. I stopped mowing, clicked my heels to attention, and threw him a smart salute, which I had just about gotten the hang of. The officer told me to go smarten myself up, as he was to escort me to see the commanding officer. My eyes popped, and a big lump went down my throat as the smile dropped off my face. What on earth had I done to warrant seeing the commanding officer?

I ran into the barracks and quickly changed clothes while the other lads asked what was going on.

"I have no idea," I said.

"I bet they want to make Les an officer," one of them shouted, and everyone laughed except me.

The officer came into the barracks and told me to get a move on.

"We can't keep the Commanding Officer waiting all day, can we Morris?"

I sprang to attention and shouted, "No sir," then finished tying the laces on my good boots.

I was then marched to the C.O.'s office as all the lads looked out the windows. I was still wondering what I had done wrong. Along the way, the officer kept asking me questions.

"Do you like the Junior Leaders, lad? Have you made many friends during your six months with us? Are you being treated all right?" As we approached the main office, he finally said, "It's all right lad; you haven't done anything wrong."

Well, that was a relief to hear, but I was still very nervous. As we stood outside the C.O.'s office, I had a flashback to the Leicester orphanage and all the times I had to wait outside the master's study to receive my punishment. The officer gave a sharp knock on the door and had just enough time to adjust my tie before a stern, "Come in" sounded through the keyhole.

I looked up at the officer, and he looked down at me. Then he said with a smile, "It's all right lad. Now in you go." He opened the door and a blast of pipe tobacco smoke rushed out. After we went through the formalities of saluting and the officer announced who I was, the C.O. took his pipe out of his mouth and told us to sit down in the chairs in front of his desk. He shuffled a few bits of paper around, picked up what looked like a memo, and studied it for a while before laying it down again. Then he looked up with a faint smile and said,

"Right, Private Morris, I expect you are wondering why I have sent for you?" He paused as if waiting for a reply, so I crisply said,

"Yes sir."

He fumbled with the papers again, gave a couple of coughs, cleared his throat, and looked at me with a friendly smile. "What this is all about, Private Morris is this memo. It includes a copy of a letter that was sent to the War Office and then forwarded to me. It is from your father."

I repositioned myself in my chair and said without hesitating, "Sir, you must have the wrong man, for I have no father."

The officer sitting next to me shook his head as the C.O. opened my file.

"I am well aware of your circumstances," the C.O. said, "and can understand why this must come as a bit of a shock to you, but..." He hesitated as he flipped through my file. "I know you have been brought up in an orphanage most of your life, and that this must be difficult for you to believe, but I can assure you that according to this letter, and from other correspondence," he fumbled with more papers, "it appears that your father has been trying to get in touch with you for some time now, and has finally traced you here."

For once I was speechless. I looked at my officer, then back to the C.O., then back to my officer, who asked, "Do you know anything about your family?"

"As far as I know, I only have my brother, Douglas, who was brought up with me," I replied.

The C.O. smiled as he re-stoked his pipe, then asked me what I thought about having a father.

"Well sir, I just can't believe it, sir." I was stuttering my words, but eventually a broad smile came to my face. "Do you mean to tell me, sir, that I have a real live father – not someone who wants to be – but a REAL LIVE FATHER?"

The C.O.'s smile grew even bigger, and as billows of smoke surrounded him. "Yes, he is your real flesh-and-blood father. The reason this has all come to my attention is that your father would like you to come home."

I got up from my chair, gasping. "He wants me home?" then sat down again.

I just couldn't believe it. Those words sounded so wonderful to me: home, father. I was 17 years old and had never heard or said the word "father" in a way that meant anything to me; now it meant everything. It was a whole new word for me to get used to: father. I kept saying it to myself. I was miles away when the C.O. spoke again, which made me jump.

"Now, the facts that your father has asked you to return home means you have two options. One is that you can go on what we call "compassionate leave" with pay, or..." He paused to relight his pipe. "The other option is to leave the Junior Leaders for good. If you did decide to leave, there would be no stain on your record. The decision to take leave or give up the army is entirely up to you."

As he took a few more puffs on his pipe, I looked over at my officer, then back at the C.O.

"Now I do not expect you to make a decision right now. You may have time to consider, and..."

"But," I interrupted.

"Just a minute," he said, holding up his hand. "Should you decide to give up your career in the army the choice must be yours and yours alone."

Without hesitating, I said, "I want to join my father."

"Well," said the C.O. "That's a very natural decision to make, but if you feel you would like more time, I strongly recommend that you take it. After all, you are giving up your whole career."

I looked him in the eye and said, "Sir, my mind is made up. If my father wants me to come home to be with him, then I must go."

"Very well, Private Morris," the C.O. said, as he closed my file and relit his pipe. "Now this will take several days to sort out. I would imagine that you would be clear to leave by next weekend, so you still have time to think about this new change in life." Then he rose to his feet and thrust out his hand. I did the same, and as he shook my hand, he said, "Well son, whatever you decide, I hope that the future will sort itself out for you. I hate to lose you, as I think you would have made a fine soldier."

With that, I thanked him and was escorted outside. The officer started giving me a sort of fatherly talk, but quite honestly I wasn't listening to a word he said. It all went in one ear and out the other, so I thanked the officer and returned to my barracks.

As I walked back, I started feeling rather proud. I threw my shoulders back and kept saying to myself, "I really *do* have a father." Although I got some strange looks, I didn't care.

My mind was racing along full speed asking questions. "What is my father like? What sort of job has he got? Does he have a car? What does his house look like?"

The ten days I had to wait seemed endless, and although some of my superiors tried to talk me out of leaving, I was quite adamant about going. I had made my mind up to leave that life and start a new one with my father by my side.

Eventually the official day of my release arrived. I looked in the mirror and saw myself in civilian clothes. I took all my uniforms back to the store. Then I went to the office to sign the necessary forms and collect my wages and savings.

All of a sudden I found I was rich: I had over 300 pounds. The paying officer advised me to put the money in my Post Office savings account as soon as possible, saying, "You don't want to lose it or have it stolen, do you?"

I told him I would put it into savings as soon as I got to my new home.

He handed me a complimentary railway pass, and then I was ready to go, though I had to wait until early the next morning to catch my train. The rest of that day seemed to take forever. In fact, I couldn't sleep a wink all night because I kept thinking about all sorts of things.

"What do I say to my father? Do I have a mother? Nothing was said about my mother. What about my brother? Has my father tracked him down as well? Is Doug living with him? It would be wonderful to see them both." I asked myself questions all night long. Why worry about sleeping at a time like this?

At last, the morning of the big day arrived. After saying goodbye to my mates, I was driven to the railway station in the Land Rover. As a big steam train slid in toward the platform I was standing on, a big smile stretched across my face. I felt like a child, for I was getting all excited.

At last, I boarded the train heading toward London. As we slowly pulled out of Newton Abbot, I felt a certain sadness about losing the friends I had made. I wondered if I would ever see any of them again. But more exciting things lay ahead, no doubt, and that thought superseded all the others.

The carriage I was in didn't have a corridor, so there were no toilets and no walking around. I put my suitcase up on the rack and then sat in a seat next to the window. At the other end of the carriage sat a man with his wife and son, who occasionally gave a glance in my direction. All I wanted to do was tell them, "I have a father!" but being very shy, I didn't know how to start a conversation. I smiled at her, but she just looked out the window. So, for some time I looked out the window at the scenery and watched the billows of smoke coming from the train.

Suddenly the man asked me, "How far are you traveling? Are you going all the way to London?" The whole family looked at me, waiting for an answer.

"No, I'm getting off at High Wycombe," I replied.

"Do you live there?" the lady asked.

"No. Well, yes. I mean..." I didn't know exactly what to say.

The lady tried to come to my rescue by asking, "Where *do* you live?"

Again, I really wasn't sure what to say. Finally I stammered, "I have a father."

All three stared at me in wonder until the little boy pointed at his father and said, "This is my dad."

Both his parents stared at him and shook their heads. All was silent for awhile. Then the mother asked in a curious tone, "Why did you say 'I have a father?' Surely everyone has a father?"

"Well," I stuttered, "I'm going...to see my father...for the very first time."

"What do you mean by that?" she asked with a frown.

I was nervous, so I started undoing and redoing my jacket buttons before saying, "I was brought up in an orphanage, and I have just been told that I have a father. So I'm on my way to see him."

Her attitude changed significantly, and she started asking more questions. But the train was pulling into a station, and I heard the porter shouting "High Wycombe," so I sprang to my feet. In a panic, I grabbed my suitcase, opened the door of the carriage, and jumped off the train without saying another word.

As I headed toward the "Way Out" sign, the train pulled out of the station. The lady stuck her head out of the window and shouted, "Good luck to you, young man!"

I simply waved and smiled. I was far too busy planning my next move.

Chapter Thirty-One

Going Home

Now that I was off the train, all I had to do was to get on a double-decker bus for the short ride that would take me to my final destination – Woburn Green, the small town where I was born. There I would finally meet my father and be able to start my new life.

I climbed onto the bus and sat on top. My mind kept asking me more questions and my heart started beating faster. I kept unfolding, reading and refolding the well-worn piece of paper that had my father's address on it, 104 Holtspur Avenue, Woburn Green, Nr, High Wycombe. As I watched the houses go by, I tried to work out what sort of house he might live in.

Finally the conductor shouted up to me, as I had asked him to, "Woburn Green."

My stomach went all funny and I hesitated before making my way downstairs. The bus slowly came to a stop, and I collected my bags. Everyone was staring at me. I just wanted to shout at them, "I have a father and he lives right here!" but I didn't have the nerve.

The conductor helped me off the bus by passing me my bags. I thanked him, and he shouted, "Cheerio chap!" As the bus pulled away, I got out the piece of paper with the address on it and unfolded it for the umpteenth time. Eventually, I plucked up the courage to ask a woman walking by if she could direct me to the address. She gave me a very long description of how to get there, which ended with her saying that it was "a hell of a long way." I told her I didn't care how far it was because I was going to join my father. "Well, good luck to you," she said, and off she went.

Woburn Green was a small town in Buckinghamshire that was spread out around a large central green. I got off the bus at the green and headed in the direction the woman had told me, lugging one large suitcase and two small bags.

Now, the thoughts pounding through my mind were, "What should I say to him? *Hello Dad I have been waiting to see you for...*No, I'll think of something. Will he have a big banner out saying 'Welcome Home Son' like those you see in American films? Will he be looking for me and come running down the street?"

As I was climbing a hill, I stopped a man to confirm the directions. He assured me that I only had about half a mile to go. I caught my breath and was off again, accompanied only by my thoughts. As people passed, I wondered if they knew my father. Whenever a man passed, I wondered if that was him, because I realized we could be walking down the same road and still pass each other like strangers. I started rehearsing what to say when he greeted me, and kept building a mental picture of what to expect, until I found myself standing at the bottom of his road.

I dropped my suitcase and gazed at the houses. They were all the same; each house identical. I hadn't imagined him living in a council house, but that didn't matter. Again, out came the crumpled bit of paper to confirm the house number, 104 Holspur Avenue. Would he have a welcome home party for me? Would he come out to greet me, would he shake my hand or hug me? All these questions were racing through my mind. I walked down the street. The closer I got, the faster my heart went. Before long, I was standing outside my father's front door. I looked at it but couldn't knock somehow. The house looked dirty. The windows were smeary, the grass was full of weeds and it hadn't been cut for some time. That worried me. Perhaps I had the wrong house. I did a final check on the house number, and it was correct. I was waiting for something to happen, but all was quiet. One or two people walked by and looked at me curiously.

I finally gathered my courage and knocked hard on the door. I adjusted my clothes. Then I heard a grumpy man shout, "Go around the back!" And then a woman's voice shouted. "The back door... whoever you are."

That was puzzling. Could that be my mother? I quickly followed her instructions and went to the back of the house, thinking that maybe I had a father *and* a mother inside. A short, dumpy, plump woman wearing a broad smile showing the few teeth she had, wearing a pinafore dress greeted me at the back door. I frowned at her and asked hesitantly,

"Are you my...mother?"

She threw out her hand and said, "Oh no. I'm Mrs. Smith. I live here with your father. You are Les aren't you?" Before I could answer, she continued, "I've been longing to meet you. What a big lad you are!"

As she beckoned me into the house, I asked her where my father was. "He's in the other room. Would you like a cup of tea? I bet you have had a long journey."

I thanked her and said I would like some tea. As she took me through the kitchen, I couldn't help noticing the dirt everywhere, and the cooking fat smell which made everything seem to be tacky and greasy. Then I followed her into a cluttered living room. She pointed to a badly tattered armchair in front of the fire, where someone was hiding behind a newspaper. Smoke rose from within. Was he suddenly going to surprise me?

"This is your father," Mrs. Smith said. Then she disappeared into the kitchen.

I didn't know what to say or do. I was about to cough to let him know I was there when it happened. The corner of the newspaper slowly came down to reveal a scruffy-looking, old man. He hadn't shaved and didn't look too clean. His hair was in no particular fashion, and it looked like no two hairs were pointing in the same direction, and he had a cigarette sticking out of his mouth. He was wearing a rough-looking striped shirt with no collar and braces that stretched over his skinny shoulders. Buttons were missing on his shirt and the top of his trousers were undone.

He focused his bloodshot eyes on me and scanned me up and down, before saying in a gruff voice, "Oh. You're here. I bet you had a long journey. Mrs. Smith will take care of you and make you a cup of tea." After a few more coughs, he disappeared behind the newspaper and another cloud of smoke.

I stood there with my mouth wide open, wondering if that was it or if there was some kind of special surprise greeting awaiting me. I looked up at the ceiling and prayed, "Please tell me I'm in the wrong house."

But no, that was my official homecoming welcome. It was nothing like any reception that I had imagined. I had gotten a far better welcome from Mrs. Smith, who was now walking in with my cup of tea.

"Come and sit down here and drink a nice cup of tea, love," she said, pointing to a chair at the dining table.

I sat down and was glad for the rest, but I just kept looking at my father, or what I could see of him, waiting for him to do something. But Mrs. Smith, who told me to call her Flo, started asking me a barrage of questions, such as,

"How old are you?" and, "What was it like in the army?"

But after ages of being pent up, I got right onto the subject of my mother. I wanted to know about her and about *him* over there whoever he was.

"Do you know what happened to my mother?" I asked, looking at Flo with keen interest. This got my father's attention. He lowered the paper and rapidly interrupted by asking Flo if I ought to put my bags in the bedroom. She immediately clammed up.

"Of course," she replied, and led the way upstairs, pointing to the bathroom as we went by. I glanced in and saw that it was in a disgusting state. Then she showed me a small bedroom. "This is where I sleep," she said, then turned around and pointed to another room. "And this is where your father sleeps."

The room had a double bed in it, with a small camp bed at the bottom. I must have looked very puzzled. She smiled and said that

I would be sleeping in the double bed and my father would sleep in the camp bed.

I shook my head and told her I would feel guilty about that, and that I should sleep on the camp bed so my father could sleep in the big bed.

"No, no," said Flo. "You see, Les," there was a short pause, "we have a lodger living with us and he sleeps in here with you. You have to share the bed with the lodger."

"The lodger?" I asked, frowning.

"Yes," she said, "we have a lodger staying with us, and this is where he sleeps. Now that you are here, this is the only place you can sleep."

I looked around the room and started to stutter. "Well, isn't there another bedroom I could use?"

She just looked at me and with a chubby smile said, "Oh no, I sleep in the other room, and well, the only other room is full of junk." She went over and adjusted the curtains. "You'll like Alan; he's a nice lad."

Whether he was a nice lad or not, I certainly was not looking forward to spending every night with him, and I had never been in a bed with anybody in my life.

She left the room. I sighed heavily and put my coat on the bed and sat down next to it. I put my head in my hands and kept saying to myself, "What on earth have I done?" After another big sigh, I thought, "Well, it's got to get better."

Funny how things don't turn out the way you anticipate. It was not at all what I had imagined, nothing like it. For one thing, I have always shared bedrooms with people, but I'd never slept in the same bed with anyone. I just couldn't get over it. My eyes were starting to fill up thinking of everything I had left, a good life with all my new mates but I didn't quite know what I was in for.

I pulled myself together and decided to unpack. There was nowhere to put my things, no chest of drawers, nothing. I had to live out of my suitcase.

"Come and have a nice cup of tea, Les," came a call up the stairs. I gave an even bigger sigh and went downstairs.

I was greeted by the smell of chips cooking in the untidy kitchen.

"Pour yourself a cup of tea," Flo said, as she tossed the chips in the boiling fat, a cigarette hanging from her mouth.

"Thank you," I said, and poured the tea into a dirty-looking cup with a crack in it. I took it into the adjoining room and sat at the table. From where I sat, I could see Flo's hefty figure tossing chips in a wire basket and giving the sausages a prod and a turn as they spat and sizzled.

I looked to my right and saw my father, who was still sitting in his chair holding the newspaper up. I think he was trying to hide. But I wanted to know more about what I had let myself in for, so I tried to make conversation by asking Flo,

"Where's the lodger, is he at work?"

"Oh, no I expect he's down at the pub, knowing him. You'll get to meet him soon enough." There was a long pause as I sipped my tea and lit a cigarette.

"You smoke then," said Flo. My father, who was also smoking, lowered the newspaper and glanced at me. "Good," said Flo, "Now there's someone else I can get cigarettes from; we're always running out of them in this house." She gave the sausages another prod.

I took the opportunity to ask my father where he worked. Flipping the newspaper over and raising it up again, he mumbled, "I'm not working anymore." End of subject. It was now deathly quiet, except for the hissing of food in the kitchen and the odd swear word from Flo.

After she got over a quick coughing attack, still with a cigarette in her mouth, Flo said, "Your father had a job at the paper mill, but they closed his department down, so he's out of work."

I sort of felt sorry for him, but I also wanted to be able to use the word "Dad." It still seemed strange to say that word, even knowing that he was my real father, so instead I asked if there was plenty of work in town. He didn't reply.

Flo suddenly said that tea was ready. As the conversation wasn't exactly what I had hoped for, I went into the kitchen and Flo thrust a plate into my hand. It was loaded high with greasy chips and two sausages that looked as if they'd been fired from a black powder gun.

She also passed me a knife and fork, which she first wiped down on her dress.

"Go and eat while it's hot, and I'll bring in the bread and butter." She told my dad his plate was ready. He muttered that he didn't want his yet, which seemed to be a habit of his. While I was eating, I looked out the window and saw the state of the back garden. It was a real mess. There was an old tin bath lying on its side next to an old dustbin with grass growing up around it, no doubt to hide it. The grass hadn't been cut for months, if that. I was about to ask Flo who cuts the grass, as I was going to volunteer to do it, when my father actually spoke to me. I swiveled around when he called my name.

Lowering the paper, he cleared his throat and said, "You know, you will have to pay rent while you are here." He paused. "As I have lost my job, I can't afford to keep you." And with that, he started to shuffle the paper some more.

"Well, that's all right," I said, "how much will you need each week?" I put my hand in my pocket.

"Well, Alan pays us eight pounds a week, so I would expect..."

I interrupted by counting eight pounds out on the table, and noticed Flo's eyes popping out at all the money I had in my hand. "I'll pay you that," I said, and gave it to him. He put the paper down and shuffled in his seat, and I think, smiled faintly. He counted the money and promptly put it in his back pocket.

"Thank you," he said, then got out of his chair for the first time and made his way to the table.

"I'll get your tea for you, Bill," Flo said. That's what she called him. Then they both went into the kitchen. I continued to eat and drink my tea but couldn't help hearing their muttering. After some discussion, my father got the money out of his pocket and peeled some notes off for Flo. I was pretending to look out the window when I saw them looking to see if I was watching. After more whispering, they came in for tea, looking far happier than they had before. Money seemed to be the problem.

I sipped my tea, which was so weak that it must have gone through the pot on stilts. The three of us sat and ate. Flo broke the silence by saying, "Did you make much money while you were in the army?"

As I finished a tough piece of sausage, I told them, "Well, the money wasn't all that good, but when you were given it there was nothing to spend it on."

"So what did you do with it all?" she asked.

"I just saved it."

My father put down his knife and fork, and said, "You mean you just stuffed it in your pocket? How much have you got now?"

"Well," I said, "there should be around 260 odd pounds. Most of it was back pay."

My father sprang to his feet and looked down at me. He stared at the money on the table and said, "What are you going to do with that money, son?"

"Well, I'll put most of it in the Post Office, but I'll need some to look for a job."

He sat down again and I noticed he couldn't take his eyes off the large amount of money.

"You know," he said, touching it, "You don't have to go all the way to the Post Office to let them look after it. I will look after it for you, son. What do you think about that?" He had a funny look in his eyes that worried me. He then pushed the money back at me in a sort of temper and said, "Well, if you'd rather trust the Post Office than your own father that says a lot about your trust in me."

All that time Flo was standing in the doorway, puffing her cigarette and staring at me and giving me a kind of nod. My father got up from the table and went to his armchair saying, "Please yourself, but you won't have to stand in line waiting to get at it or wait until they're open. You just come and ask your old dad and he will give you what you want; it's as simple as that." He promptly put his feet up on an old stool.

There was total silence. Both of them were waiting for my answer. I eventually said, "Well, if you would like to look after it, I suppose that's all right."

My father got out of his chair, grabbed the money from the table, and said, "Well son, how much do we have to look after?" as he started counting.

Flo sat down and was all smiles. "I don't think I have ever seen so much money all at once," she said, puffing away at her cigarette.

My father asked her to light him a cigarette, and finally said, "You have got 364 pounds here; what do you want me to look after?"

"Er, well just the 300, if that's all right?"

"Right," said my father. "Flo, you're a witness to what I have here to look after, right?"

Flo agreed and said, "What are you going to do with rest of the money?"

"I'll need that to look for a job, but it should last me some time. Why do you ask?"

"Well, your father is still waiting for his money to come and I haven't got a penny to my name."

So I peeled off two ten-pound notes and handed them one each. My father took his and quickly stuffed it in his pocket, saying thank you without looking at me. Flo gave me a tremendous smile, which revealed her black front teeth, and said thank you about a dozen times. As she was thanking me, the back door opened and in walked the lodger.

I looked him up and down as Flo introduced us. "This is Alan, Les." We shook hands. He was much older than I, probably in his twenties. Flo left the room, announcing she would get Alan's tea. My father rejoined his chair, and a conversation got underway between him and the lodger. I just sat there finishing my tea and gazing out into the empty garden, wondering again what I had come into. It was only then that I regretted my hasty decision to leave the Junior Leaders, for it was I who felt like the lodger.

I had a very restless night. My father and the lodger both went to the pub for a drink, and came home late. In our shared bed, Alan told me to keep still and get to sleep. He and my father snored in perfect harmony as I lay there thinking of the army and the orphanage.

Sunday came and I was up at six o'clock, a habit I had gotten into. I sat downstairs by myself. I actually felt like packing my bags and leaving. I was really depressed, but I had nowhere to go.

The local paper was crumpled up on the floor, so I spread it out on the table and scanned through it for starts, but ended up reading just about every word in it. There were one or two jobs advertised and one of them caught my eye. I can't remember the exact wording, but it was for a young man to work on the railway in a signal box at High Wycombe Railway Station.

"That's it," I thought. "I'll try that on Monday." That cheered me up a little. That Sunday was the most boring and depressing day I have ever had. It rained all day and we spent most of the time sitting and looking at each other. I noticed that every time I asked my father a question, Flo answered instead.

At tea time, which was bread and jam with a home-baked sponge that looked like someone had jumped on it, my father said, "I'm glad you decided not to carry all that money around with you. Alan gives me his to look after, don't you son?" I looked at the lodger, who was nodding his head while reading the Sunday paper. An uneasy jealous feeling came over me when I heard my father call the lodger "son." Is he his son or am I his son? I decided not to challenge him on that subject. But all of a sudden, the lodger sat up, crumpled the paper, and said in a demanding tone, "What money? Whose money? How much are we talking about?"

Everyone turned to look at him, and for awhile there was complete silence.

"Les has given his dad some money to look after instead of him putting it in the Post Office," Flo explained.

With wide-open eyes, Alan said, "How much money?"

My dad said casually, "Oh, 300 pounds."

"Wow, that's a lot of money! Can I see it?"

"No," said Flo, "it's between Les and Bill."

Suddenly, everyone started showing an interest in me. First, my father asked how much I had in the Post Office account.

"Well, I'm not sure, but it's about 200 pounds. "My father sat upright in his chair, and at the same time Alan put the paper down. They more or less said together, "Two hundred pounds! How did you get that sort of money at your age?" and eagerly awaited my reply.

"Well, I've saved as much money as I could. You see, we were encouraged to save money at the orphanage, and I don't spend very much."

Alan picked up the newspaper and said sarcastically, "I don't believe you," before burying his head in the paper.

Flo, who I think was doubtful, said, "Go and get your Post Office box, Les."

There was a lot of mutter, so, I went to get the book. When I returned, I walked into the room, thrusting the book into my father's hand.

He quickly flipped through the pages. "He's right, you know, but there's nearly 300 there." His voiced dropped as he said "289 pounds, seven and sixpence," then handed the book to Alan, who said with a smile,

"So he has. Well done, Les."

At my age of 17 years, I never twigged that you suddenly become popular when you've got something that other people want.

That night, when Alan and my father were heading to the local pub, they stopped in the doorway to ask if I wanted to go. I shook my head and declined the offer.

I told Flo that I would keep her company, but she stood up and shouted, "Hang on, I'm coming too." Before she left, she said, "You might sleep on the sofa tonight because we will be in late, and you have to be up for your job stuff tomorrow."

And off they went.

It was only later that evening that I realized their attitude toward me had completely changed since the issue of money had popped up.

Chapter Thirty-Two
Settling In

First thing Monday morning I went to the railway station to see about the job they had advertised. I was given a form to fill out, and told that they would be in touch about possible dates for interviews was soon as I mailed in the form. So, back to Woburn Green I went.

When I got home, I was introduced to a woman and her daughter, Janet; some neighbors Flo had told about my homecoming.

Janet kept glancing at me with a shy smile and offered me a cigarette. She was 16, and although attractive, had embarrassing spots on her face, which she tried to disguise with makeup. She sat down at the dining table.

"Tell me about your army life," she said.

But I was shyer than she was; telling her there was not much to say about it. Then I asked where my dad was.

"Oh, he's down at the pub, having a drink with some of his old mates and Alan."

I politely asked if they minded if I filled out a form, as I wanted to post it straightaway.

As I filled in the application form at the table, Flo produced my Post Office book. She placed it in front of me saying, "You left this down here last night; you ought to keep it safe."

Janet promptly picked it up and started looking through it, then asked what it was. Flo told her, and mentioned how much was in there.

"I haven't got one of these," she said, to which her mother snapped, "You never got any bloody money to put in." This started an argument between them. I interrupted to ask Flo if she had a stamp and envelope, which she produced after turning everything out of the sideboard drawers.

"Is there a post box nearby?"

Quick as a flash, Janet said she would run and post it for me, snatching it out of my hand as she went.

That night I went for a drink with my father and Alan, who claimed it would be good for me. I was not used to drinking, but have had the odd drink now and then. It was funny, I found out at the pub that my father was very chatty; just not on subjects concerning the family, which he completely avoided. He was also flashing a lot of money around, even though I found myself paying for most of the rounds for him and his mates

Later that week, I was very pleased to get a letter from the railway, giving a date and time for an interview. And Janet asked me if I would like to baby-sit with her that evening. I hesitated before answering, but Flo answered for me.

"Yes, it will do you good to get out and mix with someone your own age."

"I'll call for you at six then," Janet said, and off she went. Then her mother stopped by and started to gossip with Flo about people on the street. Every other word was a swear word.

That night, just before six, around came Janet. I could hear Flo telling her, "My word that's a lovely dress; you do look pretty," and when I saw her I had to admit she looked very attractive.

"Now you two behave yourselves and have a good evening together. I'll leave the door on the latch if we are in bed," Flo said.

Then Janet led me down the road to her house, which was three doors away. When we arrived, her mother was swearing as she desperately looked around for something; she kept checking the clock. After a few minutes, she finished dressing, and she also looked very smart. As she put on her gloves, she patted me on the head with a smile and said, "Help yourself to something to eat if you're hungry."

Then, pointing to Janet, she said, "And you bloody well better behave yourself tonight." The sound of a car horn made her scurry off, and the slamming of the front door drowned out her goodbye.

Janet and I sat at a small table in the kitchen. Their house looked much cleaner than mine. We both started to talk at the same time, but she allowed me to go first.

"I was just going to ask, where has your mother gone, and when will she be back?" I said. A big smile came across her face, cracking the makeup she had plastered on.

"Oh, it's all right. She won't be back until maybe early morning. You never know. But that's her new boyfriend, who doesn't like waiting, and I hate him," she gushed all in one breath. Then she placed her hands on mine and gazed at me and said, "So we have all night; what shall we do?"

Well, I had been in that sort of position with a girl before, and I still didn't know how to handle the situation.

After a short time of playing cards – yes we played cards if you must know – she stood up and said she was tired of the game and that we should go into the other room where there weren't any hard chairs. She took me by the hand and led me into the living room, then left me there, saying she'd be back in a minute.

I stood for a moment, viewing the room. There were two easy chairs by the fire, a large dining table, a sideboard, and on the far side of the room, a bed and a cot with a small baby on it, fast asleep. I sat down in an easy chair.

Janet returned with two mugs of cocoa, which she placed by the fireplace.

"Are you comfortable there?" she asked, reaching for a cushion from the other chair and placing it on the floor by my feet. "Then

I'll sit here." She made herself comfortable and rested her elbow on my knee.

As we sipped our cocoa, she tried to make conversation by asking me all sorts of questions about the girls that I'd been out with. I blushed and told her she'd wake up the baby.

"Come on," she said, looking up at me as she knelt between my legs. "You army lads have lots of girlfriends. Haven't you got a girl?"

"No," I said, reaching for my drink.

"How many girls have you been with?" she asked, raising the tone of her voice somewhat.

I remained silent, and continued to slowly sip my cocoa.

She noticed that I was blushing, and that I was shaking as well.

"You're embarrassed aren't you? You've never been with a girl before, have you?" she said, smiling and running her hands up my legs.

My word, I went hot and cold and nearly dropped my cocoa. Well, I couldn't help it; we all have to start somewhere, don't we? I quickly put my mug down and pushed myself up into the chair, claiming I had to use the toilet, which she allowed me to do. I practically ran out of the room and stood in the toilet, tightly bolted in. I looked in the mirror and saw that my face was bright red. I didn't really want to use the toilet, so I just stood there telling myself to relax, but somehow I couldn't. "It should be me doing that to her, not her doing it to me," I thought to myself. After a moment, I felt a little better. I was also getting colder; after all, it was December.

When I came back into the room, I stopped in my tracks, for Janet was sitting on the bed showing practically all of her legs.

"Come on Les; come and sit here where it's comfortable," she said, patting the area beside her. I noticed that something else was different about the room. Ah, now there was only a small bedside light on.

I slowly went over and sat a little beyond the spot she was patting, but she plunked herself right next to me and held my hand.

"Well," she said, "what are you thinking about?"

I paused and then replied, "There's going to be a sharp frost tonight."

She stared at me and said, "You are funny."

"No, I'm not," I snapped, "Go out and see for yourself; it's white with frost out there."

At that, Janet pushed me back on the bed so I was lying there on my back with my legs dangling over the side. Her face appeared over mine and she muttered something I couldn't understand. Then she pressed her lips hard onto mine, and although her lips moved, mine remained motionless. After a few moments, she raised her face and said sharply, "Well, aren't you going to do anything then?"

I remained motionless and numb. "I've never been kissed like that before," I said, swallowing hard and feeling red-hot.

"Does it do anything to you?" she asked.

"Yes, it was nice," I said.

"Is that all? It was nice?" she said sarcastically. Then she thrust her hand between my legs and grabbed my private parts, and I shot up into a sitting position. She pushed me back down again and climbed on top of me, saying, "I do have some effect on you then."

She started to simulate sex with me, but I pushed her off and rose to my feet. As I adjusted my tie, she came out with a lot of verbal abuse. She swore and said I didn't know what a woman looked like, which was very true, and how she had wasted a whole evening with someone who thought she was a man, which was not. She was really angry. Then she stood in front of me and lifted her skirt right up, showing her naked body.

"Look! Look!" she snarled. "If you ever get around to it, this is what it looks like!" With that, she stormed out into the kitchen.

I stood there in an embarrassing position, ashamed that I was 17 and here was a girl, a big girl for her age, who was only 16, but trying her darnedest to make love with me and failing. I was a failure, and I desperately wanted to change that.

I walked into the kitchen, only to find Janet sitting at the table with her head in her hands, crying.

"I'm sorry, Janet." I stood at the other side of the table, very quiet and still. She slowly raised her head. Tears were rolling down her cheeks, gathering makeup on the way down. She spluttered that it was her fault, and that she was the one who should apologize.

She told me that she started falling in love with me from the moment she first saw me, and that she so much wanted me to make love to her. "But," she sniffed, "I've spoiled it now. I just don't know what got into me." She wiped her eyes and gazed at me again. "I'm sorry, Les, really."

I told her it was all right, and that I was to blame.

Suddenly, the baby started crying. Janet got up and said she wouldn't be but a minute and went to tend the baby. I thought that it was a good opportunity to go, so I quietly went home. And it was a hard frost, just like I said it would be.

Chapter Thirty-Three

Paying Rent

On the appointed day and time, I went to be interviewed by the stationmaster, Mr. Hogg, who asked me all sorts of questions that I had no problem answering. At the end, he said with a smile that he would be in touch.

When I left his office, I saw at least half-a-dozen lads my age waiting their turn. I hoped I could get the job, as it would be a challenge for me. I remember thinking on the way home, "If I do get this job, I intend to learn as much as I can. And who knows, I could make it a career."

That weekend, my father asked me for rent money. I told him that I didn't have eight pounds on me, so would he deduct it from the money I'd given him? There was a deadly hush for a few minutes. I looked around the room and everyone just stared at me, except my father, who had his head bowed down.

Flo, as usual, broke the silence. "Your father doesn't know quite how to tell you the bad news."

I turned to look at him.

"I lost it," he said.

I was stunned, and looked at Flo for an explanation.

"Your father has been very upset over it and didn't know how to tell you."

"And you were the one who told me not to put it into my Post Office account," I snapped at him. "You were the one who said, 'Leave it with me so it's safe with Alan's money.' How much of Alan's money did you lose?"

My father stood up and started waving his finger at me in a rage. It was a side of him I hadn't seen before.

"Don't you start shouting at me, are you accusing me of something? If you are, tell me and I'll knock you right out of that door and bolt the bloody thing behind you!"

He was trembling and so was I. As he sat down with the newspaper, he started talking to himself, saying, "That's what you get when you spend your life searching for your son and try to offer him a decent home. That's the thanks. He calls you a bloody thief." He pointed his finger at me again. "You pay your way, and if you get this job you're talking about, I shall expect even more each week," he said, then hid behind the paper. I looked at Alan, who was also hiding behind a magazine. I turned to look at Flo, but she had slipped into the kitchen.

I gave a big sigh before I left the room and slammed the door behind me. Flo was peeling potatoes, not daring to look at me. I said to her, "How could he lose 300 pounds? I trusted him with it."

My father's muffled voice came from the other room, but I couldn't hear what he said.

"What did Dad...he say?"

She simply shook her head and said she didn't know. I looked out the kitchen window. It was then that I realized the sound of the word "Dad" didn't do anything for me anymore.

Flo finally spoke. "Your father is a good man, Les. With the little money he has, it is very difficult to run a house. He has a lot of worry, so the best thing for..."

The door burst open, and my father filled the doorway. "Are you talking about me?"

"No," I replied.

He fiddled with his braces and said, "If you want to eat in this house, you'd better get some money for your keep, by tonight." Then he disappeared into the other room.

I walked out of the back door. Flo asked where I was going. I merely replied,

"I have no idea."

"Will you be in for your dinner?"

"I don't know," I said, and left. I didn't know where I was going, I just wanted to walk and be alone with my thoughts. "Is he really my father?" I kept asking myself. He had shown no feeling toward me; I was only another lodger to him. I felt really miserable.

I was suddenly confronted by Janet, who had seen me coming and ran out of her house. I stopped and said hello. With a questioning look on her face she asked, "Are you all right, Les?"

"No, I'm fed up."

She started to walk along with me

"I'm afraid I'm not very good company for you Janet, especially today."

She stopped and said, "Why? And where are you going?"

With my head hung low, I said, "I've just had a row with my father, so I just want to walk and be alone to think."

"I'll keep you company, Les. Sometimes it's good to talk to someone about your problems, so my mother says. Can I come with you?"

"Yes, all right then," I looked at her and smiled.

She apologized again for her behavior the other night, then asked question after question. I poured out my troubles as we walked. I then saw a bus for High Wycombe and rushed for the bus stop, yelling "Come on! Let's go into town."

"Why?" she asked, running for the bus stop.

"Well, I have to go to the Post Office, and we can walk around town and the shops."

"But I have no money."

"It's all right."

We talked nonstop all the way into town.

"How long were you in a home?"

"Sixteen years, including the boarding-out period."

She sat and thought and suddenly asked, "How come it took your father 16 years to contact you?"

I looked at her in amazement. "You know, you're right. I never thought about that. I wonder why it did take so long." Then I started thinking that not only was she good looking, but she was quite intelligent for her age.

"How much do you pay your mum a week?" I asked as we got off the bus.

"Four pounds a week. Why, how much do you pay?"

"Eight pounds, and if I get this job he wants ten."

She gasped with disbelief and shouted, "Eight pounds! I don't believe it! I know a woman who's a bit of a snob, but she takes lodgers and charges them five pounds a week. And your dad is going to ask his own son to pay 10 pounds! I just don't believe it."

Well, I really had no idea how much everyone else paid, but that got my mind working and I started putting two and two together. "Hang on," I said as we were outside the Post Office. "I'll go and get some money. Are you all right for cash?"

"Well, yes. I mean no. I told you I haven't any." She looked confused. I smiled and went in to withdraw 25 pounds.

Over a cup of coffee, I gave her five pounds, which she passed back to me, but I insisted. "Please. Take this as a present from me; you have brightened my day, and it's nice to have a friend to talk to."

She had tears in her eyes as she took the money. "You are kind, Les, and I feel terrible, especially after what I said to you the other night." She held my hand, but people were looking at us, so I pulled mine away and started blushing. Janet smiled, and then we left.

On our way back, Janet pointed out the house that took in lodgers, but I thought no more about it. We said goodbye, and she told me that any time I wanted to come to her house for a talk or whatever, I was welcome.

I walked toward my house and actually dreaded going in, even though it was supposed to be my home. The atmosphere in the house was icy. Flo, who had woodbine sticking out of her mouth, said, "Oh, you're back. Your father was wondering where you were. Did you," she dropped her voice, "get to the Post Office?"

"Yes," I said.

Then my father appeared from the other room with a stern face. "Did you get some money?"

"Yes."

He thrust out his hand. I fumbled about and gave him eight pounds, which he put in his pocket, merely saying, "Right," before going back to his seat. Alan was sprawled out in the other chair, fast asleep.

I sat down at the table and wondered if I should say something to my father. Should I ask him about asking for so much rent? Or about the money he had either lost or spent? I'd probably never know what he did with it, but I could venture a damn good guess. I didn't like the silence. Without thinking, I said out loud, "I wonder if I'll get that job?" My voice seemed to ring through the house, but there was no response whatsoever.

Just then there was a loud knock on the door, which even woke that lazy Alan. Flo opened the door and I could hear a man's voice. Within a minute, she was leaning over my father and whispering. The very next moment, she came over to me and asked if I would go to the door with her.

Alan whispered, "Who is that, Bill?" My father muttered something, but I couldn't hear what.

When I got to the kitchen, I found two men who looked very official. One had a book open, and they both were staring at me. I couldn't think what I might have done wrong or why they should want me.

Flo, having closed the living-room door behind her, said, "Les, these men have come for a bill we can't pay. If they don't get the money, your father will be in serious trouble. Will you lend us the money to pay them?"

"But I have just given him..." I started to reply, but she interrupted.

"That's for next week's food."

"How much?" I asked reluctantly.

The man with the book said loudly, "The total is seven pounds." He looked straight at me as if it were my fault. I got the money from my pocket and handed it to him. He crossed the total out in his book and wrote "PAID," spelling it out loud as he did. Then he bid us good day, and away they went.

Flo thanked me, then popped her head around the living-room door and told my father everything was all right; the bill was paid. Then she continued preparing tea. I realized I was already sick of bread and jam.

The next morning, after another restless night, I got a letter from the railway. I ripped it open and read it to myself. "You have been selected for the position of booking boy, and will report on Monday at eight o'clock." I was thrilled to bits, and read the letter several times.

Flo crawled into the room. What a sight she was first thing in the morning.

"I have the job, Flo."

She tried to look at me with her bloodshot eyes, but all she could say as she put the kettle on was, "I suppose that means I have to make sandwiches every day?"

"Well, yes, if that's all right," I said, wondering why she wasn't as excited as I was. When my father walked in the room, I greeted him with the same words: "I've got the railway job, Dad." He just slumped into his chair and said,

"Now that you'll be earning, you have to pay more rent." He picked up the paper and hid behind it. End of subject.

After having a bit of burnt toast for breakfast, I walked round to Janet's house. Her mother let me in and told me that Janet had popped out to the shop. "Have a cup of tea," she said, pulling out a chair at the table. That's when I noticed that she only had a thin dressing gown on with nothing underneath it. I knew there was nothing underneath it because one of her "things" dropped out when she stooped over the table. I immediately blushed as she tucked it back in.

"Don't mind me," she said. "I've just had a bath and I spend hours wearing this around the house." She found some clean cups and sat down next to me. As she poured the tea, she said, "Janet told me how much your father is charging you for rent. I think it's disgusting, charging his own son that sort of money, and I shall bloody well tell him that when I see him."

I looked at her and started to say, "No, don't say anything to him," but had to turn my head away because her legs were now completely exposed.

"You bet I will. I would have you stay here, but then we would have all the neighbors talking. They already talk about us enough."

I picked up my tea without turning my head. She touched me and said, "You are a shy lad aren't you. Am I embarrassing you dressed like this?"

"Well..."

"All right, I'll go change."

"No, it's all right." I turned toward her again and she smiled and sipped her tea. Well, I didn't mind, really, if you know what I mean.

"Have you said anything to your brother? Maybe he..."

"What brother?" I interrupted, "How did you know I had a brother?"

"Well, Mrs. Smith told me. His name is Jim, isn't it?"

"Jim? No, his name is Douglas. I don't know any Jim." My shyness had completely disappeared.

"Really, I think you'll find that his name is Jim. He lives in the next town, Bourne End."

I shook my head and said blankly, "Jim? Bourne End? What does he look like?"

"Big man, a little taller than you, with a bald head."

"No, that can't be Doug; he's around my height," I thought to myself, "unless he's grown a lot."

"Do you mean to tell me they haven't taken you over there or said anything to you?"

"No, they haven't mentioned anything to me yet."

"That bastard!" she said, then apologized for swearing. "I don't know the address, but Flo will tell you, I'm sure."

I got up to leave, but she insisted that I stay and have more tea, so I did. Like her daughter, she asked me nonstop questions, and continued to reveal herself. I took one or two sneaky looks, which I'm sure encouraged her more.

"I like you," she said suddenly, "You're honest and shy, but you're clean and tidy and full of innocence aren't you?"

I blushed. "I don't know."

"You're not like the bastards around here. I could strangle half of them. I think you would have been brought up much different if you'd stayed around here, and you've got a lovely accent, which I like." All the time she was talking, she was smiling and touching me.

She quickly stood up and corrected her dressing gown because she heard Janet coming in. Then she vanished. Janet gave me a big smile and a hello, and then said, "This is a nice surprise. Has Mother been looking after you all right?"

Her mother returned dressed and promptly told Janet about my brother, swearing about it again. I stood up to go, as I wanted to get his address as soon as possible. They both insisted I stay for awhile, but I promised to come back later, after I'd been to Bourne End. They both understood, so I ran toward home.

Flo was in the kitchen, looking much better than earlier.

"Do you know my brother's address in Bourne End?" I asked in a whisper. With a quizzical look that made the long ash of her cigarette fall into the sink, she said she did and quickly told me. I wrote it on the envelope that I kept in my Post Office book.

"Thank you, Flo. I'm going to go see him."

"But..." she started to say, but I heard my father's voice and dashed out of the door.

I caught the bus to Bourne End right away. When I got off, I asked someone for directions and within five minutes was knocking on my brother's door. I suddenly got very nervous, and was rehearsing what to say to him when a woman answered the door. I didn't expect that, and was speechless for a moment.

"Can I help you?" she asked. That started me un-doing and doing up my jacket buttons, which was a habit of mine.

Eventually the words came out. "Does Jim Morris live here?"

"Yes," she replied, "but he's not here at the moment. Did you want to see him?"

"Well, yes. You see, er," I said, stuttering, "I am his brother, Les."

"Oh, why didn't you say so in the first place?" She let me into the house. The house was spotless and had a warm, friendly atmosphere, a vast contrast to my father's place.

We had tea and she asked me a lot of questions about myself. Eventually my new brother walked in. He was big and bald and much older than me, in fact, he was a foreman at the local paper mill.

After talking some, we got onto the subject of our father. Jim hadn't a lot to say about him, and told me he hardly ever saw him. "He could be dead for all I know," he said, so I got the picture. I wished I had known all that while I was still in the Junior Leaders.

After we had some more tea, they invited me to come and see them whenever I liked. As I was going out the door, Jim said, "Have you seen our other brother in Devon near Plymouth?"

I nearly fell off the front step. "I have another brother?"

He promised to tell me more about him when I saw him again. "And," he continued, "I'll tell you about our two sisters."

"Sisters!" I shouted. "We have two sisters?"

"Oh. Didn't anybody tell you anything about your family?"

"No! All I thought I had was my brother, Douglas." I asked Jim about our mother, but he knew about as much about her as I did. I found out later in life that she had passed, but never learned why I had been abandoned except that she had been in ill health.

Because they had friends coming over, I had to leave. But Jim told me to come back soon. So with that thought, I went home.

When I walked in the door, I could sense the atmosphere. I was late for lunch, so Flo told me off, but then said that there was some left in the oven. I carried a plate through to the dining room and sat down to eat. I said hello to my father, who was sitting in his usual chair, and to Alan, who was in his usual position on the couch. Neither one said a word. The food on my plate looked revolting it didn't do anything for my taste buds. It actually was foul, but I was hungry, so I picked at it.

Flo asked if I had seen my brother. I said yes and was about to tell her of my visit, but my father threw his paper on the floor, rose to his feet, and gave me a hard stare. "What's this?" he snarled as he walked toward me. "I hear you've been telling the whole bloody street how much you pay for your keep. It's none of their business, and if you don't bloody well like it, you know what the hell you can do. I fought bloody hard to get you home, and that's all the thanks I get. I wouldn't be surprised if you've blabbed everything to the whole town." He kept on. "You don't even care how many nights I've sat here with tears in my eyes, wanting you home."

I put my knife and fork down and looked him in the eye. "Why did it take 16 years to find me then?"

I wished I'd never asked him that question, for he flew over to me, and with all his force, slapped my face.

"Don't you ever speak to me like that again; you don't deserve a good home." He walked back to his chair, stopped, pointed his finger at me, and said, "You're not too old for me to give you a bloody good hiding." As he sat down, he pointed toward Alan. "I get more respect from Alan than my own son," and in a lower voice added, "I'm wondering if you really are my son."

I was very tempted to reply, but thought better of it.

Flo pointed to my food, but I shook my head and pushed the plate away. My father was still ranting on. I sat looking out the window, once again wondering what I had done. "It's me. It must be," I thought, "but where am I going wrong? I just hoped for a good home life, and this is what I end up with."

Still ranting, my father shouted, "You come home swanking with all that money and don't offer a penny to help pay the bills, and then you expect all your meals on bloody time, don't you?" He ruffled the paper.

For a moment, it was quiet. Flo asked if I would like a cup of tea. I nodded and asked if she had an aspirin, as I now had a headache.

"You'll get more than a bloody headache by the time I've finished with you."

That was the most my father had said to me since I'd been there, and it was all "bloody this" and "bloody that."

The rest of the day seemed endless. I went round to see Janet. She and her mother were preparing to go out, but I was able to kill an hour or so there while they dashed around getting things ironed and going through the usual preparations women get up to when going out. I told them I had got the job with the railway, and they were thrilled to bits with the news. It would have been nice if I had gotten that response from my father.

Chapter Thirty-Four

Working on the Railroad

On Monday, I reported for work at High Wycombe Railway Station, and was glad to get away from that depressing house.

Now, I wasn't too sure what the job entailed, but I started learning right away. I was first escorted along the tracks to the signal-box building, known as the main "North Box." You have to climb up steep wooden steps to get up to the signal box, and I was beckoned to go ahead. Because I was a young fit chap, I ran all the way to the top and Mr. Hogg came puffing up behind me.

The stationmaster, Mr.Hogg, introduced me to Percy, the signalman of the day. Mr. Hogg gave me a brief run-down on what I was supposed to do, but left me in the capable hands of Percy to fill in all the details. My correct title was "Telegraphist," but "booking boy" was easier to say and remember, so that's what I was known as.

The signal box was taken up by a uniform row of levers that practically ran the length of the building. All were colored red with the exception of two yellow ones. Above the levers was a shelf, which had a series of bell units running along it. Above the shelf was a very large display board, which fascinated me. It had the layout of the track marked on it, and red lights would appear whenever a train was positioned on the track, the signal box was one of the first to try out a new system. There were other bells and telephones opposite all the levers. There also was a bench table with a large book on top and a funny looking light hanging over it.

The bench and the book was my department. I had to record the timing of the bells in the book. For example, whenever another signal box asked us to accept a train, we had to record every movement then send those same signals to the next signal box and so on. Then the train was out of our hands and into theirs. *Are you still with me?* That may sound a little complicated, and I thought I'd never get the hang of it, but because I was interested, I learned as much as I could. I still remember most of it today.

After a couple of days, I started getting used to it. Sometimes the bells would ring nonstop, but with Percy's help, I managed to get it all booked and taken care of.

One day, Percy asked me to get a token out for a branch-line train, which I got as he watched over me. He then wrapped the token in an old newspaper, which seemed unusual to me. I looked out the window to see what was on the branch line, and spotted a small red diesel machine. I asked him what it was.

"Oh, that's a fish & chips wagon for the workers. Go give him the token and tell him I want a sixpence-worth of fish & chips, and order what you want." My eyes lit up at the thought of fish & chips for lunch. I ran down and handed the token to a crew member, then placed our order. The man smiled at me, then glanced up at Percy, who was peering out the window. Then off they went.

The first part of the morning was busy, but as soon as there was a slack period, I ate all of the lunch I had brought with me, because I was already hungry, and had a nice cup of tea that I brewed as part of my job. The rest of the morning I kept looking at the clock thinking that it wouldn't be long before I would have a nice piece of fish in crispy batter and a big bag of chips with salt and vinegar. After the food I was getting at home, it was going to be a big treat. I kept looking over at the token machine, because once that bell rang, I knew it wouldn't be long.

As I was entering some times in the book, the bell rang for the "fish & chips" branch line. I raced over to the machine, shouting,

"I'll get it Percy," and took the bell call. My mouth was watering at the thought of what was to come, and I whistled while I put the kettle on.

Before long, I could see the little red machine slowly chugging toward the signal box. I hovered near the window, watching and waiting. "Come on," I thought to myself, "you can surely go faster than that." As the machine approached the box, I ran past Percy and down the steps, nearly tripping. A man handed me the token and slowly went on.

"What about my fish & chips?" I yelled.

I don't know how many people were in that machine, but there was a sudden roar of laughter as they moved out of sight. I looked up at the signal box and heard another roar of laughter as Percy hung out of the window, wiping his eyes. Percy thought the whole thing was highly amusing, but I thought differently, for I no longer had anything to eat for lunch. I took it like a good sport, though, and he gave me one of his sandwiches.

"Well, what was that red machine anyway?" I asked. It turned out to be a mateesea wagon for dealing with the ballast around the sleepers, which go along the metal rods under the machine prod up and down, forcing the ballast around the sleepers for a nice smooth ride.

My knocking-off time was five o'clock, but I always hung around until eight or even later. If I went home on time, there wasn't a lot to do, and I still dreaded going there. But above all, I liked what I was doing and enjoyed the company.

During slack periods in the evening, one of the signalmen, whose name I can't remember so we'll call him Ron, used to train his binoculars on the house behind the box. That was because most evenings, a woman he claimed was Italian would stand naked in front of a full-length mirror brushing her long hair with the curtains wide open. Whenever he spotted her, Ron would tell me to hold the fort and then he'd gaze at her, muttering all sorts of things. If I dared suggest having a look, he would say, "You're too young for this sort of thing lad."

One day Ron arrived on shift with a large cardboard box. As many times as I asked what it was for, he always said the same thing, "All will be revealed later."

When it got dark outside, he opened the box. I smiled when I saw what it was, but I asked him what it was all the same, and he had great pleasure in telling me all about it.

"Now then, son, this is a genuine ex-naval gun-sight telescope," he said as he mounted it in record time on a tripod. "I shall even be able to see the pimples on her bum with this, it's that powerful"

A request of four bells rang. After I accepted the initial one, and started preparing for an express train, then the telephone rang, and Ron answered it. After he hung up, he told me to remember "Second carriage from the third compartment."

"What for?" I asked.

"Never you mind; just make the tea," he said. He slipped the big window open, gazing over at the marker board. Two bells rang, which I returned. Ron stood poised with the signal lever ready to pull, but didn't pull it for some reason. I looked at the board and saw no obstruction, so what was he up to?

Suddenly he pulled the lever back and took up his position at the window. Instead of the express train roaring right through the station heading for Paddington London, the train was moving slowly and just starting to pick up speed again.

Ron didn't know I was right behind him, when he shouted, "Which carriage was it Lad?"

"Second carriage, third compartment." I quickly responded.

Ron turned around and said, "Yes, right...all right...I thought you were making the tea."

"It's made," I said, looking out at the train that was now moving past us. The engine driver waved, and Ron waved back with the piece of rag that he always carried, muttering to himself "second from end."

Then I understood what was going on.

Inside the carriage in question, a couple was half-naked, making love. Ron watched them until they were out of sight, then immediately rang the next signal box to inform them. I suppose that happened all the way to Paddington, assuming the couple lasted that long.

As for Ron, well he spent most of the time hovering around the usual hot spot waiting for the Italian's light to come on. While he was pulling levers, he asked me to let him know when the lady's light came on, and in-between all that I was doing my job.

I was coming up to the end of my second week on the railway, and I loved it. When I reported to work one morning, I was given a memo that told me to catch the nine o'clock train to Paddington and report for a medical examination. Subject to getting a clean bill of health, I would become a railway man and get my uniform while I was there.

I got to work early that morning and while in the signal box, I told the signalman of the day, who was Percy, the news, and he happy for me, and he said, "I have a surprise for you too." My eyes were now wide open and he led me to the window which was slid open, and he continued.

"Ah, now, if you tell Bert over there on platform four, who's the engine driver of that train, that I sent you and that you work up here, he might let you ride on the footplate to Paddington." He said, pointing to a train with steam bellowing up around it.

"Would he?" I asked with excitement.

"Well, it's up to him, but you can ask, can't you?"

"Wow, Percy, thanks!" I said. "I'll get right over there," With a smile Percy said, "Wait a minute, give him a wave," which I did. That indicated to Bert that I was on my way over. As I had a railway armband on to show I worked for the railway, Bert invited me on board, and introduced me to his mate and before leaving showed me around that monster of a machine. The next thing I knew we were off. We both waved to Percy as we passed the signal box leaving the station.

Bert actually let me drive for awhile. I blew the whistle and shoveled coal into the fire. When we arrived at Paddington, I thanked Bert and the fireman, who said I could go with them again when it was possible. I will never forget that great experience.

I passed my examination and came home in my new railway uniform. Flo was the only one to comment about how smart I looked in it. My father and Alan just sat in their usual spots, ignoring me.

When my father did look over at me, his only words were to ask for the rent. I immediately took out my pay packet and gave him eight pounds.

"I told you when you were working you would have to pay more rent," he said sarcastically, and demanded another two pounds.

I told him I couldn't pay an extra two pounds because my bus fare for the week was just over that amount. He simply remarked that it would have to come out of my savings.

At that, I told him, "That's my money and you have no right to take any of it unless I agree."

He gave me an evil-looking stare. Alan looked at me in amazement. I was surprised myself, but felt good for saying it.

I went into the kitchen and asked Flo in a low voice, "How is it that I'm the only one working in this house, and he wants just about all I earn in rent?"

She put her finger up to her mouth and said quietly, "You don't want to upset your dad, so say no more." Then she raised her voice to a normal level and said, "I'll make you a nice cup of tea," and pointed to the living room.

I sat down at the table and listened to my father and Alan talking about a chap at the pub. After a while, they both looked at me and promptly stopped talking, so I turned to look out the window. They both got up to go to the pub.

When my father passed where I was sitting at the table, he frowned and said through his badly stained teeth, "Don't you *ever* raise your voice to me again. Do you understand?" I simply nodded. They left, making some sort of comment to Flo on the way out. It wasn't long before Flo came in with my tea and put it on the table. She pulled up a chair and looked at me.

"You know, Les, I wouldn't get on the wrong side of your dad. You see, he has what is known as a very nasty temper, and believe me, you don't want to see that side of him."

"Well," I replied, "he said he would look after my savings, so it's not for him to just help himself to it. I'm wondering if I did the right thing."

"What, you mean coming home to your dad?"

"No. Well, yes. That, too, but I meant giving him my savings. I'm just not too sure."

I think she was sympathetic, but she still was siding with my father. It suddenly occurred to me that whatever I said to her could get back to my father, so I excused myself.

I caught the bus to Bourne End and visited my brother, Jim. Fortunately he was home and we had a long chat about my other relations, along with their addresses. He wanted to know about Douglas and myself in the orphanage world and where he was at that time. I told him I had no idea, and that we simply lost contact with each other.

Jim and his wife Betty asked me how I was getting on with our father. I told him that I often wondered if he really was my father and told him about giving him my savings to look after...before I could finish, Jim said.

"I bet he told you that he lost it."

And I replied, "Yes." And Jim continued.

"He was up to his eyes in debt, and to get you home at an age where you could earn money, he sent out a sob story that he'd been trying to track you down for years. And here you are. I bet you've cleared his dept at the local pub and that worthless lodger spent the rest."

I went to say something and he again continued.

"Now that you have a job, he will have a regular sum of money coming in, plus his dole money, so he's sitting pretty now."

I left Jim with a heavy heart and went around to visit with Janet and her mother. They were both pleased to hear about my job and admired my uniform. Janet's mother apologized for the trouble she caused by talking to my dad about the amount of rent he was demanding.

"He wants more now that that I've started working – another two pounds," I said.

"I wouldn't pay him another bloody penny more," she snapped. "In fact, if I were you, I would find somewhere else to live, or you're not going to have any money at all the rate you're going."

I sat there deep in thought.

"What are you thinking about?" asked Janet.

"Oh, I was just thinking that you're not the first ones to tell me that. A couple of chaps at work told me the same thing, even my brother Jim recommended I settle somewhere else and the thought has occurred to me as well."

Janet was going out to meet a girlfriend, or so she told me, so her mother and I sat alone by the fire talking. Her mother said that Janet had gone out with a new boyfriend; she just didn't have the heart to tell me.

Although I wasn't happy about it, I told her mother that I understood, as I was hopeless with girls anyway. After that, the subject changed to sex, which seemed to be a popular subject with her. I knew nothing about all that stuff! She asked me all sorts of personal questions that made me blush. Then she asked me if I masturbated. I simply nodded, feeling ashamed, and she told me that that was good. Everybody does it, including her.

The whole time we were talking she was fidgeting with her bathrobe, and kept pulling it to one side, saying that it was hot. It was then that I noticed she was naked underneath, and when she caught me looking at her body, she smiled and said, "I saw you looking. Do you like what you see?" and suddenly opened her robe all the way.

Well, I just went bright-red in the face, hoping she wouldn't notice, but she did. I started blushing again, and then I made all sorts of excuses, and left the house with a glowing face.

I was up at six the next morning and went to work even though I had the weekends off. It was an interesting day, but it was especially long because I had no sandwiches for lunch just a Mars Bar. When it was time to go home, I was ready because I was really tired. I didn't have long to wait for the bus, a big old green double decker that would take me to Woburn Green.

I climbed the steep stairs on the bus and sat down with a big pork pie and munched into it, that was my supper. It was always handy to have a snack before facing Flo's cooking. Eventually the conductor shouted. "Woburn Green" I had just got comfortable and I reluctantly got off the bus.

Then I had a five minute walk up hill in the rain and chilly weather, but that night the bus ride seemed to take an extra long time. It was very cold, and a fine soaking rain that was making the walk from the bus miserable, I was looking forward to a nice cup of tea.

When I finally reached my father's house, it was all in darkness. I went to the back door as usual and was surprised that it was so dark and not a glimmer of light from the house anywhere. As I got nearer to the house I suddenly saw my suitcase was standing on the door step. I stood motionless, wondering what on earth was going on.

I knocked on the door, but couldn't hear a sound, so I knocked even harder and shouted to Flo to unlock the door. Nobody came, but I knew that my father and Flo were inside. I was getting wet, so I started pounding on the door, yelling, "Why are you doing this to me? What have I done?" I sat on an up turned bucket near the door and hung my head down wondering what to do now.

As I lit a cigarette, which was a waste of time because the rain soon put it out. It was when I struck my match that I noticed a paper note on my suitcase; it was a crumpled piece of paper that simply read in big letters.

DON'T WANT YOU HERE ANY MORE

So I crumpled it up and stuck it in my pocket, got to my feet, looked at my watch for I knew I could catch the next bus back to High Wycombe. I grabbed my battered suitcase and set off for the bus shelter.

As I was leaving, a curtain at the house next door lifted slightly and I could see the neighbor peeking out. She was a bit of a nosey one, and maybe I should have asked her what was going on. I paused for a moment, and then heard a noise inside my father's house. As I turned to look at the back door, I saw the curtain drop. I was just about to go give another knock on the door, but it finally dawned on me that I was not wanted. So I slowly walked away and never looked back.

I caught the last bus back to High Wycombe and went up the stairs and sat down, wondering what I was going to do, and where I was going to live, and why my father threw me out of his house when it was he who wanted me to come home. I must have looked a sight, sitting there with a blank expression on my face, soaking wet and feeling downright miserable, I just wanted to be where people weren't.

When I got off the bus, I walked around to see if there was somewhere to stay, but because it was late and I was shy in asking for help, I decided to go to the signal box and see if I could sleep in the big armchair. At least I would be warm there.

At the railway station, the public had to cross the tracks on a large bridge that spanned all the lines, but staff could cross directly over the lines. But not recommended especially at night time. It was difficult enough during the day, let alone at night. Although the lines were lit at night, with a fine rain the tracks got very slippery, and of course, you always had to be alert for oncoming trains. So there I was, feeling cold and wet and downright miserable – right down in the dumps. Not paying attention to anything, I wandered aimlessly across the tracks like I had done many times, I kept thinking about what my brother Jim had said about my father, and then it happened.

I jumped from one track to another, but slipped and fell very hard right across the tracks. I felt pain in my chest, both arms, both knees and my shinbone. My suitcase was lying wide open between the tracks, getting wet.

I just lay there, wanting to scream. I didn't care what was going on around me, even though I could hear all sorts of noises. I began to feel vibrations coming from the track that I was on, and I realized the vibrations were getting stronger and stronger, and that the noises were getting louder and louder. Then I thought I heard Percy's voice in the midst of it all, and saw a light flashing towards me from the signal box

The track was moving up and down more rapidly. Percy was shouting at me and flashed his torch which caught my eye, and with all the noise I could hear shouting from lots of people trying to get me off the line. Then I heard a couple of very scary words: EXPRESS TRAIN!

I quickly got to my feet and pulled myself together as fast as I could. I hobbled off the line while Percy stood shouting from the steps of the signal box.

Within seconds of getting off the tracks, an express train roared past me with a deafening sound, which caused me to lose my breath.

It took all of my strength to lean forward because the air was pulling me toward the train. I fell backward onto another track and hurt my bum once it had passed.

Percy was still yelling at me, so I panicked and looked in all directions to see if any more trains were coming. Grabbing my suitcase, I quickly made my way over to the signal box. It was such a relief to hear a familiar, friendly voice, although he was still shouting and swearing at me.

Climbing up the steep steps to the signal box was very difficult, although I was fit. It was as if all the energy had been drained from my body, and felt really depressed weak and hopeless. Percy put out his hand to help me and pulled me up the last two or three steps, and said,

"You could have been bloody killed out there!" he yelled. "What were you doing crossing the lines at night? I've been working here for years and you don't see me crossing the lines at night. And why on earth are you back here? You just left for home! Why are you back here?" All those questions.

Bells were ringing so Percy went back to his job but made time to put the kettle on. I took off my wet coat off and plunked myself into the large armchair we had up there, and started to feel the warmth from the stove.

When Percy got time he came and sat by me with a cup of tea and in a real fatherly tone asked me what on earth was going on? I simply produced the crumpled piece of paper from my jacket and handed it to Percy.

"This was on my suitcase at the back door to my Da...whoever he is...or was."

Percy looked at me and shook his head from side to side and stood up saying, "No true father would have done a terrible thing like that...it's exactly like I told you, you were old enough to bring money into the house...the bastard used you Les..." Then he apologized for swearing and pointed his finger at me and said. "You are the one who should be swearing...go on have a good old swear, get it off your chest."

I looked up at Percy, and said, "Yes...I ought to swear..." Percy waved his hands in the air and said, "Let it go Les, let all your anger come out at this bastard and you come out with all the foul language that you can think of…just scream it out…"

I took a large swig of tea and threw my head back and shouted, "BUGGAR…BUGGAR…BUGGAR."

Percy swung his head around at me and said while frowning, "Is that it?"

Well, I didn't know what to shout, but I did feel a little bit better and I promptly dropped off to sleep.

The next morning when I awoke it felt as if a train had hit me, what with all the scratches and bruises all over my body, I couldn't stop shivering. Suddenly a mug of hot tea was thrust into my hand. "Get that down you lad" Percy said. He was very good to me, and even wrapped a blanket around me whilst I was sleeping.

Ron arrived in to relieve Percy, and Percy took great delight in telling Ron the state of my affairs. While he talked, I pulled myself together and prepared for work, but before Percy left, he told me that I wouldn't be allowed to sleep up there again, as we would both end up in trouble. I kept wondering all day where I was going to sleep, then it was suggested that I sleep in the late train after it parks in the platform siding, and if you get in them quick enough, they will still be warm. I quickly thought about the time and that would work out, the last one comes along platform two at 11:20 pm. So that's what I did.

The worst part about it was the wait for a train that had finished for the day. And then the wait for it to drop off its carriages, so that one exhausted person had a warm place to sleep for the night. I would select a first class carriage and before long would be nice and comfortable with my large railway coat across me. It was working out well, I was having my meals in a nearby café and spent a lot more time helping and learning more about the signal box. But, alas, it had to happen.

After enjoying a really good night's sleep, I woke up to find the train was moving. My eyes shot out like chapel hat pegs, and panic set in, especially when I saw we had just passed my signal box, where I should have been right then.

I went straight to the toilet to freshen up and looked a right mess without a shave, so I decided the only thing to do is to get off at the next station and catch the next train back to High Wycombe. Now what could be simpler than that?

Of all the station to pick though, I got off at the one where I was virtually put under the lamp for interrogation. A stern little man was demanding to know why I was traveling without a ticket. He could see I was wearing a railway uniform and I tried to explain that I was sleeping on the train and had no idea it was on the move.

"Did you get permission to sleep on the train?" he asked holding his head to one side.

"Well, erm...no..." I stuttered.

The little railway official straightened his head up and without hesitation said, "I'm going to have to make a report about this." And he led me into the stationmaster's office. He sat behind his desk and dialed a number, and hearing a muffled voice he said, "I would like to speak to Mr. Hogg please?"

No, I thought, do you have to tell him? The stationmaster started moving bits and pieces on his desk while waited. "You realize you'll be in big trouble now, don't you?"

He got back to the telephone and promptly said "All right, tell him to call me as soon as he gets back, thank you."

That was the end of that. He sat back in his chair folded his arms and started to lecture me on how long he'd been working on the railway and how he expected his staff to conduct themselves. "You should be ashamed to wear a railway uniform," he said staring at me.

"Excuse me sir, what did Mr. Hogg say?" I asked timidly.

"Mr. Hogg was not available, but his secretary told me as soon as he gets in his office he will call me." So we just sat there looking at each other. I watched him rearrange the papers on his desk, and then he picked up a pencil and gave it a quick examination and produced a small penknife from his pocket and proceeded to sharpen it to a fine point, making sure that all the bits went into his ashtray.

When he had finished that little operation, he stared at me and said. "You know, I can tell by a man's appearance and his manner what sort of a background and upbringing they have had. If you had come to me for a job, I would not have given you one, let alone a uniform."

He was about to comment further but the telephone rang. It was obvious it was Mr. Hogg, so he turned his head to one side and proceeded to explain the whole story once again, dwelling on all the little details exaggerating where he could. After a short pause he slowly turned towards me and his tone changed, and after awhile put the telephone down and stood up and said,

"Right Mr. Morris, Mr. Hogg has asked me to put you on the next train to High

Wycombe and you are to report to him when you arrive." As he stood up he asked me if I would like a cup of tea. I nearly fell off my chair.

"Yes please…and may I smoke?"

"Yes of course, have one of mine." Then he left the room. I couldn't think why he suddenly changed his tune towards me, but within minutes he was back with a mug of tea and again positioned himself behind hid desk.

After a short pause, he casually asked me. "So you were brought up in an orphanage?"

From then on I think he found it difficult make conversation as he kept fiddling with things on his desk. Perhaps Mr. Hogg had been a bit more sympathetic about the whole affair.

The stationmaster produced his pocket watch from his waistcoat pocket and asked if I had finished my tea. I hadn't quite, but quickly finished it and he rose to his feet and explained that my train was due very shortly. He actually escorted me to the platform and even opened the carriage door for me when the train arrived. He sort of wished me good luck and I was gone.

Well I needn't have worried at all; Mr. Hogg even apologized for the stationmaster's dramatic behavior. He asked me about my accommodation situation and told me he would make inquiries but couldn't promise anything. He went on to tell me about how dangerous it was crossing the railway lines at night, and in future I should use the stairways.

I spent another week sleeping in the carriages…first class of course…until one of the railway chaps told me of a place that does bed & board right near the railway station. "I bet if you went around there now, they would take you in." He slipped me the address. "Tell them Mr. Hogg sent you." Although I was tired, I purchased a bag of fish & chips, sat down and ate the lot in a few minutes. After a wash and clean up at the station, I went over to check out the B & B.

Chapter Thirty-Five

Finding New Digs

I was exhausted when I arrived at the house. I gave a sharp knock on the door. Lights went on and I could just hear someone say, "I wonder who that is at this time of night?"

The door opened and a stern-looking woman looked me up and down.

"Yes, young man?" she said curtly.

Somehow I managed to say, "I understand you do accommodations."

"You're a bit late in the day for that aren't you?" she snapped, looking me over again. "But I see you're a railway chap then?"

"Yes," I said.

"Well, come in, and mind the paintwork with that suitcase."

At last, I was in the warm.

"Put your things down there and come into this room so we can have a look at you." She held the door open for me, so I thanked her and used all my best manners before explaining why I was looking for a place at that time of night.

Although she was very sympathetic, she stated right off that it wasn't her policy to take guests late at night, but because she knew Mr. Hogg wouldn't send anyone he didn't trust, I was all right. Then she put her hand out for the rent. "That will be five pounds, please." She briefly went through the house rules, and then said, "I'll show you to your room."

I looked across at a gentleman sitting by the fire, who hadn't said one word the whole time, but did manage a, "Good night."

I now had a lovely little room where I was able to sleep on my own, and so got a very good night's sleep. In the morning, I had a cooked breakfast and was handed a pack of sandwiches for work.

On the way to work it suddenly hit me that my father had actually thrown me out of the house. Why? Shouldn't I go over and have it out with him? I was so deep in thought that when I got to work, it was nice to hear the men I worked with every day say "Good morning," and comment about my uniform. Then the stationmaster spotted me.

"Ah, Mr. Morris, just the man. Will you come to my office please?"

I swallowed hard, glanced at the clock, and saw that at least I wasn't late. "What does he want me for?" I wondered. He followed me to his office.

"Come in, lad, and take a seat," he said in his usual friendly tone. He sat down behind his desk, clasped his hands together, and said, "It's been brought to my attention that you are putting in far more hours at work than you should be. Now most people here go home on the stroke of knocking-off time, but you are here all day and night. Is everything all right at home?"

I could sense he wasn't angry, so I told him about being unhappy at home and my father throwing me out, and that I liked my job and wanted to learn as much as I could. He then told me I needed to get away from the job rather than get too much of it. That didn't make sense at the time, but it does now. He knew all about my orphanage days, so I think he was sympathetic. He told me if I needed help in any way, I was to see him.

I still continued to stay at work late and work weekends, for I had nothing else to do and nowhere else to go. Janet was courting now, and judging from my last visit, I'm sure her mother would have raped me if I had gone there alone one more time. I was confined to my room at the new place, and that was very depressing. As for my father, he kept popping up in my mind, but I didn't care if I ever saw him again. He treated me like a stranger, so I dismissed him from my mind.

Chapter Thirty-Six

Christmas, Again

Eventually Christmas came around again. It was 1957, and the memories of that day still haunt me, bringing back a bittersweet tumult of emotions.

I finished work on Christmas Eve, and said my goodnights and "Happy Christmas" to Percy.

"Have a great Christmas," one of the workers said when I reached the platform.

"I reckon we shall have some snow this year," said a porter, but someone else commented,

"It's too bloody cold for snow. What do you think Les?" Although I knew the chap, I couldn't for the life of me remember his name, but I gave him a big smile and replied as I walked past,

"I don't mind what it does as long as I get to my digs first."

On the top deck of the bus, I settled in for the ride home. I had my big railway coat on, but I was still cold and couldn't stop shivering. I ate my supper, a large pork pie, on the bus. The pie was so cold I thought it was frozen, but apparently not.

As I approached the house, it suddenly struck me that the next day was Christmas Day. I wondered what on earth I should do. Then I decided that a nice long lay in bed would be a nice Christmas present to me. I forced a little smile at the thought.

It was almost 8 o'clock when I got to the front door. I was just about to open it when the landlady appeared and opened it for me.

"Oh, hello," I said with a sort of smile.

She gave me a stare and snapped, "Tomorrow is Christmas Day." As I was taking off my coat, I couldn't help thinking that she was going to somehow cancel my Christmas. As I hung my coat up in the hallway, she continued. "So tomorrow you will have to vacate your room, because I will need it."

I looked at her with a frown and said, "But..."

She interrupted me as she looked down and wiped her hands on her apron. "Because it's Christmas Day, we will be having the whole family over here, and as you are not family," she stopped when I turned to go to my room, then continued in a sheepish voice, "I will need your room for all the coats. And it's not my fault you have no family. But my family comes first."

I started up the stairs to go to bed.

"Now your breakfast will be on the table at 6:30, and I want you out of the house by seven o'clock."

"All right, I'll be..."

"I'll wrap you up some sandwiches, as everything will be closed and I don't want to see you go hungry. Er, uh, that is all, Mr. Morris." I just continued up to my room and threw myself on the bed and thought "How on earth did I know she was going to cancel my Christmas?" I was so tired and miserable that I fell asleep where I landed, with all my clothes on including my shoes.

The next thing I remember was being shaken as the landlady shouted, "Get up, get up, Mr. Morris, you're late!"

I stared at her and wondered what she was doing in my room. Then I remembered that she wanted me out of the house.

"Your breakfast has been on the table for over ten minutes."

Fortunately, I was already dressed, but my mouth tasted like the bottom of a parrot cage, so with a quick wash and scrubbing of teeth, I flew down the stairs. When I walked into the kitchen, she pointed to my breakfast and said, "There's your cold breakfast. It was nice and hot at the correct time." She pointed to the clock.

I sat down and looked at the thin film of white fat that had formed on the egg and the bacon. The fried bread was black. It too, had a white coating of fat on it, making it look like a sacrifice. I took a sip of tea, and found it was cold. I was picking at the food when she came in with some toast and stuck it in front of me. I looked at her and said I was sorry I was late, but she made no comment and went back to the kitchen. I tried to drink some more tea, but it was foul. She never could make a good cup of tea.

When the landlady came back, she slid a small package across the table and announced that she went to a lot of trouble for me, what with all her relatives coming and all the cooking and preparing of gifts. Then she said, without making eye contact, "I have made you some nice sandwiches, and as a treat, I have put in a small piece of home made Christmas fruitcake." I looked at her and thanked her, then lifted up my cup in hopes I could get a warm cup of tea.

"No more tea. You were supposed to be out of here by seven o'clock and look at the time. It's 7:20." She pointed again to the clock on the wall. "Now I have to prepare for my family, so if you don't mind," she leaned over the table and pointed to the door.

In a flash, she was standing by the front door holding my coat.

"It's a big day today for people with families. I can't help it if you don't have anywhere to go or..." she stopped when I frowned at her, and then started up again. "Now I don't want you back here before 10 p.m., and come around the back door. Do you have your sandwiches?"

"Yes," I replied, as I did up the buttons on my coat. Then she opened the door and the icy air came rushing in. I stepped outside and within seconds the door slammed behind me.

I stood on the step for a moment, pulling up the collar of my coat and putting on my gloves. It was Christmas Day. Where could I go? Everything was closed and there was no public transport. I was mulling it over when the front door opened.

"Well," snapped the landlady. "Have you forgotten something or are you going to stand on my doorstep all day?" I turned toward her but the door slammed shut again, and I could hear her muttering down the hall.

It was a bitter cold morning, the sort one sees on Christmas cards. Everything was white with the heavy frost we had gotten over the night. I started walking and noticed I was heading for the green. There was a bus shelter there where at least I could put my feet up and maybe huddle in a corner and get some rest.

As soon as I sat down, people walking by with their dogs kept stopping to explain that I wouldn't get a bus that day. One old man told me, "If you're waiting for a bus, then you've got a hell of a long wait." It wasn't long before some young chaps, who were making snowballs out of the thick frost on the green, decided to use me for target practice. After I gave them a mouthful, I decided to move on, as there wasn't going to be any peace there.

I walked slowly across the green and found myself heading for the country. I had no idea where I was going, but I had plenty of time to kill, so I just kept walking and walking and thinking, about some of the Christmases I had enjoyed and about some of the presents I had gotten, and it suddenly occurred to me that I didn't have one present that Christmas Day, or even a Christmas card. I looked at the package that the landlady had given me and thought, "Well, I suppose I can count this as a present."

I had walked several miles and had started to climb a hill that bent to the right when I heard a strange noise coming from up ahead. I tried to identify the sound and picked up my pace, and was startled to suddenly come upon a stampede of sheep, followed by a farmer.

As soon as he spotted me, the farmer shouted, "Can you stop those sheep for me lad?" So I threw my arms up in the air and started waving them around like I was trying to fly. The sheep took one look at me and stopped in their tracks.

The farmer pushed his way through them toward me and shouted, "Will you guide them back up the hill? I have to go see what my dogs are doing because some of the sheep went the other way."

"Certainly, I'll help you," I said stuffing my sandwiches in my pocket. I walked at a good pace, waving my arms and shouting all sorts of things at the sheep like I knew what I was doing, and the sheep seemed to do what I wanted them to do. Every so often odd ones wanted to wander up the grass bank, but I would shout at them and they soon got back in line.

When we reached the top of the hill, I could see what had happened. A car had skidded at the crest of the hill and went straight through the farmer's fence, allowing the sheep to escape. I herded them toward the hole and the sheep all wandered back into the field. The farmer and his dog were bringing up the stragglers, and they too slowly filtered back in.

Just inside the fence was a big blue tractor with a large trailer at the rear. After the last sheep was in, the sheep dog jumped up on the trailer, no doubt waiting for further instructions. The farmer came over to me and grabbed my hand and squeezed it tight saying, "I don't know how to thank you. If you hadn't been there, I don't know how I would have managed." Then he said, "Are you in a hurry? I have one more favor to ask you."

"No, er, no, I'm not in a hurry," I said cautiously.

"Are you sure lad? I don't want you to be late to wherever you're going on this special day."

I told him I had plenty of time, so he explained that he had to go back to the farm to pick up materials to repair the damaged fence. My job was to stand guard and make sure the sheep didn't escape again. I watched as the tractor and trailer went bouncing across the field, scattering sheep in all directions. Then it disappeared out of sight and all was quiet again. I spent my time wandering around the scene of the crime, looking at the evidence and trying to work out how the vehicle lost control at the top of the hill. Another few feet either way, and whoever it was would have struck a tree.

In no time I could hear the tractor returning. I watched the place where it had disappeared, and saw it pop up over the hill and head straight for me. I was starting to feel cold again after getting warmed up from the chase. The farmer jumped down from his tractor and immediately started unloading what he needed, throwing it all by the hole in the fence. He then got out a big wicker basket full of chicken and duck eggs, and with a big smile on his face said, "My wife and I want to give these to you for your kindness. You can take them to where you're going or do whatever with them." Then he grabbed my hand and started thanking me, ending with, "You have a very happy Christmas!"

I was stuck for words, but finally said, "I can give you a hand repairing your fence."

"Oh, it won't take me long to do this," he said, picking up fence posts. "You better get going or they will be blaming me for you being late."

But I insisted, so he explained what he was going to do.

We placed the new fence posts and then rolled out enough wire fencing to cover the area. The whole time he kept telling me how nice it was for me to stop and help him. While we were working, he finally asked me where I was going "before I ran into a bunch of sheep." So I told him what my landlady had done, and that she had given me some sandwiches and told me to stay out of the house until 10 p.m. because her family was coming over for the day.

When he heard that, the farmer threw down his hammer and shouted, "She WHAT? She threw you out of the house on Christmas Day?" He went into a rage, shouting words I couldn't understand. After a long pause, he apologized. "I'm sorry, that was my native tongue cursing that landlady of yours." Then he walked over to me with a big smile and put his hand on my shoulder and said. "It's all right, I'm not from a far-off distant land, I'm from Wales originally, and that was what you call the Welsh language. Every time I get upset or lose my temper it automatically pours out."

The farmer went to turn around but stopped and cocked his head to one side and said, "How would you like to spend Christmas day with us here on the farm?"

I stood with my mouth wide open. I suddenly felt warm and wanted inside.

"Look, we have plenty of food, and there's just my mother-in-law, my wife, and my daughter, who just turned 14." He smiled and raised his hands in the air and said, "Right. That's settled.

Let's get this hole fixed up and we can go in and have a nice hot drink."

With the two of us working on it, it didn't take long to finish the fence. After a final check and a good shaking of the whole structure to test it, he said, "That's fine. Now let's get out of here."

He threw the leftover bits onto the trailer. I climbed on the trailer with the dog and away we went. It was very bouncy ride, but it was fun. I'd never been on a farm trailer before, and come to think of it, I had never been to a farm before, so it was all new to me. It wasn't long before we got to the farmhouse, where we were greeted by his wife and an old chocolate Labrador, who came bounding up to me in slow motion.

The farmer introduced me to his wife. "This is Pat, and by the way, my name is Ted. I never thought to introduce myself because so much was going on." As I was shaking hands with Pat, Ted was trying to get into my pocket to get my sandwiches.

"Where are those sandwiches? I want to show them to Pat." With a little help, he tugged them out of my coat and thrust the now-crumpled brown bag under his wife's nose. She had no idea what was going on, and was probably wondering who on earth I was.

"What is it?" she asked.

Ted took great pleasure in unwrapping the sandwiches, and saying, "Look what that bitch of a landlady of his has wrapped up for this young lad's Christmas dinner. Just look at it."

We all stared at the meager offering.

"Corned-beef sandwiches. Just look at that. You think she would have at least wrapped up some turkey or chicken sandwiches, but not bloody corned beef."

As he was telling Pat all about my landlady, the farmer was breaking the sandwiches up, and throwing them to the chickens parading around. That brought back fond memories of Mrs. Woodley and her hens.

"Come inside," Pat said. "You must be quite cold out there." As I walked into the back of the big house, I could feel the warmth of the place and an aroma of home cooking that made my mouth water. I was introduced to the older lady who was waiting inside.

"This is my mother, Flo," Not another Flo I thought, but she was very pleasant. As I took off my coat, I was thinking of the other Flo at my father's house, and in a daze, wondered what I would have been doing if...

"Are you all right...? Oh, you know, I don't think I got your name! And here we've been working together for about an hour." Everyone was waiting for me to announce my name, so I threw off my daze, threw back my shoulders, and said,

"My name is Les Morris."

"Welcome to our home, Les," Ted said. "We want you to be one of our family today. And speaking of family..." He looked around the room. "Where is Diana?"

Pat, who was making her way to the kitchen, said, "Oh, she's upstairs getting smarted up because she heard we had a visitor."

"Let's get rid of that coat and fix ourselves a nice hot cup of something," Ted said, taking my coat to the hallway.

We were standing in a big dining and living area, very spacious, with low black beams stretching across the expanse. The windows were quarter-light leaded triangles. I had never seen such a big fireplace – it was large enough to hold whole tree branches, and made a comforting roaring fire. There were two huge easy chairs and a big sofa that was currently occupied by one of the dogs.

It wasn't long before Pat came in with two large mugs of hot tea, which looked like they were made with real tea and were very welcome. I was just beginning to feel warm again after my Christmas walk through the English countryside, and as we sat down at the big bleached wooden table, who should walk in but the daughter.

Ted got to his feet, and said, "Ah, there you are. We have an unexpected guest here today, and his name is Les. Les, this is our daughter, Diana."

Diana walked straight over to me and thrust out her hand. I shot mine out to meet hers and she squeezed it hard, saying, "Hello, Les, pleased to meet you."

Diana was beautiful. She was wearing a red polo-neck sweater that went well with her lovely long black hair, and she carried herself well. I didn't want to let go of her hand.

"Now that you've met the whole family, let me quickly show you around." He pointed in the direction of the front hall, and I walked ahead of him. But as I left the room, I turned my head around for another quick look at Diana. As soon as our eyes met, she gave me a lovely smile, so I gave her one back.

We were now standing in a huge entranceway that had a tremendous front door of solid oak. A majestic staircase led to a landing, which was where we went next. As we climbed, Ted explained a little about the place.

"This farmhouse was originally built during the 12th century. It's been in my family since the mid-18th century, when my great-, great-, oh, I can never remember how many greats there were, but Pat and I came here in 1939. We were the ones to introduce sheep here."

We stopped outside a bedroom door. Ted leaned over to me and said, "You will like this room."

My eyes opened wide when I saw the room's main feature, a heavily carved four-poster bed with a red-velvet canopy and draft curtains. The whole room was paneled in oak, and had six leaded windows. The floor was covered by a deep oriental carpet. Ted saw me gaping and said, "Well, what do you think of our grand bedroom? The bed is Tudor, I am told." That didn't mean anything to me at the time, but later in life when I studied the kings and queens of England as a tour director and public speaker, I understood how rare and valuable that bed had to be.

"There are five bedrooms here, but one is converted into an office," he said as we headed downstairs. Pat overheard his comment and said,

"What he really means is that bedroom is full of junk!" And they both laughed.

"Will you two be long? We're just about ready to serve lunch."

"We'll just be a minute. Come on, Les; let me show you the lounge."

The lounge was breathtaking. It had another roaring fire, with a great big Christmas tree tucked in the corner. Just above the fireplace, the Welsh flag was displayed with pride.

"Okay," said Ted, "We had better get ready for our meal before the ladies get on to us." And into the large kitchen we went to wash our hands and carry food into the dining area. And what a spread was laid out on the table! I don't think I'd ever seen so much food for one family. Ted carved the roast turkey and we all passed our plates around. There were roast potatoes, mashed potatoes, Brussels sprouts, stuffing, turnips, and nice thick gravy.

"Well," Ted said, "this is better than your corned-beef sandwiches. Eat as much as you like; you're very welcome on this festive day."

Pat spoke next. "I still haven't heard how you two met."

Ted took great pleasure in explaining how the sheep happened to escape and run into me, and if I didn't happen to be wandering the back roads of the shire, goodness knows where the sheep would be now. He and his wife both thanked me again.

After politely wiping her mouth with her Christmas napkin, Diana asked, "Um, what do you do for a living, apart from saving sheep?" She finished the question with a lovely smile.

"I work for the Great Western Railway at the High Wycombe railway station."

Ted's eyes lit up at that. He put his knife and fork down and said, "You work for the railway?"

I nodded.

"Oh, you will have a friend for life if you work for the railway," Pat said with a laugh.

Everyone was staring at me and I started to blush. I stopped eating and said, "Oh, I just work in the main signal box. It's nothing special. I'm known as a booking boy."

Ted said, "I have always been fascinated by the railways. I love to see those big old steam engines plodding along."

"If I can't find him, I know that he will be at a station or a crossing looking for the trains," Pat added.

So we had quiet a chat about my job and then I asked about the farm and Ted happily told me everything.

It wasn't long before lunch was over, and although I offered to help clear up, I was told, "No, you are our guest, and you follow me."

I thanked Pat and her mother for the wonderful meal, and they set about clearing dishes. Ted and I went into the lounge, where he told me to sit in the big chair while he poked the fire and tossed another tree trunk on.

When he settled down in the chair opposite, he noticed me looking at the Welsh flag.

"Ah," he said. "Do you know the history of the Welsh flag?" I told him I didn't.

"Well, most people have no idea why we have a dragon on our flag, or that it goes way back to King Henry Vll." He leaned toward me. "He was King Henry the VIII's dad, and because he was born in Wales – at Pembroke Castle, in fact – he was a great believer in King Arthur, and that other famous king who was born in Wales, Uther Pendragon."

Ted suddenly stopped and looked me. "Do you know anything about King Arthur? You're looking at me like you have no idea what I'm talking about."

I shook my head and said, "I'm sorry, I don't have any idea. History wasn't my favorite subject, and I thought King Arthur was just a fairy tale."

"Oh no, Les. He was real. In a nutshell, the dragon got on our flag because of the Welsh king, Uther Pen*dragon*." He emphasized the word *dragon*, but that was the end of that. Today as an expert on the subject, I can talk for ages about King Arthur and King Uther.

Pat, Flo, and Diana joined us, and I felt very comfortable, what with the tremendous company and such wonderful surroundings. We all sat and talked about just about everything except the railway, because Pat said once Ted got on the subject there was no stopping him, and after all, it was a family day.

Since I didn't want to overstay my welcome because, and as Pat had said, it really was a family day, and I decided this wonderful family needed to finish it without a stranger in their house. So I stood up and announced, "I would like to leave now, so you good people can be a family again."

Ted suggested that I stay because I couldn't get into my room until 10 o'clock and it was only 8:45. Everybody agreed, but I raised my hand and said, "Thank you kindly, but I feel I should leave. It's dark, and I have to find my way home, because I, er, don't know where I am."

They all tried to convince me to stay, but I thanked them with all my heart and told them, "This has been the best Christmas of my life, and I will never forget your friendship." I got my railway coat and all the family gathered around me and wished me well. Ted announced that he would run me home, which made me feel special.

As I went to the back door, I could hear Pat and Diana whispering to each other. Then Diana asked, "How many presents did you get for Christmas, Les?" It sounded lovely when she said my name.

"Oh, well, I didn't get any presents."

"What about a Christmas card? How many of those..."

I interrupted her by saying, "No, I don't usually get cards or presents. I don't really know anyone who would send me one."

There was more whispering between Pat and Diana, then Pat disappeared and returned with a Christmas present all wrapped up and Diana gave it to me. My eyes lit up and I said "This is for me?" just as Ted pulled up with his Land Rover.

"Open it when you get to your little room at the top," Diana said.

I walked out to the car and thanked everyone as I got in. Then Pat raced up and snatched the label off the present.

"This was for Ted," she explained, turning to see if anyone was listening. "It's a present from Flo. Every year she gives him the same thing, a new pair of slippers, and he never wears them, so he has boxes of them upstairs. So please take this as a present from all of us, all right?" I thanked her again, and she gave me a hug. "We didn't like the idea of you not having a gift at Christmas, of all days. And good luck to you in the New Year."

As we pulled away, the three women waved and shouted, "Happy Christmas, and a wonderful new year!"

"I can't believe I have a present on Christmas Day," I said as we started down the driveway.

"Well," said Ted, "You're very welcome to those slippers. They're expensive ones – she buys the same bloody thing for me each year."

He paused to ask if I would get the gate. It wasn't far from the repair job we did that morning, and Ted commented, "Well, the fence is still standing, thanks to you."

I tried to say I didn't do much, but he wouldn't listen and kept thanking me, and before long we were approaching my road. Ted said he was interested in seeing the house I lived in because he would, "pay that woman a visit and give her a piece of my mind." I tried to say something, but Ted continued. "No, no. I'm going to find out what sort of woman would throw some young man into the streets on Christmas Day. I mean, of all days."

I told him which house it was and he pulled up outside. There were lots of cars outside and people inside and Ted looked around with his lips pursed, making a sort of humming noise.

"All right, I will remember this place, and after Christmas I will pay her a visit."

I got out of the Land Rover, proudly carrying my present, and thanked Ted several more times, then told him that he could come and see me in the signal box and I'd show him what goes on there. Ted raised his hand and said,

"Yes Les, I'd love that..."

All of a sudden, the front door opened. My landlady was seeing some guests out of the house. She had a smile on her face until she saw me heading up the walk, then frowned and looked hard at her watch. I could hear her mumble to her guest, "Oh, it's only the lodger, and he's early."

In a loud voice I shouted, "Thank you Ted, and good night!" and off he drove. I was waiting for the visitors to pass before going in when the landlady, in her usual commanding voice, said, "You're early young man. Go around the back and wait for me."

So I walked around the back of the house and within seconds she was there.

"I thought I told you not to be back until 10 o'clock. It's," she looked at her watch; "it's only 9:15."

"I haven't got a watch, and it's very cold out here."

She relented and opened the door wider. When I was inside, she said, "Well, who was that who brought you home? Didn't he have a watch?"

"I don't know," I said and started to take off my coat.

"Keep it on," she snapped, then went to see if any of the guests were visible. "Quickly, run upstairs before you're spotted, and don't let me see you until the morning."

And run I did. She was still saying something to me as I was going up the stairs, but all I wanted to do was open my present. Before I even took off my coat, I sat on the bed, ripped off the fancy wrapping paper, opened the box and pushed the lid off. I let out an involuntary, "Wow!" which I'm sure the remaining guests and half the town heard.

Inside the box were indeed slippers, but not just slippers – leather ones with a fine plush lining. I took my coat off, then took off my right shoe, and tried one of the slippers on. It fit like a glove, so I put the other one on and walked around the bedroom a couple of times. After having spent a jolly good Christmas, I went to bed beaming. It was even better knowing that that night my feet would be warm, because I was wearing my brand new slippers in bed.

The next day – Boxing Day – I went happily to work, spent most of the day there again. After treating myself to some fish & chips, I got on my bus and headed to my digs.

Ted must have come around to the house while I was gone and given the landlady a piece of his mind, because the next morning I was told to leave at the end of December. I don't know what he said, but it must have upset her. She told me, in a roundabout way, that she wanted my room for somebody else.

Chapter Thirty-Seven

Back on the Line

After chatting with some of my coworkers, I found that I could get accommodations, if only a temporarily. Even that was a great relief, and when I told my landlady I would be leaving in a week, I'm sure I caught sight of a faint smile.

The room I moved into was in High Wycombe, close to my work. It was even smaller than the one I had left though. To make things worse, the room was filled with boxes and bits of spare furniture, which the landlords were reluctant to move out because, as they pointed out, my stay was only temporary until I found another place.

It was sparsely decorated, with only one small picture, a photograph actually, hanging on the wall at a pronounced angle. I went over to it and was about to straighten it, but had second thoughts because I wouldn't be looking at it long.

I used to lay and gaze at the picture; it was a lonely little thatched cottage with a beautiful garden, surrounded by huge trees. There was a little old lady standing on the front porch gazing out across a wheat field dotted with red poppies. She stood there wiping her hands on her piney. I would lie on my bed ignoring the clutter around me, and look at the picture, wondering what she was looking at. What was she seeing that I couldn't see? I took that picture off the wall and looked at it for hours, just wondering.

Then one night while looking at it, I noticed the left part of the picture was curled back. Straightening it out, I could make out a dark shadow in the shape of the head of a horse. I hung the picture up on the wall at that same angle again.

Finding another place proved more difficult than I had imagined. For the next two weeks I hunted all around, but couldn't find any other accommodation. One morning, halfway through the third week, my new landlady told me I had to go, and her *husband started giving me looks that had a hint of violence in them. I told them I would* go on Saturday morning, whether I had new digs or not. It gave me two days to find a place. They agreed.

That very night, when I came home after work, it was the old familiar story: My suitcase was on the doorstep, and knocking on the door was a waste of time, as they both completely ignored it.

Once again, I was tired and hungry with nowhere to go. I picked up my case and headed for the railway. By now it was chucking down with rain and it didn't take long for me to get soaked. That didn't worry me, but where I was going to sleep did, and the only place I could think of was the railway carriages, first class of course.

As I crossed the platform, Don, a porter I knew said jokingly, "Are you off on holiday then, Les?" I kept on walking, but looked back, and said,

"I wish." It was then that I had an idea; I called back to Don, the railway porter, "Don, can I leave my bag in the porter's cabin, until later?"

"Hey Les, are you back to the railway carriages again?" Don said in a sympathetic tone, and then he looked at the big railway clock, and said, "Bloody hell, it's only 7:45. Your train doesn't come in till 11:30-ish."

"I know, I'm going to get something to eat and that will kill a bit of time." Don reached out his hand to take my worldly goods, and said, "Yeah, give it here, I'm going that way." And I thanked him. "I'll stick your name on it. It'll be all right."

At the café, I ate a plate of steak & kidney pie, with chips, peas and nice hot rich gravy. Then had large slice of apple pie, with thick custard for my pudding, and to top it all off, I had a nice cup of tea.

Now all I wanted to do was sleep. My waitress kept asking me if I needed anything else, but I just kept shaking my head, and ordering more tea. Then the owner, who was a big chap, gave me one of those looks and towered above me with his arms folded. I think he wanted me to clear out.

Dropping the money for the meal on the table, I simply got up and walked out without saying a word. "Now, what do I do?" I thought to myself. I didn't want to go back to the railway station, so, I walked along a street away from the station and saw a place that I could rest and get dry. The light in the big old red telephone box attracted my attention and within minutes I was inside. "This will keep me dry for a while," I thought.

Unscrewing the light bulb was impossible, unless you were seven feet tall. So, with my big railway overcoat I crouched down on the floor and got nice and comfortable. Although there were a couple of spiders swinging around on their ropes, I left them alone, and they did the same for me, and eventually was feeling quiet snug.

I had just dozed off when I heard a rat-a-tat on the glass of my phone box. I looked up and saw and old lady waving her brightly painted, carved duck handled umbrella on the glass, and shouting something that I couldn't hear. So I arose to my feet and pushed the door open and asked her if she wanted to use the telephone.

"No, I don't want to use the telephone, but if I did I shouldn't have to wake somebody up to do so." I went to answer but she continued. "This is a public telephone box, not a place for sleeping or any other cavorting activities that I very often see going on in here…if it was an emergency what is one to do…?"

I stepped outside and told her it was all hers, but she just walked off muttering to herself. I shook my head in disbelief, and back in the telephone box I went, to try and get comfortable again. Would you believe, I just got into a good position, when the same rat-a-tat came upon my telephone box. I glanced up and immediately got to my feet because the same little old lady was standing there, but that time she had a policeman beside her.

She pointed to me with that daft duck handled umbrella, and said, "That's him officer, he keeps sleeping in our telephone box, and when I approached him about it, he shouted at me using such foul language, and I certainly don't deserve that."

"Would you step outside please, sir." The policeman asked. As I was stepping out the old lady was waving her hand carved duck handled walking stick at me, saying,

"I bet he won't swear at me while you're here, police officer."

"All right, aright, madam, you can leave now." And the old lady hinted that she wanted to stay, but the policeman pointed to her, asking her to leave, and saying that he would handle it from there.

Once again she went off muttering to herself, and the policeman turned to me and asked, "Can you give me a good reason why you were resting in this telephone box?" He then noticed my railway uniform. "Do you work at the local station?"

I told him, "Yes, and I did not swear at that old lady, I only asked if she wanted to use the telephone...that's all."

"Oh I believe you, she's nothing but a nuisance that old lady, she's always looking for trouble and she happened to come across you."

"The reason I was in here is that I have no bed to go to, so I have to wait until 11:30-ish for my train to come in and be parked in the siding platform so I can get to sleep."

With a frown on his face, the policeman said, "You're waiting for your bed to arrive on platform one?"

"Yes, and if I can just make until 11:30, the carriage will still be warm, and I snuggle down in a first class carriage."

"First class, but of course," said the policeman.

While we had a cup of hot tea in a small café that he knew, I told him my saga of being thrown out of three houses in a month's time. After hearing the whole story, including rounding up sheep in the country on Christmas day, he said, "You seem like a decent chap, and very polite, and with the story you've told me most young lads would have acted in a different manner. He suddenly looked at his watch and said. "Hey we better get back to the station your train should be arriving."

The policeman walked with me to the High Wycombe railway station and low and behold the train was just backing in and who should be there? Yes Don, who was seeing my carriage back. He saw me with a policeman and said he could vouch for me. He blasted his whistle, and my hotel carriage was there at last. Don said, "Would you like me to bring your case to you?"

"No thanks Don, I'll pick it up tomorrow."

"Why the police escort Les? Have you been in trouble?"

The policeman said, "No, I just came to make sure that he gets a nice clean first class, comfortable carriage."

Don looked at the policeman, and asked, "Is that you Dick?" And the next thing we all shook hands and into my hand-picked first class carriage I went, while Don and the policeman walked off chatting together. I never even took my shoes off before I went straight to bed in my nice, warm carriage.

The next morning I awoke, but was starving, so I went to the café and had a large breakfast. I was allowed to spend another week in the railway compartment – first class of course – until I was once again summoned to see Mr. Hogg.

The stationmaster, having seen my expression, smiled and told me not to look so worried. After giving me a little talk about how well I had been doing at work, he produced a telegram, from which he read aloud. It was from the Society. "A Colonel Bernie is concerned about you, and I quote what he has written: "Report to Hunstanton, where accommodations and clothes will be provided to you, for a fresh start."

Mr. Hogg rose from his seat and said, "Well lad, it looks to me as if you are to get a fresh start. I wish you well." He stretched his hand out toward mine. "I have a ticket for you, and you may leave whenever you are ready." Well, I was very relieved that I would finally have a place to live. I loved the railway, but with no accommodations to be had in the area, I looked at the move as a blessing, but was totally bewildered at the sudden and frequent changes of circumstances in my life. I spent that night in my first class carriage, but before I settled down for the night, I had to find something out.

I went the few blocks to the house that left my suitcase on the doorstep, and knocked on the front door; the landlady recognized me and said, "What did you want? It was my husband who insisted on putting your case…"

I put my hand up to stop her and asked her a question, "That picture hanging at an angle in my room, can you tell me anything about it?" The lady looked surprised and with a faint smile asked,

"Why do you want to know about the picture?" I explained how I used to look at it for hours, and wanted to know more about the lady wiping her hands and looking across wheat field. "Was it the horse she was looking for?"

"Wait here," she told me, and upstairs she ran to get the picture. "Well young man you have got a good eye, this is an old photograph of my mother. She used to wait outside the cottage door for my father who was reaping the wheat with a horse drawn combine machine, and when he saw me come outside, he knew that it was time for lunch."

"Wow." Was all I could come out with, she then said,

"Is that what you thought?"

I replied, "No, I had no idea, but I knew there was a horse there, so did the horse get lunch too?"

"Yes he would put a feed bag over his mouth and my Dad would bring his helper along and we would all have lunch together. Those were some of the fondest memories of my life." The lady squinted and said. "Did you find accommodation?"

"I've been sleeping in the railway carriages when they park up at night." She frowned and said it was her husband who gave the orders there.

"So what are you going to do?"

"Oh it's all right, Mr. Hogg got a telegram from the orphanage in Hunstanton, and they told me to return to the home in Norfolk…so I'm leaving tomorrow…but the picture was worrying me."

The landlady was crying, saying, "I can't believe my husband threw out an orphan."

"It's all right, this is the third time this month, I'm getting the hang of it," I said with a smile.

"Will you forgive me…"

"Of course I will."

She hugged me and asked if I would like to have the picture?" She gave it to me and said she had to leave me. I thanked her again.

The following morning, I got up early and said goodbye to my workmates, who all wished me well, then said goodbye to Mr. Hogg, who I found was responsible for contacting the Society. He gave me a reference to show that I left in good character and saw me onto the train. I wonder if he ran up the platform clicking his heels when the train was out of sight. No, of course he wouldn't...would he?

Chapter Thirty-Eight
Saved by the Society

That was the end of Buckinghamshire. I was back in Hunstanton, Norfolk, where not much had changed. Uncle gave me a room in the attic, where I was very comfortable.

Job-hunting was my main concern, and I ended up at a nursery in Heacham. No, not looking after children. Greenhouses and plants, you know. Uncle recommended me to the owner and he told me that it would be a good job. I used to ride my bike there and back. It was no problem going, but it was a long climb up the hill on the way back.

After having one or two piddling jobs to do, which at least gave me some variety, I found that my main job consisted of sorting out tray after tray of silly little plants, with one stem and two leaves, and transplanting them into another tray. There were thousands of the things. It wasn't but a couple of days, before the job became boring.

The women who worked with me in the large greenhouse used to pass the time with women's talk and generally sorting out everyone's problems in Heacham. As for me, I had no one to talk to, and quickly got fed up to the teeth. As soon as I had finished one tray of mustard and cress, another would be plunked down in front of me. When no one was looking, I used to grab a handful of the plants, rip them out, and throw them under the bench.

At lunch I would sit in the greenhouse all on my own, as everyone else went home for lunch, and eat my sandwiches and drink coffee from a flask. I often would sit and stare at the plants I was working on, muttering to myself about them. Then I would spring to my feet and snatch another handful from the tray and discard them like many a handful before. I was never so bored with work in my life. It was repetitive, the same thing day in and day out, the same faces, and same conversation and gossip from the women. I even fed the same mouse at lunchtime. However, that soon came to an end.

One day, when I rode my bike into the nursery I was stopped by the boss, Mr. Simmons. That was not normal, as I hardly ever saw him while I worked there. I had to stop a bit sharply as I was going rather fast, and I honestly thought he was going to tell me off about it. Or maybe he found the handfuls of those stupid little plants I had thrown under my bench? When the dust finally settled from my braking, he came up to me and said, "Master Morris." It used to annoy me when people used that phrase as if I was still a little Home Boy. "The rest of the staff is going with me to the Chelsea Flower Show in London, and I want you to keep an eye on things here. Now carry on with the work at hand and take messages if there are any phone calls."

Just then a coach (tour bus) arrived and all the staff, and many strangers, family I suspected, scrambled aboard. I stared at the coach, fiddling with my handlebar grips, and thought, "Why can't I go to London? Even just for the ride? I'm not interested in the stupid flowers."

"Are you listening to me?" my boss shouted.

"Oh. Yes sir," I said as I pulled my thoughts together.

"Now don't forget to keep your eye on the soil sterilizer. You must watch the temperature gauge," and with that, he walked toward the coach. I watched as the coach drove off. A couple of hands waved at me, but I was jealous I couldn't go, so I half-heartedly waved back and slowly made my way into work.

For a while, I stood looking at all the seed trays they had put out for me to sort; tray after tray of little green plants that were all in need of transplanting. I grabbed a whole tray, ripped out all the plants, then ran outside to some waste ground and threw them as far as I could.

"Now you lot can become self setters; you'll like that," I yelled.

When I got back to the greenhouse, I heard the phone ringing. I rushed over to a shed that had an extension, but the phone stopped. As I came out, a van pulled in to deliver some goods. After the man unloaded, he thrust an official-looking paper under my nose.

"Sign here please," he said, so I nervously scrawled my name on his paper. The look he gave me told me I had signed on the wrong line, but he simply muttered something and got back in his van. I didn't have time to think about it, as the phone started to ring again, so back in the shed I went. Then I hesitated. I was not used to using a phone. I finally picked it up and nervously said hello. A voice demanded to speak to the boss. "He's not here," I said. The voice got louder and demanded to know where the boss was and what time he would be back. As I was trying to tell him, he interrupted and asked if anyone else was there that he could talk to. When I told him I was on my own, he slammed the phone down.

I went back to the greenhouse and decided I would have an early lunch. I left bits of my sandwich on the floor for the mouse, but there was no sign of him. I looked at the remaining plants and thought I ought to make an effort, so I started doing some transplants. I managed to do three trays, and then got thoroughly fed up. I went outside for some fresh air and started fiddling with my bike. Before I knew it, I was on it, riding around the greenhouse, skidding around the corners, and occasionally knocking over plant pots, which I quickly stood up again.

There were several greenhouses spread over a large area, and as I hadn't explored the grounds before, I thought it was about time I did. I rode in and out of the greenhouses, killing time, and it wasn't long before I started racing around them, kicking up a trail of dust. I was going as fast as I could alongside a large greenhouse, when it happened.

There was a very large explosion, which rang in my ears, followed by the sound of a great pile of glass crashing down. I turned in the direction of the sound with my mouth wide open. "What the hell was that?" I thought, and then suddenly remembered the soil sterilizer. I found myself plowing through a small bush and on to some freshly dug ground because I wasn't looking where I was going. I didn't fall off, but decided to go back a different way. Then I found myself pedaling like mad toward the main gate.

It was sheer fear that gave me the energy to peddle the way I did. Before going through the gate, I glanced back toward the smoke and the hissing sound. Oh, what a sight. The greenhouse near the sterilizer had completely collapsed and there were bits of broken glass everywhere. I peddled straight out of the gate and didn't look back.

I had, as you might say, sacked myself from a job I hated. I knew I was wrong to leave the way I did but, well I bruised easily, and I knew I would be in serious trouble when the boss came back. I just kept pedaling as fast as I could to the orphanage. I don't even remember riding up that steep hill; normally, I had to get off my bike before reaching the top.

Uncle greeted me as I walked in the back door. Looking at his watch, he said, "You're early aren't you?"

"Well, yes. You see, Uncle, I ...er...sacked myself from the job." I waited for a reaction, but he must have thought it was one of my jokes, so he simply smiled and said, "Yes, but why have you come home early? Isn't there much going on down there?"

"A lot was going on a few minutes ago," I thought to myself, but said, "No, you see Uncle...." By this time we had walked through to the kitchen, where Auntie had flour all over her hands.

"My word you are nice and early. To what do we owe this honor?"

"That's what I'm trying to find out," Uncle said.

"Well it's like this: I sacked myself." Again I waited for a reaction.

All of a sudden, a large puff of flour rose from Auntie's mixing bowl as she turned to give me one of those matronly looks. "You mean you've walked out of your job?"

Uncle, who was topping up the Aga cooker, dropped the lid.

For the rest of the day and evening, I was a nervous wreck every time the phone rang or someone knocked on the door. I would tremble and wait for someone to call me. Late at night, when we were having supper around the kitchen table, guess what the subject was? Yes, the sacking of Master Morris by himself.

It was decided that I would get in touch with my boss in the morning, as it was coming on 11 o'clock. All of a sudden, a loud knock echoed through the house, which not only sent shivers through me, but also made me dribble cocoa down my shirt. Uncle and Auntie both went to the door and led Mr. Simmons into their study.

I just wanted to hide. The assistant matron told me to face them like a man, and the general assistant said she would hide in the boiler room – a thought that had crossed my mind. My hands became sweaty and I was literally shaking.

"Drink your cocoa," said the assistant matron. As I picked up the cup, I could hear someone coming through the dining room. The kitchen door opened and Auntie stood in the doorway.

"Come on," she said. "He's not very happy, but if you just tell him the truth – that's all you can do – and of course, apologize."

We seemed to arrive at the study in seconds. The door was open and I could hear the two men talking softly. Auntie stood aside so I could go in and gave me a smile. It felt like I was walking into a dentist's surgery.

"Er," I squeaked.

"Ah. Master Morris, I believe you have some explaining to do," Mr. Simmons said in a stern voice. "Do you realize how much it has cost me to leave you in charge of my nursery? Literally thousands and thousands of pounds and all you can say is "Er?" Well, that's not good enough. I want to see you in my office at nine o'clock sharp. By then, you may have a little more to say to me than "Er," because I certainly have more to say to you." He stood up and Uncle saw him out of the home.

Do you think I could sleep that night? I tossed and I turned, as I kept rehearsing what I was going to say, but before I knew it, I was standing in front of Mr. Simmons in his office at nine sharp. He was talking on the telephone to his insurance agent by the sound of it, so I just stood there, very nervous, fiddling with my cycle clips. He pointed to a chair and quickly said, "Sit."

I sat and watched him doodling on an old bit of blotting paper as he spoke, changing the phone from one hand to the other. I couldn't help noticing that he soon had a smile on his face. He was smiling, not at me, but at something that was being said on the phone. The fact that he was smiling at all sort of eased me a bit. After what seemed an eternity, he put the phone down and apologized for being so long.

"Well now, Master Morris," he said, as he walked around his desk and sat on the edge of it in front of me. "First of all, I want to apologize for losing my temper with you last night." I stopped twiddling with my clips and stared at him. "You see, having thought and slept on the matter, I realize I never gave you proper instructions. And it's been pointed out to me that you never have had any dealings with the soil sterilizer, have you?"

"No," I said quickly.

"And," he continued, "I also realized that a man with little experience shouldn't have been left in charge of the whole nursery. So," he paused and moved to the other side of the desk, "having had words with my insurance agent, who doesn't think there's going to be a problem replacing the damaged items, I think this whole affair can be forgotten." He ended with a smile, which made me feel much better. "Now what have you got to say about that, Master Morris?"

I simply stuttered, "Thank you, sir, and I am sorry for the trouble I have caused you."

"That's all right," he said, "and I want you to forget the whole incident. Now, as regards to your position here," he continued, fixing his eyes on me, "your job is still open if you want it."

I sprang to me feet and said in a determined voice, "No, thank you, sir, I think it would be best if I left."

"But you can carry on as before. I am not sacking you."

"But I don't want to stay."

"Look, go home now and think about it, have a word with Uncle, and if you want to start back, come in the morning as usual, but if not, ring me and let me know, okay?" Then he escorted me to the door, and as I left, pointed to my cycle clips. "I suggest you buy a new pair."

I looked down and saw that I had twisted one wide open.

So, I smiled and rode back to the orphanage, feeling relieved that I didn't have to go back to the nursery.

The next week, I rode my bicycle all the way to Kings Lynn, which was 16 miles away. The reason: I wanted to join the Royal Air Force. After the necessary interview and the verification from the home that I had informed them of my decision, they said I would hear from them soon, and that they would send me a railway warrant to take me northwest of Birmingham to RAF Cosford, the big Air Force base. Once I was there, I would have further interviews, and then they would decide in which department of the RAF they would like me.

Well, after telling Uncle and Auntie all about the interview, they were quite excited about the whole business, and so we waited for the RAF to make contact.

After only a week, I got a letter from the War Department, so I tore it open. Inside was a letter telling me to report to RAF Cosford, and enclosed was a roundtrip railway ticket from Hunstanton. There would be a shuttle lorry to take me from the station to the base. Everyone at the home very pleased with me for making the decision, and Uncle was giving all the advice he could dish up.

"Now remember," he said in a regimental way, "when you go for the interview, you only get one chance for a good first impression, so walk tall, throw your shoulders back, firm hand shake and show them how proud they would be to have you in the RAF." Pointing to my shoes, he said, "Make sure your shoes are nice and shiny, trousers pressed, and tie on straight. Look in the mirror before you get off the train to see that you are presentable."

I thanked him for his advice, and Auntie asked if I wanted another cup of tea.

With three days to kill before my interview, I had told just about everyone I saw during that time that I was going to join the RAF. I got all sorts of comments and advice, including some from George Raines, the chap who owned the green grocery. He told me that the most important thing to remember was to be honest and truthful. He then said, "You are making a wise choice young man, and I'm sure St. Christopher's will be proud of you."

He gave that big smile of his and put his hand on my shoulder and thrust out his other hand, and with a firm shake told me, "When you get your uniform, you come and see me. I want to be one of the first to salute you. Now don't you forget, come to see me, Master Morris."

The day for me to go, I was very excited. I stood, looking at the big steam railway engine, which was letting out all sorts of hisses. The driver of the engine gave me a smile and a wave and said, "Good morning." I shouted the same back, and told him I was going to join the RAF. Why I said that I do not know.

"Good luck to you son," he replied.

The whistle blew, so I quickly jumped on the train. I sat in a carriage that didn't have a corridor; just individual compartments. There was a gentleman reading a newspaper and a lady with her daughter. Nobody said a word, so I said "Good morning." The mother and the child acknowledged me, but the gentleman hid behind his newspaper. And off we went. The lady broke the silence and asked me where was I going.

I spoke clearly. "I'm going to RAF Cosford, because I am joining the RAF."

The gentleman briefly lowered his paper and gave me a little smile. Before we arrived at Kings Lynn, which was my first change, my carriage was almost full. I heard someone saying it was market day there.

I was waiting till the other passengers got off, when the gentleman tipped his hat to me and said, "Good luck with the RAF. I spent ten years of my life in the RAF myself. Goodbye."

It turned out to be a long journey. I had to change trains again at Birmingham Snow Hill. Then we finally pulled into RAF Cosford. The base was so big it had its own railway station. As I had been told, there was a lorry waiting. Five of us young lads were all there for the same reason, and we all seemed to be on the nervous side. I know I was. After we formally exchanged names, we all climbed into the back of the lorry.

When we arrived, we were greeted by a smart-looking sergeant who told us all to dismount and form a line. After all the formal greetings, we were led to a large building and brought into a room and told to take a seat. An officer was introduced to us, and after a brief talk about the RAF, he told us that we were going to take a brief test.

A TEST?

As soon as I heard those words, I went all funny inside and started sweating even though it was cold. The lad next to me asked if I was all right.

"Yes, yes, I just didn't know there would be a test. I hate tests."

"Well, you will have to get used to them if you join up."

The officer told us to stop talking. The sergeant came around with the test papers and pencils and put them in front of each person. I must have given him a pathetic look, because he said, "Are you all right lad?"

"Er, yes sir."

He pointed to his stripes and said, "Sergeant, if you don't mind."

The officer gave us our instructions. "There will be complete silence," he said, looking at me. "There will be no set time to complete the test, but as soon as you have completed it, please raise your hand. The sergeant will collect your papers. Any questions? No? You may start your test now."

All the time we were taking the test, the sergeant was walking around the tables, keeping an eye on us. I was in a complete dither. I looked through all the questions, and wrote the answer down for one or two, but my hands were all sweaty and for some unknown reason I could not concentrate. Whenever I take tests, I get very nervous and often cannot complete them. One by one, the other lads were raising their hands. The sergeant collected their test papers and handed them to the officer, who checked and marked them accordingly. Soon everyone else was finished and had gone into the next room for a cup of tea. As for me, I was still struggling. The sergeant came up to me and said, "I want to remind you that your train will be arriving very soon."

The officer asked if there was a problem. I looked up at him and in a panicked voice said, "Sir, I freeze up when taking tests."

He picked up my paperwork and after a quick look said, "Well, if you cannot complete this test, the RAF will not take you." Then he said in a lower voice, "Why don't you give the Army a try, they will take you."

That made me feel a little bit better, so I stood up and said, "I'm sorry I wasted your time sir. I will try the Army as suggested." He thrust out his hand and shook mine, saying "Good luck to you."

The sergeant escorted me in to join the others and the chap I sat next to earlier asked, "How did you do on the test?"

Before I could open my mouth, the sergeant said, "Oh, he did very well. Now we must get all of you to the railway station, as your trains will be here very soon."

I thanked the sergeant and shook his hand and he winked at me, saying quietly, "I know how you feel; I hate tests as well. Good luck," and into the lorry we jumped.

During the ride in the lorry, I was quizzed nonstop by the other chaps about how I had done on the test. I didn't tell them that I fouled up. One of the lads said, "I bet he did very well to have the officer chatting to him like that," and another said,

"And the sergeant was taking an interest in him." At the station, we split up and went to our different destinations.

It was a very long, depressing day for me. I didn't get home until late that evening. Uncle and Auntie had kept my food warm and were waiting to hear the results of the day. I slumped down onto a chair in the kitchen, where the greeting committee was anxiously awaiting the news. All they had to do was look at me to know something had gone wrong. Auntie very sympathetically asked me, "Did everything go all right? I mean, are you in the RAF?"

I gave a big sigh and said, "No. I didn't pass the test. And yet it was a simple test. I just couldn't pass it."

One of the lads, Peter, waved my plate of food in front of me and said. "Hey, get stuck in this, you look hungry." I looked up and thanked him, for I was really hungry, and it was one of my favorites – cottage pie.

Everything seemed to sort itself out though, and my main priority was still getting a job. I also had to find accommodations, as the orphanage was only a temporary solution. I heard that the cinema was looking for someone, and although I wasn't keen on the idea, Uncle made the necessary arrangements for an interview.

So there I was, back at the cinema as assistant projectionist. What a change there was. Mr. Large happily showed me the two new projectors, which looked very complicated to me. And what about those electric curtains! No more running down to the stage and pulling all sorts of ropes and things. So for a couple of days I was shown how to operate all the new-fangled equipment. It didn't take long, owing to my previous experience, and it was quite interesting.

I also got fixed up with accommodations quite quickly, all arranged by the home. They were just around the corner from the home. The landlady, Mrs. Davis, showed me to my room, which was about 18' x 18'; just enough room for a single bed and a chest of drawers and that was it. The wallpaper was that pre-war stuff, badly hung, with bumps in it. I had a window that looked out onto the back garden, but it was difficult to see out, what with the heavy white-netting curtain. But it was sort of home for awhile.

I'm sure Uncle and Auntie were glad to see the back of me for awhile, but I used to visit them during the day, as my work was at night. Everything was going well at the cinema, but something was wrong with me and I just didn't know what it was. Oh, I had a job, which was okay but more or less repetitious, and my digs were okay, but I felt really depressed when I was in the house. Like the others I had lived in, the only rooms I could use beside my own, were the bathroom and the kitchen at breakfast. I wanted something else in life, but didn't know what or where to look.

When I talked with Uncle and Auntie, they would simply ask, "What do you want to do?" Now that I knew I didn't have a good enough education to get a good job, I had no idea. The RAF rejection proved that. After three or four months of that, I got to the stage where I was absolutely sick of everything. It was early on a Sunday evening. We weren't allowed to show films on Sunday, so that was always my day off. I decided to go for a walk along the beach. The tide was well out, so I aimlessly walked out toward the water, my mind a complete jumble. I looked out at the sea and saw a large merchant ship heading for goodness knows where. I stopped walking and thought, "What about joining the Merchant Navy?" That way, not only could I travel to some great countries I had read about, but I could even go around the world. Then I started thinking about what would happen if I got seasick or didn't like it, and that I wasn't that good a swimmer, so what if the ship sank? That put paid to that idea. I was getting nowhere at all.

There were several people just strolling along the sand. I wondered if they had problems and were here trying to sort out their lives too. "No, they're all right," I decided. Some were running around laughing and joking and even the dogs looked happier than I was. I stopped in my tracks as looked all around.

"That's what it is," I thought, "all these people are with other people." Everyone was with someone, including the dogs. Everybody needs company. I scanned the beach as far as I could, and started talking to myself aloud.

"Do you know, Master Morris, you're the only person on this beach alone. Why is that? I don't know; I just don't." I stopped talking when I noticed a dog running toward me wagging his tail. When he reached me, I said, "Hello, little chap," and patted his head, but the owner whistled for him to return, and I was back on my own again. I made my way toward a shelter to sit and have a smoke. As I sat watching the people walking by, I started wondering what some of the other lads that had been in the homes were doing. I hadn't been there long when an old man with a stick came up, raised his hat, and said,

"Good afternoon. Do you mind if I join you?" and sat down. Although I was happy with my own company, I couldn't very well tell him to shove off, so I said,

"Yes, that's quite all right."

I had seen the old man several times around Hunstanton, and although I had never had a conversation with him, he would always raise his hat and say hello and I would say hello back. He made a comment about the weather, then turned to me and said, "You're one of the ex-Home Boys, aren't you?"

"Yes, I am," I said, thinking it had been a long time since I heard that phrase. It didn't upset me; I just wondered how long I would be branded with that label. He sat there for some time talking about the orphanage and the various masters that had run the place, and said that although he didn't know the present master, he understood he was a very good man for the job, to which I agreed. We ended up talking for a long time, mainly about me. He asked question after question, and I ended up telling him my life story, or very nearly. He genuinely seemed interested.

"Now what of the future?" he asked. "Where do you go from here?"

I looked at him hard and wondered how he knew that was why I was there. I just shrugged my shoulders and said, "I have no idea. That's why I'm walking along the beach today, searching my mind and trying to find answers."

He smiled, and said, "Well, the first thing you have to do is find out what you would like to do, and then establish if you can do it. For example, suppose you thought you might like to become a doctor. It's no good thinking about it if you haven't got the qualifications. So, the first job is to get those qualifications – without them, you're not going to become a doctor."

I sat gazing into space thinking about what he said. I knew darn well that my education level was nil, that I had no qualifications whatsoever. I had lost a hell of a lot of schooling during all that moving around, with different schools and teaching levels, and not being able to catch up what I had missed. That made me feel even more depressed.

After explaining to the old man about my education problems, he gave me that friendly smile of his and said, "A lot of people have made it in life with no education, and I know you can make it, but you have to help yourself, especially as you have no one to guide and advise you." He rose to his feet and adjusted his coat. Before he left, he said, "The finest thing for you, my lad, is to join the Army. Whatever you have in you, they'll bring it out. And they feed you and clothe you. You'll have a roof over your head, and they pay you and give you the chance of traveling the world."

When I heard that, I threw my shoulders back and said I would.

He raised his hat and bid me good day and then simply disappeared. I immediately stood up and looked around the shelter and even shouted, "Hey, old man, where are you?" I got some strange looks from people and asked a couple if they saw the old man leave. They shook their heads and said that said they had been standing and talking close by, but never saw an old man – just me talking to myself. I sat back down for a few minutes to go over what the old man had told me, and kept thinking about the Army bit. Then I shot to my feet and went straight to the orphanage and asked Uncle and Auntie what they thought about me joining the Army.

"I think it would do you good," said Uncle. "The one thing about the forces is you get a roof over your head, you get clothing, travel, and you get paid for it."

"That's what the old man said; the exact words."

"What old man?" Uncle asked.

I just shook my head and said, "Oh, he was someone I spoke to on the beach."

Uncle said, "In my opinion, I think it's an excellent idea." Auntie agreed, so Uncle and I sorted out the address of the Army Careers in Kings Lynn. I told him that I would cycle there Monday morning to make the arrangements.

Having gone through a medical exam and various tests (my IQ test came in negative), I had to wait and see if I had been accepted or not. During that time, I carried on as normal, working at the cinema and hovering around the letter box each morning looking for that important letter. One morning I was awoken by my landlady, who handed me an official brown envelope saying, "I think this is what you've been waiting for, it's from the War Office." I sat up in bed and ripped it open. The letter said I had been accepted in the Royal Artillery and was to report to basic training in Oswestry, Wales. A railway warrant was enclosed.

I leapt out of bed and got dressed, but before putting on my shoes, I read the letter again, and was thrilled to bits. I wanted to open the window and tell everyone that I had been accepted, but settled for running downstairs and telling my landlady, who was pleased for me and wished me well. I told her I couldn't stop, as I had to go tell Uncle and Auntie, and they, in turn, said that, "It would be the making of me," and wished me well.

Chapter Thirty-Nine

Army Life

Little did I know what was in store? On the train, I looked through the pamphlets I had on the Regular Army. After seeing the colorful photographs of army life, it looked great. I would have been called for National Service the next year anyway, so instead of going for two years, I signed up for three.

On arrival at Owestry, I found out I was not the only one joining, and once again, we found a military truck waiting for us. Finding it difficult to climb up in the back, especially with someone in authority shouting at me, I was given a hand by Max, a chap of my own age.

It seemed we had only just gotten comfortable in the truck, when we were out and in formation, having our names checked. After queuing up for our kit, which included clothing, etc, within minutes we were being led off to our billet like a pack of mules. Home for the next six weeks was an old war hut that slept about 14. We each got an iron bed and a steel locker, and that was that.

Having dumped my equipment on the rolled-up mattress, I sat down and thought that the pamphlets hadn't shown it like that. Suddenly, a roar sounded through the billet. It was our drill sergeant, who came in to introduce himself, and by heavens, didn't he do just that. Everyone stood like statues by their beds as he came around to each of one of us and had us shout our names and numbers.

Now have you ever seen the size of those military numbers? There are eight digits all together, and you were expected to remember them straight off. After the drill sergeant had asked everyone else their name and number, he finally came up to me and caught me glancing at a piece of paper with my number on it.

"What's your name, you 'orrible, man who can't keep still?"

"Morris, sir," I replied.

"What's your number?"

"Uh...two, two, nine..." I just couldn't remember it. When the sergeant spoke to me again, his mouth was only an inch or so away from my nose and he shouted at the top of his lungs, "Your number is 22983839. Now, what is it?"

"Two, two, nine..."

"I've just told you, you 'orrible man."

My mind went blank, apart from getting a vivid vision of an old man talking to me on the beach at Hunstanton. If only I had kept walking that day.

For the first week, I was fed up to the teeth and wished I hadn't joined, for the training sergeant really put us through our paces. He woke us up in the early hours of the morning to get dressed and double around the parade ground.

Although it was possible to leave the Army within a certain time, we all managed to stick it out. After the second week, we were allowed to go off the base. The novelty was to walk out in your uniforms, but ever since I had put my feet in those big heavy boots, I just couldn't get the hang of them. My feet wouldn't go where I wanted them to.

Having been let out, and having to go in uniform, I found myself on my own and ended up heading for a café, which had tables and chairs outside. That was a fatal move on my part. There were one or two girls sitting outside who looked at me as I approached the white metal chairs. For some reason, instead of going down the path to order my coffee, I decided to cut through the maze of furniture. Now remember those boots? I must have kicked every chair I went near, and managed to knock over two. Then my hat fell off. I picked everything up, and the girls thought it highly amusing. My face was as red as a beetroot, and I felt really embarrassed.

As I tripped into the doorway, the woman behind the counter commented, "It's a good job those chairs are metal." Having got a coffee and a sticky bun – yet another fatal mistake – I went outside to enjoy it. I decided to go to the far end of the girls, so I carefully made my way through the maze of tables and chairs. No, I didn't hit too many, but when I reached my table most of my coffee was in the saucer. What a relief it was to sit down. I poured the contents of my saucer back into my cup, and began to relax a bit. I threw my right leg over my left, and in the process of doing that, kicked the table, which upset my coffee. I continued by knocking over a chair, eliciting bursts of laughter from you know who.

Although my coffee had been in and out of the saucer, it was still very hot. As I brought the cup up to my mouth, it got stuck to the plastic bill of my hat, which meant I couldn't move for a few minutes. As I tried to release it, coffee spilled down the front of my uniform onto my trousers. I finally managed to free the cup and decided to make a hasty retreat. I left the café the same way I came in – knocking tables and chairs as I went, and leaving the other patrons in fits of laughter.

Basic training continued for what seemed a lifetime. We trained on ack-ack guns and L-70s, which were interesting. We had drill parades and more drill parades, assault courses and route marches. I was absolutely exhausted, and it was always nice at the end of the day to put my feet up and take those damn boots off.

Most of the lads got a lot of mail and spent some of the little free time they had writing to their loved ones. All through the training, I didn't receive one letter, which I really would have liked.

Max had a photo of his girlfriend stuck to his locker, and showed it to me with pride. "How about that then?" he said with glee. "Have you got a picture of yours?" I simply said I hadn't got one, which he couldn't understand.

When we were almost through with our basic training, we all started wondering where we would be dispatched. Max and I hoped we would be together. We had our final pass-out parade, and all went well. We gave a big sigh of relief when it was over.

When we received our transfer orders, Max and I found that we were both to join the 42nd Field Regiment in Plymouth. There was some celebrating that night, I can tell you.

Chapter Forty

On Leave

Before going to Plymouth, I had a short time off on leave. As I had nowhere else to go, I went back to Hunstanton to spend some time at the orphanage. I traveled by train and had to change trains at Paddington Station in London. I had almost an hour to spare, so I went to the railway café for a cup of tea and a sticky bun. The café was quite busy. Once I got my tea, I looked for somewhere to sit. There were only one or two seats vacant, so I decided to sit with a little old lady at a table for two. It looked like I was going back in time for she looked and acted very Victorian.

The old lady simply smiled when she saw me heading for her table. I politely asked if I could join her, and she smiled again and said, "But of course." I sat down and started working on giving my tea a good stir. Then I cut my sticky bun and was about to put some in my mouth when I saw the old lady staring at me with a frown. I put my head down and continued eating. Suddenly, I realized what was wrong.

She was staring at my hands, which had several warts. I put my food down and apologized to her, saying, "I'm sorry. I normally hide my hands when I'm with another person," and promptly put my hands out of sight under the table. She sipped more of her tea with those thin wrinkly lips, which had a very faint smear of lipstick and replied,

"No, no, I don't mind seeing your hands; they don't worry me." She wiped her mouth very daintily with what looked like an embroided hanky, and gave me another smile. She was quite frail looking, the wrinkly fur hat matched her wrinkly complexion. She also had a *Road Kill*, or rather a fox-fur stole, wrapped around her neck, which I couldn't help but stare at since it still had the head on it. There was just a dab of powder on each of her cheeks. No, not the fox... her face. When she smiled, she showed her slightly tarnished teeth, which looked like they were all hers.

She had another sip of her tea, then smiled again and asked, "Have you ever tried to get rid of those warts, young man?"

"Yes. I have tried all sorts of cures, but they look as if they're here to stay."

She smiled and reaching her hand across the table, said, "Show me your hands." I was reluctant to show them, but she insisted, so I held one out for her to examine.

"Well," she said, "you have some really big ones on this hand. What about the other one?"

I showed her my other hand.

"Well, well. You have several warts that need to be taken care of. Now," she said, shuffling closer so the people at the next table couldn't hear. She looked into my eyes and continued softly, "Now this is what I want you to do." She flipped my hands over to see where all the warts were and stared into my eyes, "I want you to count how many warts you have. Then I want you to sell them to me."

I just smiled and took another bite of my sticky bun.

"I'm serious, you know."

I smiled and repeated what she said, "You're saying that if I count my warts, you will buy them from me?"

The old lady looked from side to side to see if anyone was listening and said again, "Now remember, for this to work you must count every wart, not just the big ones, but every last one."

I cocked my head to one side and said, "All right...I'll count them all and you will..." before I had finished she said again staring into my eyes.

"I will buy them from you."

I had a quick sip of my tea and realized there was no sugar in it, but while the old lady was drinking hers, I counted all my warts. "All right," I said, "I have got 13 warts. How..."

She interrupted me. "I want you to double check to make sure you have the right number. Go on, check them again."

After checking again, I announced that I still had 13 of them. I sat back in my chair and folded my arms together and smiled then leaned forward and softly asked, "Right. How much are you going to give me for 13 warts?"

I was starting to drink more tea and frowned, no sugar. Then she announced, "Young man, you are the one selling, so you have to tell me what you want for those warts."

By now, the people at the next table were smiling at me.

"Well, what about you give me a halfpenny for them all."

A man at the next table pursed his lips and nodded in approval, then got up and left. The old lady brought her crocodile-skin handbag up to her lap and started digging through it. She finally produced and old penny saying, "I don't have a halfpenny, so I will pay you one penny for your 13 warts." She put the coin down on the table and slid it in front of me.

I started to feel around in my back pocket but she pushed the penny toward me and said, "No, please take the penny. Now." Then she held both my hands. "I want you to forget all about those nasty warts." She tightened her grip and said again, "Forget all about the warts and forget all about me. Now I have to go and catch my train." The old lady rose to her feet and adjusted her fox fur, then put on her leather gloves and carefully placed her crocodile handbag over her arm. She shook my hand and again reminded me to forget all about the warts and her.

As I reached over to the next table to get the sugar, and turned back to say goodbye, she was gone, just vanished. I was going to walk her to her train. I finished my sticky bun and my tea, then my eyes fixed onto the penny coin on the table, it happened to be a 'Victorian Penny Bun' coin, which, after all those years, I still have.

Two years later, when I was on leave and eating dinner at the orphanage, Uncle and Auntie both asked at the same time,

"How did you get rid of those warts?"

And that was the very first time I noticed they were completely gone. There was no trace of them. I had completely forgotten about them and the old lady with the road-kill. I felt for my wallet and dug around and produced the penny coin she gave me.

Auntie said, "I have heard of many ways to get rid of warts, but not this one, I must remember it." She held my hands and carefully examined them and just shook her head in disbelief.

On my first visit to the orphanage since joining the Army, Uncle and Auntie could see a dramatic change in me already, and agreed that joining the Army was the best thing for me. I was proud of myself, and walked around the town wearing my uniform, but still knocked the hell out of anything that came close to my boots. Local people would stop me and say hello. "You were one of the Home Boys weren't you?"

The ladies would say, "Well, they have turned you into a nice young man. I'll bet they're proud of you."

Mr. Raines, the greengrocer, gave me a smart salute.

Feeling things were beginning to come together for me, I decided I would push it to the hilt, and pay a visit to the orphanage in Leicester, the worst of all the orphanages that I had stayed. I traveled by train to the railway station that I had tried to run away from all those years ago. When I arrived, it brought back a lot of memories. I paused at the police office, but then decided to get to the orphanage because I didn't have much time.

When I caught the bus, I couldn't remember what to ask for, so I just said, "I want to get off at the end of Victoria Park." The conductor obviously knew where I wanted to go and produced a ticket. The bus, of course, reminded me of the time I traveled with the master. I wondered if that was the same bus. Then I realized I was sitting in the same seat I had then.

The master and matron who were at the home when I was there had been fired, or so I was told, but I was still hesitant to walk down the driveway. I plucked up courage and walked up to the big house. As I got nearer, I heard a lot of children giggling and laughing and shouting and generally making a lot of noise. That was not how I remembered the place. I rang the front doorbell and within seconds the door burst open. I was confronted with all these children: young boys and girls, some saying hello and others shouting at the top of their voices to the staff, "There's a soldier at the door!"

The next thing I knew, the matron, or Auntie, as she was called, came toward me with a big smile on her face.

"You must be an old boy from here."

"Yes," I said as she beckoned me in. She raised her arms in the air and told the children, "Quiet down a bit please. Another old boy has come to see us." Turning to me, she said, "And what's your name?"

"Er, Les Morris," I said.

"Ah yes, I have seen your name in..." she paused, and then continued, "the old punishment book." I didn't know whether to smile or hang my head in shame. I stood staring at the famous staircase, which had been strictly out of bounds, yet here the children were running up and down on it and having great fun. I pointed to the stairs and said, "When I was here, we were not allowed on the staircase unless we had the job of cleaning it. You could be sent to the master's study just for thinking about sliding down the banister."

Auntie pulled a face and said, "You must have been here during the Fletchers' reign."

I nodded.

"So you were also deprived of sliding down the banister?"

I said that was true.

She then herded the children like sheep from the stairs and told me to take off my military belt because it had big buckle on it, and announced; "Now children, Mr. Morris is going to slide down the banister."

I couldn't believe it. I pointed to myself, and said, "Me? I can slide..."

"Yes you, Mr. Morris. Come on," she said pointing to the top.

It felt great walking up the stairs knowing that what I was about to do would have gotten me into big trouble at one time. But here I was standing on the landing, looking down at all the children who were now cheering me on to slide down the banister. I got into position and automatically looked across to the master's office, expecting him to come out at any time screaming. But he didn't, so with a big smile on my face, I let go and flew down the banister to an almighty cheer from the children.

It brought tears to my eyes. I had always wanted to do that, and now I had achieved it. Auntie was still clapping.

"Go and do it again, Mr. Morris! Go on."

So I ran up the stairs and flew down again.

"Wonderful," I said to Auntie, exhilarated.

As we pushed past the children, she said, "I bet you would like a cup of tea now."

"Oh, thank you," I said, and off we went to the kitchen for some home-baked cakes and a nice cup of tea. I was introduced to other members of staff and we talked about my time at the home. I told them I couldn't believe it was the same miserable place. Auntie showed me around, and it was very strange to look at some of the rooms that I had to suffer in, especially the boiler room, and the shoe room, and the hallway where I had been beaten senseless after the time I ran away. It made me feel sick.

So that was enough of that.

"Well, I have achieved two things here today; I slid down the banister, and I have seen what the place can be like with the master and matron gone. I'm very grateful, Auntie, for your help," I said.

"I'm only too pleased to meet lads who have been here before," she said with a smile. "Have a safe journey back." We shook hands and I was given a rowdy send-off by the children. Then I got onto a train to go back to Hunstanton with a huge smile on my face.

The time flew by and before I knew it, I was back on a train, heading for Plymouth.

Chapter Forty-One
The Royal Citadel Plymouth

It was a nerve-wracking experience to report to the 42nd Field Regiment, Royal Artillery, at the Royal Citadel, in Plymouth. It was now to be my home. I went to the guardroom, and was told to report to the New Zealand Battery, where I was then shown to my billet. When I got there, who do you think was already settled in? Yes, Max. He immediately put me right on the dos and don'ts, and believe me, there were plenty of them.

The Royal Citadel was a fortress, with a battlement surrounding it and cannons protruding out towards the "Hoe" and Plymouth Sound. It was a very historic place, but we did not appreciate that at the time. In fact, at first it was just another barracks, but as Plymouth was a large town, there were always places to go and a lot of people to see. Mostly what we saw was a lot of women, especially when the Navy wasn't in town.

I remember nearly every night the lads would come into the barracks and start talking about the girls they'd been out with, what they did with them, and what they intended to do the next time they met. Very often, they would look across to my bed and ask me who I went out with. I would tell them a young blonde, etc. They knew damn well I was lying, and told me so.

I was still very shy and just didn't have the nerve to approach a young lady, let alone ask her out. I would go for walks or into a coffee bar for hours, but most of all I used to hide in the cinema. I envied the lads talking about their night out. How dull and uninteresting my night's were. I met a gentleman at the coffee bar who was an architect and lost his wife and now lived all alone. He asked me one day, "If you picked up a young lady and you wanted to spend some private time with her, where would you take her?" I told him.

"Up on the Hoe or in a park, why do you ask?" I replied.

"I have a house not far from here and I would like you to have a look at it with me." So, while we were walking towards his house, I asked. "Why do you want me to show you your house?"

"I don't know you that well, but you seem like a reliable chap and as I was talking to you, I had this idea come into my head." I must have given him a strange look because he suddenly said, "No…No… don't get the wrong idea, I'm not a queer…I'm not like that." That was a relief because the next thing I knew we were at the house.

As we walked up the terraced steps to the front door, he said, "I am away from here most of the time and the place is getting untidy with weeds front and back and the lawn." He stopped when the front door opened. "I was wondering if you would like the job of looking after the place, staying here now, and even bringing your young ladies here to entertain, if you like." He smiled and continued, "That beats the Hoe, etc…what do you say?"

"Well, I'd love to," I said with excitement. He handed me the keys and showed me around and gave me his card with a number that I could call if at any time there was a problem. Suddenly he said, "I don't know your full name and you don't know mine. So everything was sorted out and I couldn't wait to tell Max.

My not being able to meet a women problem was on the way to being solved. One day, I accidentally fell off the top of my truck which I was working on. To be honest, I was fooling around. I reported to the sick room and was told I had a sprained ankle and that I was to be on light duties, so I changed all the light bulbs for instance. For a couple of weeks, my job was to work in our battery office. (No, not vehicle batteries; instead of platoons, divisions, and so on, in the artillery we had batteries.) I had numerous little jobs to do, such as sorting mail, delivering notices, and answering the telephone.

It was through the telephone that I got involved with the first woman in my life. What I mean by "first woman" was the one that introduced me to sex, and I took to it.

Sometimes the telephone would ring all day; other days it was very quiet. On one of the quiet afternoons, the phone rang. A woman asked to speak to Gunner (Private) Watkinson. I checked with some of the office staff to see who the chap was, as I certainly hadn't heard of him. They returned with the same verdict: "Never heard of him." I told her, and she made one or two comments as if to make conversation, but I was being summoned, so I said I couldn't help her and forgot all about it.

The following day, the same woman rang and asked for the same person. "Can I speak to Gunner Watkinson?" With a frown, I told her that as far as I knew, there was no one in our regiment with that name. In fact, I continued, "I doubt if there was anyone in the whole British Army with that name," but she insisted that there was.

It became a regular ritual. Sometimes she called twice a day, and of course I ended up having a quiet conversation with her. After that, she used to ask for me when she rang.

One of the lads suggested that I take her out, but I dismissed the idea, saying I just wasn't ready for that. Well, to be honest, I didn't know how to ask her. She saved me the embarrassment by asking me out, and I stuttered out my acceptance. Her name was Lorie. I told her to go to the address at Rex's house, and to meet me at 6:30pm.

After we hung up, I danced all around the office with excitement, and a limp, and couldn't believe that I had been asked out. What made it even better, our date was for that very evening.

After soaking in a bath for an hour, I put my best clothes – blue blazer, gray flannel trousers, with checkered shirt and shiny shoes. I practically used a full bottle of aftershave and a whole tub of cream on my hair. Before I left the barracks, all my mates wished me well and told me to use the Black Magic Touch.

So off I went to Rex's house complete with a box of Black Magic chocolates. Like the commercial said, "The way to a women's heart is Black Magic Chocolates." When I arrived at the house, I went in and put the chocolates on the coffee table by the sofa, and turned on the television. They took a long time to warm up in those days. I checked everything, went over what was to play out, and as I always did when I was nervous, undid my blazer button and did it up again. I didn't realize I did that until it was pointed out to me. Then I started the rehearsing stuff, by pacing up and down the hallway looking through the peep hole then saying.

"Hello Lorie, I am Les, and am very pleased to meet you."

"No...No...No..." I said to myself and went back and started over again. I looked at my watch. Only five minutes! It was panic time!

I walked briskly up to the front door. "My name is Les and you must be..." I looked through the spy hole and my eyes sprang wide open and stuck out like chapel hat pegs. "Bugger...Bugger...Bugger, she's here."

I undid my blazer buttons and was doing it up again when the doorbell rang. I quickly did them up again and without thinking just opened the door. Before I could say anything Lorie walked up to me with a wonderful smile and pointed to my jacket button which was buttoned wrongly. I looked down and re-buttoned it for at least the hundredth time.

"You must be Les," said Lorie."

"Erm...yes I must be, I mean yes I am." I could feel my face burning then I shook Lorie's hand. We both walked into the lounge, and I took her coat which she bent down to put it on a chair and the front of her blouse revealed how hilly she was.

After hanging it up out came the famous words, "Would you like a cup of tea?"

"If you are going to have one, I will as well." she said. While making the tea Lorie was asking me about the house and I was going on about it when she suddenly said, "Let's go and sit down for a minute." And she led me by the hand into the lounge. She sat right up against me on the couch, and asked me questions, and I asked her questions.

"How old are you Les?"

"I'm…er…18." Then she told me she was 37 married to an RAF chap who was in Singapore and they are both waiting for the divorce to go through.

I stared into her eyes and she asked, "What are you thinking Les?"

I casually said, "So you are the mystery voice…I can't believe this is happening?"

She smiled and said, "Well, there's nothing happening, I've been here seven minutes and neither had a cup of tea, nor a Black Magic Chocolate." We both laughed and I said I'd get the tea.

"Let's have tea later…come here." Her hands started wandering all over me. "Oh what a big fellow you are," she kept saying.

And what was I doing? Well, I was up to my old tricks of getting redder and redder, with all too familiar beads of sweat rolling down my face. I didn't know what to do, and she knew it. She kept rubbing her hands all over my body as I kept thrusting the box of chocolates under her nose, hoping she would calm down a bit. I joked around and told her not to take any chocolates with teeth marks on them because they had hard centers, but she wasn't interested, and finally took them out of my hand, putting them out of my reach.

She turned my face toward hers, and said softly, "Have you ever done this before?" I dropped my head in shame and said in a shameful way. "No…I haven't."

Lorie gave a hearty laugh and told me to relax. By now, my tie was off and my shirt unbuttoned. I must admit I was feeling a little more relaxed, but I was still worried about what was to come.

And then it happened.

The real action started. She literally tore off my trousers and pulled me onto the floor and rolled on top of me and rubbed herself all over me. I lay there helpless. Honestly, once again I still didn't know what to do. But boy, she was a good teacher, and certainly knew what she was doing.

Without going into a lot of details, I had my very first sexual experience, and simply exploded with excitement. After the third time,

I was feeling really, really great. In fact, I was quite pleased with myself and was looking forward to going back to the barracks and reporting my progress. I felt that I had at last become one of the lads, and now I was a man. But reporting to the chaps was not happening at that moment – the night was not over.

Lorie left the room to make some coffee while I sat on the sofa rolling a cigarette, glowing like the one-bar electric fire that was taking the chill from the room. While we both sipped our coffee, I went to reach for the chocolates, but she said, "To hell with them," and pulled me on top of her. "Now it's your turn," she said with a shine in her eye. I didn't mind, but I hadn't finished my coffee.

I made a right pig's ear of it, so Lorie, my new sex teacher, started giving me instructions on how a woman likes a man to perform. As I was in the Army, I was used to taking orders and did as she commanded. For a beginner, I think I did rather well, because she ended up lying beside me glowing and smiling, just like me.

After a gloriously long while, it was time for her to leave. I offered to escort her home. As we came through the park, with the moon shining down like daylight, she stopped and we sat on a bench with me tucked in close. Squeezing my hand, she gazed into my eyes and I watched her ruby lips move as she said, "What a romantic night this is." Without any more warning, she smothered my face with kisses, and yes, she was off again. She made love to me on the bench and when we walked away, my legs were uncontrollable. It was difficult to walk.

Climbing the stairs to her flat seemed like hard work. When we got inside, she shouted out to her flat mate, Ursula, but there was no reply.

"So Les, we've got the place to ourselves," she said with a smile, and would you believe it, she was at it again. Before I knew it, I was on her bed and she really got me going. Although I was very fit, I ended up feeling absolutely exhausted, and just lay there limp and sore.

When I eventually hobbled back to the Royal Citadel, it was half past three in the morning. I crept into my barracks and went over to Max's bed, which was next to mine. I woke him up to tell him about my adventures. He said in a drowsy voice, "Tell me in the morning, its bloody 3:30 am!" And he promptly went back to sleep.

I felt like throwing all the lights on and announcing to the whole room that I had at last done it. I crept into bed and for some time lay there reminiscing about the night's activities before dropping off to sleep.

The next morning, I think I told everyone I met. Max, who was now more than in the mood to listen, was very pleased for me, and said he wanted to know every morsel of information. At break, a gang of the lads from my billet surrounded me and wanted to know all. And I was thrilled to tell them.

One of the lads got to his feet and pointed his finger at me. "He dips his bread for the very first time, and gets what we all dream of – a bloody nymphomaniac!" We all laughed. Then I thought to myself, what the hell is a nympho-whatever?

I was finally truly accepted as one of the lads because after all that time I had "dipped me bread." I stood up and threw my shoulders back and felt really good. Then Max stood up and shouted. "Let's take Les to the Barbican tonight to celebrate." There was a thunderous roar of agreement.

Now today, the Barbican is a big, clean tourist area, but in those days it was full of bars, clubs, and lots of women of "ill repute." After my experience, I felt more confident going there, especially with all my mates. As we wandered around laughing and joking, I stopped short in front of an antique shop and stared into the front window.

"Come on Les, there's nothing in there but junk. We're looking for something much better," Max said.

"I'll catch up in a minute," I replied. As he went off, I resumed looking at the big penny-farthing bike on display, daydreaming about that eventful day in my life at Ashdon orphanage all those years ago, hearing the humming of the big wheel and recapturing those memories of long ago, but was interrupted by the lads calling me.

The celebration of my initiation went well, and I threw my shoulders back and now considered myself a man.

THAT'S AS THEY SAY, IS IT!

Woody

As mentioned in the beginning of my book, Mrs. Woodley (known as Woody only to the adult world) was like a "Fairy Godmother" to my brother and I. As children we always referred to her as Mrs. Woodley. Even when we became adults we still referred to her with her full title.

During my adult years, when I visited my brother Doug who lives in Chelmsford Essex, we would drive out to the village of Ashdon and visit Mrs. Woodley in her house near to the church. Her house was only one up and one down, with no bathroom. You had to walk down to the bottom of her garden to use the toilet.

A galvanized bath hung on the wall outside, but she claims to have never used it because it was cumbersome and she would settle for a strip down wash at the kitchen sink whenever she felt like it. So, the galvanized bath ended up in the garden alongside the wooden out-house half filled with soil. It made an ideal mint garden.

My brother and I always kept in touch with Mrs. Woodley by tele-phone or letters, sending her birthdays and Christmas cards. Even when I moved to the United States in 1984, I kept in touch and when visiting England I would stay with my brother and I would look forward to visiting dear old Mrs. Woodley.

One year she was very sad because they told her she could not sing in the choir because of her poor eyesight. Then another visit revealed that she was not allowed to ring the church bells. Then the key to the church was taken from her, and that really upset her. You see, the church was locked for various reasons and because her house was right by the church she would unlock the church for visi-tors, etc.

Mrs. Woodley couldn't understand that she was now in her 90's and that she could not function like she used to. So, she got bored and took up knitting, but the thing that really upset her was…she couldn't do the gardening anymore. She told me, "I had a man come and weed the garden, when he pulled out a weed, he threw to one side of the garden."

I asked her, "What was wrong with that?"

"I told him you put them in the galvanized bucket, so that they DIE," she shouted.

One memorable visit to Mrs. Woodley was the year she turned 100 years old and there she sat in her wing-backed chair with that lovely smile she had but showing her rotted teeth exposing one large tooth that proudly hung from her top jaw. Doug and I presented her with flowers. One of her village friends took them from us to put in a vase and I made a comment to Doug that we would have to change Mrs. Woodley's name to one-eater because of her tooth. That got us both giggling.

Mrs. Woodley pointed proudly to the large card standing on the mantle shelf which was the telegram from Her Majesty The Queen. The Queen congratulated Mrs. Woodley for reaching the ripe old age of 100 and every person who manages to reach that age gets the famous telegram from Her Majesty.

Dear Old Mrs. Woodley was moved to a nursing home in Cambridge, against her will, but it was no longer safe in that cold old cottage, and because she never had a television, she had no idea what differences there were now in the world. The reason I mention this is that all during her life she had never seen a black person. The story goes that an African black nurse attended Mrs. Woodley and she frightened Mrs. Woodley to such an extent that she hid under the sheets and wouldn't come out, telling her to leave her alone. No not race related, but ignorance of the people of the world because she was confined to the little Village of Ashdon Essex.

She married in 1929 and he died 1935. This chap was from another small village called Castle Camp, about three miles from Ashdon. He was buried in the local church after only four years of marriage; he died of a heart attack.

Constance Gwendolyn Woodley (Woody) passed away in December 2009 at the ripe old age of 103 and is buried on top of her husband in Castle Camp. Together again after 99 years apart.

I miss seeing and talking to:

"My dear old Mrs. Woodley"